D0933973

A
HISTORY
OF HAVING
A GREAT MANY TIMES
NOT CONTINUED
TO BE FRIENDS

଼ଡ

A
HISTORY
OF HAVING
A GREAT MANY TIMES
NOT CONTINUED
TO BE FRIENDS

ℰᴧ

Patricia R. Everett

University of New Mexico Press
Albuquerque

Library of Congress Cataloging in Publication Data

Luhan, Mabel Dodge, 1879-1962.
A history of having a great many times not continued to be friends:
the correspondence between Mabel Dodge and Gertrude Stein,
1911-1934 / Patricia R. Everett. — 1st ed.
p. cm.
Includes bibliographical references (p.).
1. Luhan, Mabel Dodge, 1879-1962—Correspondence.
2. Stein, Gertrude, 1874-1946—Correspondence.
3. Intellectuals—United States—Correspondence.
4. Women authors, American—20th century—Correspondence.
I. Stein, Gertrude, 1874-1946.
II. Everett, Patricia R.
III. Title.
CT275.L838A4 1995
818'.5209—dc20
[B]
95-4345
CIP

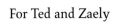

For Ted and Zaely

$\mathcal{P}\mathfrak{d}$

CONTENTS

$\mathcal{L}$

ILLUSTRATIONS

꽃ə

ACKNOWLEDGMENTS

THIS PROJECT HAS SPANNED MORE THAN A DECADE AND HAS BEEN a consistent presence in my life, keeping me company throughout all the changes during those years, a companion surprisingly effortless to return to each week on my designated writing day. My involvement in the letters between Mabel Dodge and Gertrude Stein has brought me into contact with many people who have been generous with their time and interest. Warm acknowledgment goes to Bruce Kellner for his continued support, enthusiasm, helpful criticism, and insights. He always shared his seemingly boundless knowledge of the period and graciously allowed me to carry him in my head as my mentor. His letters in themselves are treasures to read and collect, and I am grateful to have been the recipient of so many and of his friendship. Barbara Mathes also deserves special recognition for being the first to be responsive to my curiosity about Mabel Dodge and then providing me with an opportunity to organize an exhibition of work by the artists in Dodge's circle. Her early confidence in me contributed to the initiation of this project in important ways.

For time to write, I am indebted to many people. I am particularly grateful to two pairs of friends, Tom and Claire O'Connor and David White and Sophia Wheelwright, who lent me their summer houses for a week at a time, providing me with the delicious isolation and proximity to the ocean that seemed so necessary for immersion in my work and the space to be creative. Tom O'Connor was also very helpful with a difficult French translation. I am thankful for the flexibility extended to me by Susan Sussman at the New York Psychiatric Institute and by the Jewish Board of Family and Children's Services that enabled me to devote time to writing during my internship and first job after graduate school. I am grateful to the American Council of Learned Societies for a grant that helped me take a month off from work in order to pursue my research. I owe an enormous amount of thanks to Kerri Parker, who provided the loving and consistent daycare for my son Zaely that allowed me to finish this book during the first year of his life. Without the confidence in the environment she provided for him, I could never have found the rare freedom for a new mother to focus and return to writing. And for his curious affection for the sound of my printer and his fascination with my study, I am grateful to Zaely for keeping me company during the tedious task of printing out the final draft of my manuscript.

For feedback on my writing, I greatly appreciated Robin Karson's gentle and detailed comments and her willingness to be the first person to read even a part of what I had written over the past ten years. For their quick and thorough responses to my many questions, some of them quite last-minute, I am very grateful to Bruce Kellner, Ulla Dydo, Leon Katz, Donald Gallup, and Robert Wilson. Donald Gallup's transcriptions of Gertrude Stein's letters to Mabel Dodge at the Beinecke Library were a much appreciated resource. I thank him also for his early and inspiring enthusiasm for my project. I appreciated Mary Maguire's help in generating ideas at the beginning of my search for a publisher.

Always a highlight of my research were my visits to the Beinecke Rare Book and Manuscript Library at Yale University. I never failed to feel energized by my conversations with Patricia Willis, and I am very grateful for her generosity with her time, enthusiasm, and permissions. Much appreciation goes to the staff at the Beinecke Library for making the Mabel Dodge Luhan and Gertrude and Leo Stein Archives so available. I want to extend special thanks to Danielle McClellan for her patient assistance with the photograph orders and to Steve Jones and Lori Misura for their help and interest over the years.

For permission to publish these letters, I am grateful to the Yale Collection of American Literature, Beinecke Rare Book and Manuscript Library, Yale University, and to Calman Levin as administrator of the Gertrude Stein Estate. I want to express appreciation to the following for their permission to reproduce photographs: Beinecke Rare Book and Manuscript Library; the Regis Collection, Minneapolis; Museum of Fine Arts, Boston; Metropolitan Museum of Art, New York; the New York Public Library; Albright-Knox Art Gallery, Buffalo, New York. The New York Public Library was a continual source of discovery and pleasure. The Amherst College Library served as an unexpected and welcome haven for my research, and Ann Maggs at the Music Library enthusiastically joined me in a search for a minute piece of music history.

Soon after I completed the manuscript for this book, my friend Julie Westcott interviewed me about the process of writing for an article for our high school alumnae magazine. The hours of talking together about my book and how it got written during the various phases of my life—changes in career, marriage, leaving New York, becoming a mother—were moving and inspiring for us both. I am grateful to Julie for her perspective on being both a mother and a writer, the support and generous interest that she consistently extends, and for our friendship, which always enriches me.

I wish to thank my editor, Dana Asbury, for her immediate and enthusiastic response to my manuscript and for her patience and guidance throughout the final stages before publication.

I am very grateful to my parents, Jean Halverson and William Everett, for providing me with an education that opened up so many doors and for their love and faith in me beyond this project. Barbara and Lew Ellenhorn and Gintare Sileika Everett also have given to me in important ways with their enthusiasm about this book. My friends, both old and new, have warmed me with their sustained interest. Finally, my husband, Ted Ellenhorn, has been an unfailing source of encouragement and support and a real champion of the priority and sanctity of my writing time. I continually feel blessed by his belief in me.

PATRICIA R. EVERETT

ℒℴ

PREFACE

This collection of letters represents the complete and unedited extant correspondence between Mabel Dodge and Gertrude Stein, encompassing the years from 1911 to 1934. There are 104 letters from Dodge to Stein and 31 from Stein to Dodge. It is possible that some of Stein's letters to Dodge from before 1914 were among those destroyed when the Villa Curonia was vacated by Edwin Dodge and piles of papers designated to be sent to Mabel Dodge in New Mexico were inadvertently burned. I have inserted in chronological order three letters written by Mabel Dodge to Alice B. Toklas that were included among the letters in the Gertrude Stein papers, as well as one letter from Toklas to Dodge that was found among the letters in the Mabel Dodge papers. All of the correspondence is located in the Collection of American Literature, Beinecke Rare Book and Manuscript Library, Yale University.

I transcribed Mabel Dodge's letters from the originals. While I gratefully relied and drew upon Donald Gallup's transcriptions of Gertrude Stein's letters to Dodge, I also transcribed the letters anew from the originals.

In my transcriptions, I have sought to remain loyal to Dodge's and Stein's original written word. I have not corrected or deleted misspellings, inconsistent spellings, typographical errors, grammatical errors, or repeated words. Dodge had idiosyncratic ways of spelling and was not always a good speller. She wrote "Dam" for "Damn," "tradgedy" for "tragedy," and in her contractions used a single "l" instead of "ll," as in "you'l." She regularly did not capitalize certain words, such as "english" and "german," and wrote "americain." Stein's style of handwriting, with its casual indication of many letters by a seemingly random line that peaks and dips, makes it difficult to distinguish individual letters and thus to evaluate her skill as a speller. For example, her writing style makes it almost impossible to guess if she wrote "know" or "known." In these instances, if one word makes more sense than another and it is plausible that Stein wrote it, I have selected the word that better fits the context. Occasionally, however, it is clear that Stein did misspell a word, such as in leaving out "ed" or "ing" at the end. As with Dodge's writing, I have not corrected these errors. One consistent pattern of Stein's idiosyncratic spelling is her use of "x" in place of "ex," as in "xhausted" and "xcept."

In the case of misspelled proper names, I have corrected them in brackets with the correct spelling preceded by "i.e.," following the style used by Edward Burns in *The Letters of Gertrude Stein and Carl Van Vechten, 1913–1946* (1986). When a person's name has been abbreviated or only the first or last name is supplied, I have furnished the missing information in brackets, except in instances where either the person is so well known that his or her last name suffices as identification, such as Picasso or Matisse, or the person is so frequently mentioned that his or her first name is clearly identifying, such as with Leo Stein, Alice B. Toklas, Edwin Dodge, Paul Ayrault (a lover of Mabel Dodge's for a time), and John Evans (Mabel Dodge's son by her first marriage). In her letters, Mabel Dodge sometimes referred to others by a single initial after she had already mentioned them once, for example "C." for Constance Fletcher. In writing to Gertrude Stein, she almost always referred to her husband Edwin Dodge as "E." and her lover Paul Ayrault as "P." Although Dodge herself had three different last names during the period of her correspondence with Stein, a result of her marriages to Edwin Dodge, Maurice Sterne, and Antonio Luhan, I have referred to her as Dodge throughout, because that was the name that she bore during the central years of their friendship from 1911 to 1914. In all footnotes and endnotes, "Stein" refers to Gertrude Stein and "Dodge" refers to Mabel Dodge, unless otherwise indicated.

When a word has been omitted, I have inserted the missing word in square brackets. I have not altered the original punctuation, thus retaining Dodge's frequent dashes and omissions of apostrophes, as in "thats" and "todays." Stein also often omitted apostrophes, as in "lets" and "its," and rarely used commas. She always punctuated her inquiries with a period, never a question mark. Stein used a very thin and scratchy fountain pen and her ink has often grown pale. It is possible that some of her periods may have faded away, as in a number of instances where they are called for but do not appear. There are also some apparently haphazard marks on her stationery that may be commas or apostrophes, although it is difficult to tell. In these cases, I have indicated the punctuation if it makes sense and omitted it if it seems like a random mark. Only when a punctuation mark is needed for the sake of sense have I supplied it in square brackets. In instances in which I have been uncertain of a word and have made my best guess at it, I have inserted a question mark in square brackets following the word. When Dodge's spelling has made word recognition difficult, I have followed the word with my own interpretation and a question mark in brackets, as in "beareded [berated?]." In instances where the text is indecipherable, I have written "illegible" in brackets in place of the word or words. I have translated all foreign words and phrases in footnotes.

Mabel Dodge had a number of personalized stationery styles throughout the period of her correspondence with Gertrude Stein, and her letters were almost always written with a thick fountain pen. Two styles predominated during her years in Italy, each of which has three versions of ink color and paper combinations. The first features a monogram of her initials, "MD," surrounded by a circle inside of which run the following words from Walt Whitman's "Song of Myself": "Do I contradict myself? Very well, then, I con-tradict myself." This monogrammed stationery with the Whitman motto appears in three varieties: lavender and silver monogram on lightweight cream-colored paper; gold and blue monogram on medium weight light blue paper; and silver and bright blue mono-gram on thick cream-colored paper. The second form of stationery presents Dodge's telephone number and address in all capital let-ters printed in a sans serif style: "TEL.:19-94./VILLA CURONIA/VIA DELLE PIAZZOLE/ARCETRI." This writing paper appears in three versions: dark gray ink on lightweight pale gray paper; dark gray ink on white lightweight paper; and navy blue ink on me-dium weight gray paper. Only one letter provides an example of Dodge's stationery from New York, white paper with deckle edges and "23 FIFTH AVENUE" engraved across the top in dark navy blue capital letters.

When she moved to Taos, New Mexico, and became Mabel Dodge Luhan in 1923 through her marriage to Antonio Luhan, a Pueblo Indian, Dodge had several kinds of writing paper. One is domi-nated by a thick line drawing of her adobe house, with a mountain in the background and roosters on either side, done in orange, black, and green and most likely by the scenic designer Robert Edmond Jones, as suggested by the initials "R.E.J." in the lower right corner. Underneath the drawing is written in all capital orange letters "LOS GALLOS, TAOS/NEW MEXICO," the name given to her house because of the ceramic roosters decorating the roof line. Another style of stationery on gray and white thinly striped paper with dark navy blue ink displays her monogrammed initials "MDL" on the left side, with the "L" large in the center, and on the right, "TAOS, NEW MEXICO" appears in all capital letters. A third example reads "MABEL DODGE LUHAN/ TAOS . NEW MEXICO" in simple capital black letters embellished slightly with modest serifs. Mabel Dodge occasionally wrote on plain white bond paper, often indicating the location and date at the top. She also corresponded on hotel and ship stationery and from time to time sent postcards.

Gertrude Stein's range of stationery when writing to Mabel Dodge was by comparison quite limited. She wrote all but five of her letters on cream-colored lightweight paper engraved with "27 RUE DE FLEURUS" in bright red ink. Three letters were written on the same paper printed with dark navy blue ink, and two appeared on hotel stationery. The remainder of Stein's correspondence to Dodge consisted of seven postcards and one telegram.

In transcribing the correspondence between Dodge and Stein, I have included the address information handwritten or printed on the stationery and have supplied in brackets the writing paper used for each letter if it is not apparent from the transcription, for example "[Whitman motto]." For the sake of both design and consistency, throughout the correspondence I have presented the printed addresses, such as "VILLA CURONIA" and "27 RUE DE FLEURUS," in all capital letters, with initial full caps and subsequent small caps, except in the case of "RUE" which is not capitalized in French addresses and thus appears in all small caps.

Dodge did not regularly supply days of the month on her letters to Stein and, with one exception in 1917, never noted the year. Sometimes she indicated only the day of the week. Stein never furnished dates on her letters to Dodge. In order to date the Dodge letters, then, I have relied first upon the handwritten notes of months and years that appear in the upper right corner of many of the letters, although internal evidence has sometimes led me to alter the date. With two exceptions, these notations were provided by Donald Gallup and arrived at in his research for his edited collection of letters to Gertrude Stein, *The Flowers of Friendship* (1953). Twelve of the letters from Dodge to Stein were undated, and internal evidence pointed to approximate dates in ten of them. Two remain unable to be dated and are included at the end of the letters section. For the Stein letters to Dodge, Dodge guessed at the dates, writing these on blue notepaper that she attached to each letter. Telegrams and postcards usually displayed postmarks indicating the day of the month and year. Where a date is provided by a postmark, I have indicated so in brackets, as in "[postmark: 6 July 1913]." When dating is reliant upon the month and year notations on individual letters, I have included these dates in brackets. Where the year is certain but the month is not, I have noted approximate dates with "circa" preceding the date in brackets, as in "[circa April 1911]." In three instances in which the year was not certain and I inserted the letters into the body of the correspondence where sense indicated, I have followed the year with a question mark and enclosed it in brackets, as in "[1915 ?]." I have also used evidence contained within the letters as well as the sequence of information to inform the placement of each letter and arrive at approximate dates. For this purpose, I have checked dates of ship arrivals and departures, obituaries and wedding announcements, and biographies of those individuals mentioned in the letters.

A number of these letters have been published elsewhere. Donald Gallup included eleven of Dodge's letters to Stein in *The Flowers of Friendship*, although they are not all quoted in full and are not annotated in detail. Dodge herself included ten of Stein's letters to her in the third volume of her autobiography, *Movers and Shakers* (1936), but some include deletions and none is annotated. In her biography of Mabel Dodge (1984), Lois Rudnick quotes briefly from several of Dodge's letters to Stein and does not include any of Stein's replies to Dodge. In *Charmed Circle: Gertrude Stein & Company* (1974), James Mellow quotes from a number of letters from both Stein and Dodge to each other, although none is printed in full.

Because Stein's work was frequently published out of sequence or many years after it was written, I have supplied two dates immediately following the first mention of each of her titles, using Bruce Kellner's system that he employed in *A Gertrude Stein Companion: content with the example* (1988). The first date or dates indicate the time the work was composed and the second date is the year that it was first published.

In this collection, the correspondence between Mabel Dodge and Gertrude Stein is presented chronologically with introductory paragraphs to individual letters or groups of letters. In my interest in

ℰᴓ

INTRODUCTION

Mabel Dodge's early support and promotion of Gertrude Stein's writing was most likely enormously strengthening for Stein, serving to link the two women in a mutually beneficial way. In *The Making of Americans* (1903–11; 1925), Stein had written:

> You write a book and while you write it you are ashamed for every one must think you are a silly or a crazy one and yet you write it and you are ashamed, you know you will be laughed at or pitied by every one and you have a queer feeling and you are not very certain and you go on writing. Then some one says yes to it, to something you are liking, or doing or making and then never again can you have completely such a feeling of being afraid and ashamed that you had then when you were writing or liking the thing and not any one had said yes about the thing.[1]

Mabel Dodge said yes to her writing, as had Gertrude Stein's loyal companion Alice B. Toklas before her, thus assuring for herself an important role in the development of Stein's confidence about her work. Stein regularly sent samples and news of her writing to Dodge, while Dodge continually inquired about her work and exuded praise.

In the early spring of 1911 in Paris, Mabel Dodge accompanied a friend to 27 rue de Fleurus, where she first met Gertrude Stein. The two women, both of whom were inspired collectors of creative people, soon arranged to have lunch and to get together in Florence during the coming summer. The Buffalo-born, already widowed and remarried Dodge was immediately drawn to the innovative writer originally from California. She recalled the beginning of her connection with Gertrude Stein: "She and I had taken to each other in Paris. I seemed to amuse her and she was always laughing her great, hearty laugh at me."[2] As Mabel Dodge was leaving Paris to go south to Italy, Gertrude Stein entrusted her with a manuscript of her lengthy novel, *The Making of Americans*, still in progress. Dodge's reading of this work and her unbridled praise for its revolutionary form—"To me it is one of the most remarkable things I have ever read. There are things hammered out of consciousness into black & white that have never been expressed before"[3]—marked the beginning of an important fit between the two women. Gertrude Stein came to believe in herself firmly as a genius, and Mabel Dodge was unwavering in her recognition and support of her distinctive writing. Throughout her life, Dodge imbued others with larger-than-life attributes, a tendency that fit perfectly with Stein's conviction of her own unique talents.

The friendship between Mabel Dodge and Gertrude Stein followed a pattern common to many of Stein's friendships, particularly after Alice B. Toklas entered her life in 1907. There was the initial warming up, then a more intense connection that threatened Alice B. Toklas, who slowly began to sever the tie. Stein's part in this process seems more difficult to establish. However, it is clear from the extant letters that Stein's correspondence with Dodge drops off sharply after 1914, and the tone of her subsequently shorter letters is removed and unengaged. It appears that their estrangement was significantly enough pronounced that Stein included Dodge in her 1924 prose piece, "A History of Having a Great Many Times Not Continued to Be Friends." Stein writes: "No names mentioned. / Mable able able Mable Mable able too."[4]

Besides documenting the progression and later cooling of the friendship between Mabel Dodge and Gertrude Stein, their letters to each other offer glimpses into a wide range of social and cultural activities and details of their daily lives. The two women arrange lunch and dinner dates and make summer plans. They trade stories and inquire about their mutual friends and acquaintances, including the American painter Marsden Hartley, the art historian Bernard Berenson, the novelist and playwright Constance Fletcher, and the tenor Paul Draper and his wife and salon hostess Muriel. They introduce their friends to each other. Stein suggests Dodge look up the journalist and author Hutchins Hapgood, and Dodge provides Carl Van Vechten, a critic and writer, with a letter to Stein, both introductions resulting in lifelong friendships. Dodge appeals to Stein for direction and help in the matter of a love affair and later offers Stein advice about her relationship with her brother Leo. The letters provide details about Stein's process and progress of writing, her searches for a publisher, and Dodge's informal role as her agent. Dodge offers her enthusiastic support for Stein's writing, and Stein encourages Dodge in her proselytizing efforts. The two women communicate about current art exhibitions, including the Armory Show in New York, the first showing of Futurist art in Paris, and the exhibitions at Alfred Stieglitz's 291 gallery. They frequently mention artists, publications, and who is writing articles about whom. They send each other clippings from magazines and newspapers. And they exchange news of books, such as Frederic W. H. Myers's *Human Personality* (1903) and Henry James's *The Outcry* (1911), and current movements such as psychoanalysis.

The entire correspondence between Mabel Dodge and Gertrude Stein offers its own illustration of the development and later deterioration of their friendship. Dodge's salutation "Miss Stein" gives way to "Gertrude" at the end of 1911, the year they met. In 1912 Dodge has become sufficiently familiar with Stein to plead with her to pay a visit in the fall to her palatial home outside of Florence, the Villa Curonia, and then to beg her to return after she has come and gone—"if you love me you'l come back. I can't do without you. . . . Pleaaaaaaase say yes."[5] At this point, Dodge has engaged Stein as her confidante with regard to her tumultuous affair with her son's twenty-two-year-old tutor. In her letters to Dodge from this time, Stein encourages further communication and inquires specifically about the ends of incomplete stories. During her fall visit, Gertrude Stein wrote "Portrait of Mabel Dodge at the Villa Curonia," an abstract word portrait that generated much publicity about both its author and subject.[6] Dodge believed herself perfectly described in the portrait, as she relates to Stein:

> I consider the "Portrait" to be a masterpiece of success from my (& your) point of view as a portrait of me as I am to others! . . . Some days I don't understand it, but some days I don't understand things in myself, past or about to come! When I tell people that my "precious coherence" is in it they roar never having perceived any in me![7]

In 1913, the year of the Armory Show in New York that provided Americans with their first startling view of the revolutionary art being produced in Europe, the correspondence between Mabel Dodge and Gertrude Stein includes lively discussion of the controversial show, gossip about shared friends and acquaintances, and mutual support and praise. In New York, Dodge was actively drumming up publicity for Gertrude Stein with her article about Stein's writing that was published in *Arts & Decoration*, a magazine sold at the Armory Show.[8] When she received a copy of Mabel Dodge's celebrated article, Stein wrote: "I am delighted and more than delighted. I expected to be pleased and I am really stirred."[9]

At this time, the relationship between Mabel Dodge and Gertrude Stein was as close to mutual as it was ever going to get, with Dodge continuing to be more emotive in her expressions of affection and need for the friendship. When it appeared that Dodge would not be coming over to Europe for the summer because of personal matters, Stein wrote, in an uncharacteristic display of concern: "I am awfully sorry that we are not going to meet this summer. What are the private complications and what is the present state, can you tell me or would you rather wait till we meet. I would like very much to know what is happening to you."[10] During the spring and summer months of 1913, Gertrude Stein was feeling very appreciative of Mabel Dodge for all the exposure she had secured for her in New York in connection with the Armory Show. She wrote to Dodge, "You have made an audience for me alright, its been a real triumph. I can't thank you enough."[11] This was the last expression of grateful or enthusiastic feelings toward Mabel Dodge that Gertrude Stein was to display in her extant letters.

Although Dodge continued to effusively express her admiration for Stein, she began to sense that something was amiss in their friendship. On 8 July 1914, Dodge observed in a letter to Stein, "Did you ever get my long letter from Atlantic City? You never said. Your letters sound very cold & faraway."[12] Dodge's letters to Stein were more often than not met by silence. A rare letter from Stein in 1915 was cold and factual, reading like a telegram. Despite this tone, Mabel Dodge did not give up. And when Stein sent a letter on 2 June 1922 that seemed mocking in its request—"Don't you want to send me a photo of yourself being an Indian"[13]—Dodge still persevered. Then in Taos, New Mexico, Dodge and the Pueblo Indian Antonio Luhan, whom she would marry the following year, were lovers, while Stein and Carl Van Vechten were viciously gossiping about her involvement with Indians.

Mabel Dodge's efforts to get a response out of Gertrude Stein continued to be met with silence. She closed one letter: "With the same affection as ever (in spite of the <u>terrible</u> things you said to Neith [Boyce] & Hutch [Hapgood] about me—that I was a 'sweet woman from the middle west.'"[14] Stein finally responded, albeit rather impersonally, with her final extant communication, a postcard that offered holiday greetings and depicted a group of formally clad hunters with a dead deer at their feet. Finally, in 1934, when Gertrude Stein and Alice B. Toklas were in the United States making their celebrated lecture tour that included stops in New York, Chicago, Detroit, and Pasadena, Mabel Dodge attempted one more reconciliation, writing from Taos: "You must bury the hatchet (if it is a hatchet) & come for a good visit, you & Alice. . . . Maybe you are not mad—anyway you've never answered me for ages!"[15] This appeal did not work, and Dodge's final existing letter ends pleadingly, "We must meet <u>some</u>where!"[16] After Gertrude Stein's visit to the United States, there is no evidence that the two ever had further contact before Stein's death on 27 July 1946. Mabel Dodge was to outlive Stein by almost twenty years, as she died on 18 August 1962, still married to Antonio Luhan, her fourth husband.

In a number of important ways, Mabel Dodge and Gertrude Stein shared similar backgrounds and developed in parallel directions. Although Dodge grew up an only child in a wealthy Buffalo family and Stein was the youngest of five children born to a well-to-do middle class family that eventually settled in Oakland, California, both women were raised with absent and inconsistent fathers. Mabel Dodge remembers feeling "cold as ice" as her father was dying and describes his funeral as "infinitely boring and rather disgusting to me. I had no other feelings."[17] When Gertrude Stein's father died, she reports, "Then our life without a father began a very pleasant one."[18] Both Dodge and Stein, then, seemed to fashion their own lives in reaction against the failed patriarchal authority in their families. Dodge set out to raise herself, and Stein bound herself to her brother Leo, the two of them together resisting the influences of their older siblings and parents.

In their adolescence and early adulthood, both Mabel Dodge and Gertrude Stein had at least one important sexual experience with a woman that each later wrote about. As a seventeen-year-old young woman on her first trip to Europe, Dodge had a spiritually and sensually charged relationship with Violet Shillito, a young woman whom Dodge idealized and endeavored to model herself after. Together they read aloud George Sand, Gustave Flaubert, and Honoré de Balzac. Dodge describes their affair in *Intimate Memories: Background* (1933), her memoirs from that period:

> I reached out my hand and laid it shyly upon her left breast, cupping it with my palm. Instantly it was attuned to a music of the finest vibration. From between her young breast and the sensitive palm of my hand there arose all about us, it seemed, a high, sweet singing. . . . We needed no more than to be in touch like that with each other, just hand and breast, to make our way into a new world together.[19]

This new world included the discovery of an "exquisite and commendable"[20] sensuality. Dodge's further adolescent explorations of sexuality with other girls at boarding school failed to replicate the emotions she had experienced with Violet. "There was no fire there,"[21] Dodge admitted of one of her later encounters.

When she was in her mid-twenties and still at Johns Hopkins half-heartedly pursuing a medical career, Gertrude Stein began attending regular meetings of a group of liberated female graduates of primarily Smith and Bryn Mawr. There she met May Bookstaver and became involved in an intense affair with her. May loved another woman as well. This love triangle was the subject of Stein's autobiographical novel *Q.E.D.*, written in 1903 and put away in a cupboard, reportedly forgotten until 1932. While looking for an unpublished manuscript to show to the historian Bernard Faÿ and the writer Louis Bromfield, Stein discovered this first novel and "was very bashful and hesitant about it, did not really want to read it."[22] It remained unpublished until 1950, four years after her death.

For both Mabel Dodge and Gertrude Stein, sexual expression was an integral part of their identity. However, they approached the business of discussing it with others quite differently. As Christopher Lasch puts it, Mabel Dodge "may be regarded as a pioneer in the cult of the orgasm."[23] (She even had a dog named Climax.)[24] In her memoirs, Dodge frankly reports the details of a number of her sexual experiences while she openly sings the praises of sexual excitation, exalting it to a level far superior to thinking. She recalls her first orgasm during rushed and spontaneous intercourse with her first husband, Karl Evans, in her parents' house:

> I had never heard of that gentle transformation . . . as though the nerves expressed themselves in the manner of silent, fiery fountains falling on black velvet. My body had

burned with high fires but had never penetrated this far, strange other world. No one had ever told me about this definite, so definite and surprising thing. And I had never read of it.[25]

In an account of her medical history, "Doctors: Fifty Years of Experience" (1954), Dodge recalls her first orgasm as having occurred under quite different circumstances. At the time, she was infatuated with her gynecologist, Dr. Parmenter, with whom she would soon have an affair. During lovemaking sessions with Karl Evans, Dodge reports: "I invented a new method for myself. I closed my eyes and pretended it was the doctor I was with. And for the first time since we had been married the strange, unknown miracle occurred in my body. Such sweet sensation permeated me all over, up and down the nerve stems."[26] Dodge makes no further record of such sensual pleasure until her encounter with Antonio Luhan in Taos.

In contrast to Mabel Dodge's memoirs, Gertrude Stein's overtly autobiographical works, such as *The Autobiography of Alice B. Toklas* (1932; 1933) and *Everybody's Autobiography* (1936; 1937), do not contain the particulars of her sexual involvement with either Alice B. Toklas or May Bookstaver. In her poetry and fiction, however, Gertrude Stein displays a talent for the erotic, often thinly disguised, as she celebrates her relationship with Alice B. Toklas. In "Didn't Nelly and Lilly Love You" (1922), Stein relates her marriage proposal to Toklas and refers to them as husband and wife: "I am a husband who is very very good I have a character that covers me like a hood and must be understood which it is by my wife whom I love with all my life . . ."[27] The title of Stein's poem "Lifting Belly" (1915–17) clues the reader into its highly erotic suggestions:

I said it I mean lifting belly.
Don't misunderstand me.
Do you.
Do you lift everybody in that way.
No.
You are to say No.
Lifting belly.
How are you.
Lifting belly how are you lifting belly.
We like a fire and we don't mind if it smokes.

And:

> Lifting belly patiently.
> Can you see me rise.
> Lifting belly says she can.
> Lifting belly soundly.
> Here is a bun for my bunny.
> Every little bun is of honey.[28]

In "A Sonatina Followed by Another" (1921), Stein plays with the same metaphor of honey: "You are my honey honey suckle. / I am your bee."[29]

In her novel *Q.E.D.*, Stein limits herself to descriptions of passionate embraces and kisses to illuminate the sensuality of the central lesbian relationship: one woman "felt herself intensely kissed on the eyes and on the lips" and another kiss "seemed to scale the very walls of chastity."[30] The novel contains daring passages such as the following, in which the main character's moral objections to lesbian sex are implicitly debated: "'You are so afraid of losing your moral sense that you are not willing to take it through anything more dangerous than a mud-puddle'" and "'I don't know on what ground I am objecting, whether it is morality or a meaningless instinct'" and "'she may be interested in seeing how far I will go before my principles get in my way.'"[31] In one of the most forthright passages, the central character offers her willingness to explore her sexuality with another woman: "'I could undertake to be an efficient pupil if it were possible to find an efficient teacher.'"[32]

Mabel Dodge and Gertrude Stein were both salon hostesses who succeeded in creating a lively atmosphere that lent itself to debate, controversy, and the formation of new connections between people. Both enjoyed collecting others around them and gloried in the various combinations that resulted. They loved gossip and sent it back and forth in their letters to each other. Each was intensely involved in the relationships among their groups of friends and acquaintances. From contemporary accounts, it appears that Dodge and Stein had similar styles of presenting themselves at their salons. Mabel Dodge describes Gertrude Stein's presence at the early salons hosted by herself and Leo: "Gertrude used to sit silently in the background and listen like the others. Sometimes she had a little puzzled look in her eyes. I believe by puzzlement and wishfulness she finally arrived at a way of doing something new too."[33] In *The Autobiography of Alice B. Toklas,* Stein describes herself as having "sat peacefully in a chair."[34] In his novel *Peter Whiffle: His Life and Works* (1922), in which Mabel Dodge appears as Edith Dale, Carl Van Vechten recounts her role at her New York salon:

> Sometimes she was not even at home, for the drawing-room was generally occupied from ten in the morning until midnight. Sometimes—very often, indeed—she left her guests without a sign and went to bed. Sometimes—and this happened still oftener—she remained in the room without being present.[35]

Mabel Dodge's silences are legendary. The writer and editor Max Eastman complained that "for the most part she sits like a lump and says nothing. She seems never to have learned the art of social intercourse—a rather dumb and stumpy little girl, you would say, and move on to someone who at least knew how to make conversation."[36] Although Eastman considered Dodge's silences a social handicap, others marveled at the confidences they engendered and the power they bestowed on her, much in the way that Gertrude Stein was empowered by her own silences. Lincoln Steffens remarked that "Mabel Dodge managed her evenings, and no one felt that they were managed. She sat quietly in a great armchair and rarely said a word; her guests did the talking."[37] In Max Eastman's novel, *Venture* (1927), Dodge is the character Mary Kittridge, who is portrayed in the following passage: "The will to be a sphinx in one whose eyes are calf-like / Would describe the ardor of it. / Sit silently and secrete intensity."[38] And Van Vechten further describes Edith Dale: "She sat quietly with her hands folded, like a Madonna who had lived long enough to learn to listen."[39] Muriel Draper remembers Dodge's silences from her visits at the Villa Curonia:

> Mabel did not move. She did not have to. She was everywhere. Mabel did not speak. Words were too slow for her. She went quickly into where you lived and found you there, while you were still in the first throes of verbal communication. She was patient. She would wait for you. If you wanted to catch up another time, you would find her there, sitting.[40]

The English actor Robert de la Condamine inscribed in a book he gave to Dodge: "'To Mabel Dodge, who has the courage to sit still and the wisdom to keep silent.'"[41]

As art collectors, Mabel Dodge and Gertrude Stein were both important early patrons of the new art, with Dodge purchasing works by the American modernists and Stein, together with Leo, buying European art. It was reportedly Leo Stein who was the mastermind behind their early and daring collection of works by Cézanne, Renoir, Picasso and Matisse. Gertrude herself, as Leo tells it, did not initiate a purchase of art until "1911 or 1912 [when] Gertrude bought a cubist Picasso, the first picture for which she was responsible to come to 27 Rue de Fleurus."[42] Gertrude Stein later confesses her lack of discernment in collecting:

> Once an oil painting is painted, painted on a flat surface, painted by anybody who likes or is hired or is interested to paint it, or who has or has not been taught to paint it, I can always look at it and it always holds my attention. The painting may be good it may be bad, medium or very bad or very good but any way I like to look at it.[43]

Mabel Dodge remembers:

> Gertrude didn't care whether a thing was *bon gout* or not, or whether it was quattrocento or not, unless it affected *her* pleasantly, and if it did please her she loved it for that reason. . . . It made her daring in a snobbish period of art. I remember she adored those ridiculous miniature alabaster fountains, with two tiny white doves poised on the brink, that tourists bought at the shops on the Lung'Arno, and she had a penchant for forget-me-not mosaic brooches.[44]

Mabel Dodge, on the other hand, played a very active role in her own art collection. She became involved, albeit quite late in the game, in raising money for the 1913 Armory Show, which exerted an important influence on the development of abstract art in America by exposing artists to the new expression currently gaining force in Europe. She was a regular visitor to Alfred Stieglitz's 291 gallery and thus had direct access to the new trends in art. Dodge collected works of art by several of the artists in her circle, testament to the support she extended to the new art. Among the works she owned was Marsden Hartley's 1913 *Portrait of Berlin* (Collection of the Beinecke Rare Book and Manuscript Library, Yale University). This abstract portrait of a German officer was included in an exhibition of Hartley's Berlin paintings at 291 in January 1914. The catalogue for the show included a foreword by Mabel Dodge, excerpts from Gertrude Stein's play *IIIIIIIII*, in which Hartley is the character "M——N H——," and remarks by the artist, all of which were published in the January 1914 issue of

Camera Work. In 1913, Mabel Dodge purchased two works by Max Weber, which he describes in a letter to her dated 22 January 1913: "The pastel study of the Chinese vase with geranium leaves is $40, and the gouache drawing of the interior with the nudes is $60."[45] In addition, she owned a 1911 painting by Weber entitled *Three Witches* (Collection of the Beinecke Library). She also owned an abstract portrait by Andrew Dasburg entitled *The Absence of Mabel Dodge*, whose current whereabouts are unknown. In *Peter Whiffle*, Van Vechten mentions that Edith Dale displayed paintings by Marsden Hartley and Arthur B. Davies in her apartment.[46]

It may be that these parallels between Dodge's and Stein's interests, passions, friendships, and roles as salon hostesses and art collectors created an atmosphere of competition between the two women that led Stein, probably with the goading of Toklas, to feel threatened by the enormous amount of publicity that Dodge received due to her connection with Stein. Dodge offered this possibility for the dissolution of their friendship in *Movers and Shakers* (1936): "Once I asked Leo why she had changed towards me, and he laughed and said because there was a doubt in her mind about who was the bear and who was leading the bear!"[47] Stein's friendships seemed to work best when she was the only genius and could usually count on being the focus of attention. Although in many ways Dodge behaved in accordance with these unspoken rules, promoting Stein's writing and continually expressing interest, she also came to be a personality in her own right, not just an appendage of Stein's. Dodge generated her own following and had independent reasons for at times being the center of media attention and curiosity. These factors may have been responsible for the beginning change in the relationship between the two women, a shift that seemed to have its origins in Stein's response to Dodge.

During the years 1911–14, when the friendship between Mabel Dodge and Gertrude Stein was at its height, the literary and art worlds in Paris and New York were virtually exploding with innovation and renewed creativity as they shook off their ties to the past. At the turn of the century in Paris, Montparnasse emerged as a vital center where artists, including many Americans who heralded the new modernism, such as Jo Davidson, John Marin, Elie Nadelman and Edward Steichen, lived.[48] The Café du Dôme and Café de la Rotonde provided opportunities for the members of the new avant-garde to meet and exchange their revolutionary ideas. By the fall of 1905, Gertrude and Leo Stein's home at 27 rue de Fleurus was becoming a place where their artist friends Henri Matisse and Pablo Picasso brought visitors to see the paintings on the walls. Inspired by the 1904 Salon d'Automne in Paris, with its display of canvases by painters such as Edgar Degas, Paul Gauguin, Édouard Manet, Pierre-Auguste Renoir, and Vincent van Gogh, Leo Stein had begun his and Gertrude's daring joint collection of modern art in the fall of that year. He purchased works by Cézanne, Gauguin, Matisse, Picasso, and Renoir. Relegating to his study the Japanese prints that had previously decorated the living room, Leo covered the walls, eventually up to the ceiling, with paintings. In 1907, the Steins organized the haphazard visits by artists and friends into regular Saturday evening gatherings; their more intimate artist friends were invited to an early dinner. From nine o'clock in the evening on, others were free to drop by for art viewing, conversation, debate, food and drink, and gossip.[49] Besides Matisse and Picasso, regulars to the salon included the poet Guillaume Apollinaire, the painter Marie Laurencin, the Fauve painter André Derain, the poet Max Jacob, and the Russian patron Sergei Shchukin. A number of American artists who had traveled to Paris to study also became steady attendees at these Saturday evenings, among them Patrick Henry Bruce, Charles Demuth, Marsden Hartley, Maurice Sterne, and Max Weber.[50]

In Paris, art galleries as well as cafés and salons provided crucial meeting grounds for artists, writers, and collectors. With their idiosyncratic personalities, dealers created different atmospheres at their galleries. Ambroise Vollard was secretive and elusive, hiding his collection of Cézanne paintings away until he found someone he wanted to sell them to. Gertrude Stein described her first visit to his gallery on the rue Laffitte:

> It was an incredible place. It did not look like a picture gallery. Inside there were a couple of canvases turned to the wall, in one corner was a small pile of big and little canvases thrown pell mell on top of one another, in the centre of the room stood a huge dark man glooming. This was Vollard cheerful. When he was really cheerless he put his huge frame against the glass door that led to the street, his arms above his head, his hands on each upper corner of the portal and gloomed darkly into the street. Nobody thought then of trying to come in.[51]

Also on the rue Laffitte was the gallery of Clovis Sagot, a former circus clown turned art dealer who showed works by Picasso. It was at Sagot's gallery that Leo Stein purchased their first Picasso, *Young Girl with a Basket of Flowers* (1905), over Gertrude Stein's objections, as she tells it:

> Gertrude Stein did not like the picture, she found some-thing rather appalling in the drawing of the legs and feet, something that repelled and shocked her. She and her brother almost quarrelled about this picture. He wanted it and she did not want it in the house. Sagot gathering a little of the discus-sion said, but that is alright if you do not like the legs and feet it is very easy to guillotine her and only take the head. No that would not do, everybody agreed, and nothing was decided.
> Gertrude Stein and her brother continued to be very divided in this matter and they were very angry with each other. Finally it was agreed that since he, the brother, wanted it so badly they would buy it.[52]

Daniel-Henry Kahnweiler had a gallery on the rue Vignon, where he exhibited the work of the Cubist painters, including Picasso and Braque. As Stein explained: "They all made contracts with him and until the war he did everything for them all. The afternoons with the group coming in and out of his shop were for Kahnweiler really afternoons with Vasari. He believed in them and their future greatness."[53]

In New York, the central meeting place for the avant-garde in art was Alfred Stieglitz's Little Galleries of the Photo-Secession at 291 Fifth Avenue, cofounded in 1905 with the photographer Ed-ward Steichen. When the gallery moved in 1908 to 293 Fifth Av-enue, it changed its name to 291, the name by which it had already been commonly called. Hutchins Hapgood had first taken Mabel Dodge to 291 at the end of 1912. She returned frequently to the gallery, drawn to the atmosphere Stieglitz created and the com-pany he kept:

> It was one of the few places where I went. It was always stimulating to go and listen to him [Stieglitz] analyzing life and pictures and people. . . . I owe him an enormous debt I can never repay. He was another who helped me to See—both in art and in life. His belief was that he never gave in to anything except what he believed to be the best; . . . that he cared only for what he called the spirit of life, and that when he found it,

he fostered it. If, like the rest of us he was in the dark regarding the masks of his colossal egotism, what of it? Only so could he get things done.[54]

It was at 291 that Dodge met both Marsden Hartley and Andrew Dasburg, who were to be her friends for years.

Gertrude Stein and Stieglitz had first corresponded in early 1912 regarding the publication of Stein's word portraits of Matisse and Picasso in Stieglitz's magazine *Camera Work*. These appeared in the Special Number August 1912 issue accompanied by reproductions of paintings and sculptures by both artists. In one of her letters to Stieglitz, Stein emphasizes the importance of careful proofreading of her work: "You will be very careful, will you not, that no punctuation is introduced into the things in printing. It is very necessary as I have put in all of it that I want and any that is introduced will make everything wrong."[55] Stein never visited 291, as she did not make a trip to the United States until 1934. However, she and Stieglitz maintained a connection for several years in their mutual interest in and support of Hartley.

For its supporters, 291 was a sanctuary, a hallowed place of learning, a community that opened its arms. For its detractors, 291 represented a misguided and incomprehensible display of eccentricity, naïveté, and madness in art. The gallery began as an extension of the Photo-Secessionists, a group of photographers, named by Stieglitz in 1902, who were dissatisfied with the lack of recognition traditional art institutions paid to photography as a valid art form. The Photo-Secessionists included Gertrude Käsebier (who took a celebrated photograph of Mabel Dodge on a roof-top that was published in the May 1915 issue of *Vanity Fair*), Steichen, and Clarence H. White and advocated that photography be considered as important a form of art as painting. Early exhibitions at 291 featured the photographic prints of members of the Photo-Secessionists, as well as works by French, British, German, and Austrian photographers.

Stieglitz boasted that 291 drew 167,000 visitors between 1905 and 1912 (an average of 92 people a day).[56] Over the years, the unheated rooms at 291 displayed works by the early American modernists, including Arthur Dove, Marsden Hartley, John Marin, Alfred Maurer, and Max Weber. After visiting 27 rue de Fleurus in 1909, where he saw the Steins' impressive collection of paintings, Stieglitz also championed the cause of the French moderns, devoting exhibitions to Cézanne, Matisse, Picasso, Auguste Rodin, and Henri de Toulouse-Lautrec, among others.[57] At other times, the walls at 291 were hung with the caricatures of Marius de Zayas, the stage designs of Edward Gordon Craig, or art by children.

Stieglitz provided a lively running commentary on the art and was always a dominant presence with his lectures, questions, and parabolic manner of speaking.[58] The painter John Sloan remarked that Stieglitz "talked one ear off. It has grown back pretty well, but I never returned to 291."[59] Stieglitz would not sell art to just any-one; he had to feel convinced of the buyer's commitment and ap-preciation.[60] He offered devoted emotional support and occasional financial advances to the many artists whose work he exhibited. The collection of regulars at the gallery often crowded into 291's back room to warm themselves around the wood stove and to gather for the daily noontime lunch ritual named The Round Table, the meal paid for by Stieglitz. This group included the artists Dove, Hartley, Marin, and Weber, the authors and critics Charles Caffin, Benjamin de Casseres, Sadakichi Hartmann, and J. Nilsen Laurvik, and those involved in promoting and developing the gallery, in-cluding Paul Haviland, Agnes Ernst Meyer, and Marius de Zayas.[61]

An influential and related player in the crusade for modernism was the magazine *Camera Work*, edited by Stieglitz and published from 1903 to 1917. The magazine featured superb reproductions of photographs by the Photo-Secessionists in their new role as art-ists as opposed to illustrators. Paintings, drawings, and sculpture by artists such as Picasso, Matisse, Marin, and Rodin were also reproduced. *Camera Work* published theoretical articles with com-pelling titles: "The Unconscious in Art" by Benjamin de Casseres, "What is the Object of Art" by Henri Bergson, "The Esthetic Sig-nificance of the Motion Picture" by Sadakichi Hartmann. It of-fered quotations from James Whistler, Plato's "Dialogues," and Van Gogh's letters, Gertrude Stein's abstract word portraits of Matisse and Picasso, and Oscar Wilde on "The Artist." *Camera Work* also reprinted articles by art critics about exhibitions held at 291.

In 1914, Stieglitz asked artists, writers, visitors to the gallery, the building's elevator operator, and others to respond to the ques-tion, "What is 291?" He devoted the entire July 1914 issue of *Cam-era Work* to printing in unedited form the many responses he received. Mabel Dodge furnished a poem she wrote called "The Mirror," which is one of the few entries that does not directly address Stieglitz's question. The poem begins:

> I am the mirror wherein man sees man,
> Whenever he looks deep into my eyes
> And looks for me alone, he there descries
> The human plan.

Dodge ends the poem with:

> I am the alternating peace and strife—
> I am the mirror of all man ever is—
> I am the sum of all that has been his—
> For I am life.

Hutchins Hapgood wrote:

> "291" to me is a "Salon," a laboratory, and a refuge—a place
> where people may exchange ideas and feelings, where artists
> can present and try out their experiments. . . . I go there when
> my irritation is intense—as to a cooling oasis. I go there to
> meet a rare human group in which is nourished a strenuous
> love for human expression.

Marsden Hartley replied:

> When I think of what America has been with "291" I am
> thinking how strange it would have been without it. It stands
> unique—by itself. There is nothing anywhere—not in Europe
> even—that is the equivalent of it. . . . It has been and still is a
> kind of many headed creature standing firm for every variety
> of truth and every variety of expression of the same.

The scenic designer Lee Simonson offered: "'291' is a man who
lives through a company, a crowd busy expressing a man; a room
and a shrine; an adventure and a dream; a pageant of critics, proph-
ets and fools; a drama of creators; the lure of yesterday, the men-
ace of tomorrow."[62] Clearly, 291 was broad in its impact and
generous in its support.

Newspapers and magazines energetically and often disparagingly
reported on the controversial exhibitions of modernist art at 291,
generating much free publicity for the gallery. Some reviewers
outdid themselves in finding creative ways to attack the gallery:

> As for the wild, weird things disclosed by Alfred Stieglitz . . .
> well, they represent the turkey trot, the grizzly bear and
> bunny hug of pictorial art. This is no place for the placid,
> home-loving citizen who swears by Bouguereau and the

Barbizon landscapes. . . . Mr. Stieglitz has just put over the Arthur B. Carles show without police interference, and will now defy the elements with Marsden Hartley.

Another wrote: "We are not at all persuaded that Mr. [Max] Weber is on the right road or that humans can ever lay aside their consciousness of pain at the sight of malformed bodies long enough to enjoy his canvases." One writer directly criticized Stieglitz for his vision:

The more the work is strange, crude, awkward, appalling, evidently the more it is in favor with him. The present display [a Max Weber exhibition] marks the high-water mark of eccentricity. If it has any reason to exist, then the eyes of the world in general are wrong, which, by the way, is just what these men insist.

Other reviewers blended an appreciation of the new art with acknowledgment of its initial difficulty: "Mr. [Arthur] Dove . . . is another of the young American artists who have seen a new and strange light, and have come out with something absolutely original and quite incomprehensible." Some critics, however, were unflaggingly laudatory: "Come, all ye, whose souls are famished. A banquet has been prepared for your delectation. . . . If you are alive, whoever you be, go to the great little Photo-Secession Gallery at 291 Fifth Avenue, where the Marsden Hartley masterpieces will be on view."[63]

In addition to her support of the new movements in art heralded by Stieglitz, Mabel Dodge was a pioneer in her early fascination with psychoanalysis. At her home at 23 Fifth Avenue, she held a Psychoanalytic Evening around 1915 at which A. A. Brill, a psychiatrist who had met Sigmund Freud in 1908 and had trained with Carl Jung in Zurich that same year, spoke about Freudian theory. In her memoirs, Dodge reports that several guests walked out in the middle of Brill's talk because "they were so incensed at his assertions about unconscious behavior and its give-aways."[64] The author Lincoln Steffens credits Mabel Dodge with providing some guests at her Evenings with their first glimpse of psychoanalysis:

It was there and thus that some of us first heard of psychoanalysis and the new psychology of Freud and Jung, which . . . introduced us to the idea that the minds of men were distorted by unconscious suppressions, often quite irresponsible and incapable of reasoning or learning. The young writers saw a new opening for their fiction, the practical men a new profession. . . . There were no warmer, quieter, more intensely thoughtful conversations at Mabel Dodge's than those on Freud and his implications.[65]

In 1916, Dodge began analysis with Brill and maintained a frequent correspondence with him until his death in 1944.

Freud's historic lectures at Clark University in September 1909 marked a crucial moment for psychoanalysis in the United States, as they formally introduced his revolutionary theories to an American audience. Freud's ideas about the unconscious, hidden motives driven by primitive or sexual desires, and dreams as conveyors of meaning were of enormous appeal to the avant-garde in the United States, who were in search of the newest trends in thinking and of underlying meanings.[66] Mabel Dodge was an outspoken example of the American intellectual who embraced this new way of thinking to examine her own psyche, as her memoirs and letters are filled with interpretations and analyses of the thoughts, feelings, and behaviors of both herself and others. To those so inclined, Freud offered a way of explaining how hidden motives affected an individual's way of thinking and acting through concepts such as condensation and symbolization as revealed in dreams and slips of the tongue. In condensation, a number of ideas are compressed into one expression, such as in Freud's example of his dream of the botanical monograph: "'Botanical' was related to the figure of Professor *Gärtner* [Gardener], the *blooming* looks of his wife, to my patient *Flora* and to the lady . . . of whom I had told the story of the forgotten *flowers.*"[67] In symbolization, one image or idea in a dream represents another, as in the classic example of a snake standing for a phallus. Mabel Dodge writes about one way she understood these concepts in *Movers and Shakers*, explaining that her first psychoanalyst, Smith Ely Jelliffe, "had taught me the close connection between excrement and gold in the symbolism of the psyche, and I had observed the relationship between our money-making fixation and the great signs advertising all kinds of laxatives that decorated the billboards of our country."[68]

How did Americans learn about this new movement? Its popularization began soon after Freud's Clark lectures, although the fields of medicine and psychology had been generating articles about psychoanalysis from as early as 1895. In the 1895 *Boston Medical and Surgical Journal*, Robert Edes spoke of Freud's theories in laudatory terms in his article "The New England Invalid." Havelock Ellis widely quoted Freud in his *Studies in the Psychology of Sex* (1899) and also referred to Gertrude Stein's experiments with automatic writing while she was a student of William James's at Radcliffe. In 1902, James published *The Varieties of Religious Experience,* in which he discussed the various therapeutic techniques popular at the time, including Freud's "cathartic method." James Jackson Putnam published a paper in 1906 in the *Journal of Abnormal Psychology* that Sanford Gifford asserts "deserves to be called the first analytic paper in English." Its title in full was "Recent Experience in the Study and Treatment of Hysteria at the Massachusetts General Hospital: With Remarks on Freud's Method of Treatment by 'Psychoanalysis.'"[69] In the aftermath of Freud's 1909 visit to the United States, a number of psychoanalytic institutes began to be established. In 1911, Putnam became the president of the American Psychoanalytic Association. In the same year, A. A. Brill founded the New York Psychoanalytic Society.

The first significant popularizations of Freud's ideas were concentrated in the year 1915. A study of the *Reader's Guide* and its listing of articles on Freud and psychoanalysis shows that ten articles appeared in 1915, whereas in each of the previous five years, there had been between one and five. In 1915, Max Eastman published two articles in *Everybody's Magazine:* "Exploring the Soul and Healing the Body" and "Mr. Er-er-er—Oh! What's His Name?" In the same year, *Good Housekeeping* printed "Diagnosis by Dreams," by Peter Clark Macfarlane. Three books on psychoanalysis that were not targeted to scientific readers also came out in 1915: Putnam's *Human Motives,* Edwin B. Holt's *The Freudian Wish,* and Isador H. Coriat's *The Meaning of Dreams.*[70] In Mabel Dodge's role as a biweekly columnist for the Hearst newspaper chain from August 1917 to February 1918 (a job begun at Brill's suggestion that she become a writer for therapeutic reasons), she added to the popularization of psychoanalysis with articles such as "Mabel Dodge Writes About the Unconscious" and "Consuming Energy is Keeping Well." In the latter article, she takes Freud's idea about the toxic effect of pent-up instincts[71] and writes:

> If you do not use your energy it turns bad in you. But when the frozen energy melts and evaporates, when you are turning out every bit of energy that you have, in some form, externalizing it in some way, then you are at your best. At your happiest and healthiest![72]

Many American intellectuals fervently adopted Freud's view of the world and set about analyzing everything about themselves and others. The aim of such activity was often the discovery of a real or authentic self, stripped of dishonest facades and hypocritical stances.[73] The influence of the teachings of psychoanalysis was inescapable in the Greenwich Village of the teens. As the writer Floyd Dell recalls, "Everyone at that time who knew about psychoanalysis was a sort of missionary on the subject, and nobody could be around Greenwich Village without learning a lot about it."[74] On a different note, Hutchins Hapgood describes the climate of often excessive analysis that developed out of enthusiasm for the new psychology:

> Psychoanalysis had been overdone to such an extent that nobody could say anything about a dream, no matter how colorless it was, without his friends' winking at one another and wondering how he could have been so indiscreet. Freud's scientific imagination certainly enriched the field of psychology and was a great moment in our knowledge of the unconscious. But every Tom, Dick, and Harry in those days was misinterpreting and misapplying the general ideas underlying analysis.[75]

Although Hapgood claimed he had no use for his own psychoanalysis, he reported that "Mabel, of course, tried it, as she tried everything."[76] In addition to her extended analysis with Brill, Mabel had undertaken an earlier analysis in 1916 with Smith Ely Jelliffe that lasted about six months.

The Provincetown Players, some of whom were associated with Mabel Dodge (who spent several summers in Provincetown, Massachusetts), incorporated the ideas of psychoanalysis into their plays, often parodying them. George Cram Cook and Susan Glaspell's play *Suppressed Desires* is a satire of the blind faith adoption of basic Freudian principles and shows the trap of rigid application of psychoanalytic mechanisms.[77] In the play, Henrietta, an indefatigable proselytizer of the science of psychoanalysis, counsels her sister Mabel to discover her suppressed desires so that she can act on them, thereby avoiding the possibility of going insane:

> It's like this, Mabel. You want something. You think you think you can't have it. You think it's wrong. So you try to think you don't want it. Your mind protects you—avoids pain—by refusing to think the forbidden thing. But it's there just the

same. It stays there shut up in your unconscious mind, and it festers. . . . It breaks into your consciousness in disguise, masks itself in dreams, makes all sorts of trouble.[78]

However, when Mabel enters therapy with Henrietta's psychoanalyst to uncover the meaning of a dream, the interpretation pronounces that Mabel has suppressed desires for Henrietta's husband. Henrietta then abruptly abandons her previously unbendable belief in the meaning of all utterances and dreams and dismisses the interpretation as stemming from a "coincidence."

The correspondence between Mabel Dodge and Gertrude Stein reveals the intricacies and changing moods of their relationship while providing lively glimpses into the social and cultural climate of the time. Although the existing letters date from 1911 to 1934, the height of their friendship was between 1911 and 1914, during the time of Stein's "Portrait of Mabel Dodge at the Villa Curonia," Dodge's article on Gertrude Stein distributed at the Armory Show, and Dodge's informal role as agent for Stein's writing. Theirs was a friendship that was generally unbalanced in areas of focus and affection, although it met mutual needs. Stein needed someone to admire and promote her without any wavering in commitment. Dodge served well in that role, consistently providing encouragement, readership for Stein's writing, and enthusiastic praise for her genius. Dodge, on the other hand, continually searched for others to help define her identity and to fill in the empty spaces she so painfully experienced in her daily life. In Stein, Dodge found both inspiration and validation, gaining through her celebrated association with the controversial writer a purpose and an increased belief in her own importance. With the dissolution of their friendship, marked by Stein's prolonged silences and cool communication and Dodge's continued efforts to reengage her, Dodge was left hurt and somewhat puzzled. For a time, however, through their friendship and contacts, Dodge and Stein had helped catapult each other to fame and popular recognition.

THE LETTERS

~

1911

Mabel Dodge first met Gertrude Stein in Paris in the early spring of 1911. Like so many others before and after her, Dodge was taken to the apartment at 27 rue de Fleurus, the home of Gertrude Stein and her brother Leo, by a regular attendee of the weekly gatherings. Although Dodge claims in her autobiography that "I forget who took us,"[1] accounts by both Gertrude Stein and her companion Alice B. Toklas identify Mildred Aldrich, an American writer living in Paris, as the one who introduced Mabel Dodge to the Steins.[2]

In *The Autobiography of Alice B. Toklas,* Gertrude Stein describes her initial impression of Dodge on that first Saturday evening meeting: "She was a stoutish woman with a very sturdy fringe of heavy hair over her forehead, heavy long lashes and very pretty eyes and a very old fashioned coquetry. She had a lovely voice. She reminded me of a heroine of my youth, the actress Georgia Cayvan."[3] In *European Experiences,* her memoirs of this period, Mabel Dodge describes Gertrude Stein as "prodigious. Pounds and pounds and pounds piled up on her skeleton—not the billowing kind, but massive, heavy fat. She wore some covering of corduroy or velvet and her crinkly hair was brushed back and twisted up high behind her jolly, intelligent face."[4] Dodge continues, portraying Alice B. Toklas, who had lived with Gertrude Stein since the late summer or early fall of 1910:[5] "She was slight and dark, with beautiful gray eyes hung with black lashes—and she had a drooping, Jewish nose, and her eyelids drooped, and the corners of her red mouth and the lobes of her ears drooped under the black, folded Hebraic hair, weighted down, as they were, with long, heavy Oriental earrings."[6]

Mabel Dodge describes the now-famous and widely illustrated

studio that she saw on her first visit to 27 rue de Fleurus: "A large, rather bare room and a few good chairs and tables and *those pictures* on the walls."[7] That evening she was undoubtedly exposed to the paintings by Picasso and Matisse that hung crowded together with works by Cézanne and others on the walls of the Steins' living room. Picasso's *Gertrude Stein* (1906) occupied an important place on one wall. Other paintings in the Stein collection that Dodge would likely have seen on her first visit were Picasso's *Young Girl with a Basket of Flowers* (1905) and *Young Acrobat on a Ball* (1905), as well as Matisse's *Music* (1908). Leo Stein, an artist and enthusiastic scholar of many disciplines, including aesthetics, philosophy, and history, was a serious and intense presence at these evenings, as he often stood and lectured on the new developments in art with, as Mabel Dodge observed, "an obstinate look on his face that so strongly resembled an old ram."[8] Dodge explains Leo's role at the weekly gatherings:

> In those early days when everyone laughed, and went to the Steins' for the fun of it, and half angrily, half jestingly giggled and scoffed after they left (not knowing that all the same they were changed by seeing those pictures), Leo stood patiently night after night wrestling with the inertia of his guests, expounding, teaching, interpreting, always the advocate of tension in art![9]

The first extant letter from Mabel Dodge to Gertrude Stein seems to follow an early visit to 27 rue de Fleurus in the spring of 1911. Dodge planned to spend the rest of the spring and summer near Florence at the Villa Curonia, her palatial residence in Arcetri, with her husband Edwin and son John. Gertrude Stein intended to rent a house in Fiesole that summer, the Casa Ricci, with Leo and Alice.✲

[Whitman motto]*

[CIRCA EARLY SPRING 1911] [PARIS]

Dear Miss Stein—

I want to thank you again for your charming kindness to us in letting us come & pass an evening with you & the pictures. Don't forget us when you come to Florence.

Very sincerely yours—
Mabel Dodge

⌒Mabel Dodge arranged to have lunch with Gertrude Stein in Paris before leaving for Nice on her way to Italy for the summer. Dodge's stepfather, Admiral Reeder, had recently died and she was traveling to visit her mother in Nice. Charlotte Becker, an American poet, illustrator, and playwright who was later to become book reviewer for the *Buffalo Evening News,* was staying with Dodge in Paris before accompanying her to Italy.[10]⌒

TUESDAY [CIRCA APRIL 1911] HÔTEL ASTORIA
AVENUE DES CHAMPS-ÉLYSÉES
PARIS

My dear Miss Stein—

Thursday will do just as well, so meet me at Lavenue's† at half after twelve—I have with me a friend whose verse is rather well known in America, Charlotte Becker, & I should so like you to know each other.

Most cordially yours
Mabel Dodge

I am leaving Thursday night for Nice.

*One of Mabel Dodge's styles of stationery contained her monogram "MD" surrounded by a circle containing a quotation from Walt Whitman's "Song of Myself": "Do I contradict myself? Very well, then, I contradict myself" (Walt Whitman, *Leaves of Grass,* 34).

†According to the 1913 Baedeker guide to Paris, Lavenue's was a "1st class" restaurant in the Hotel Lavenue on the Rue du Départ in Montparnasse. In *European Experiences,* Dodge identified Lavenue's as one of her favorite restaurants (400).

〜By the time she left Paris for Florence, Mabel Dodge had established a close connection with Gertrude Stein, despite Alice B. Toklas's increasing importance and presence in Stein's life that was later to crowd out many friendships. As Dodge recalls in *European Experiences:*

> Alice was making herself indispensable. She did everything to save Gertrude a movement—all the housekeeping, the typing, seeing people who called, and getting rid of the undesirables, answering letters—really providing all the motor force of the menage. . . . And Gertrude was growing helpless and foolish from it and less and less inclined to do anything herself, Leo said; he had seen trees strangled by vines in this same way.
>
> Gertrude was still able, however, to form attachments and she and I had taken to each other in Paris.[11]

At this time, Stein entrusted Dodge with her manuscript of *The Making of Americans,* a lengthy prose work that was initially designed as a psychological exploration of one family and "had changed from being a history of a family to being a history of everybody the family knew and then it became the history of every kind and of every individual human being."[12] In her memoirs, Dodge recalls transporting the thick manuscript:

> When I left Paris to go back to Florence I had her manuscript of "The History of a Family," pounds and pounds of it, and in the station I dropped it getting on the train, and all the pages flew in every direction with everybody stooping on the platform and under the wheels to recover the white leaves![13]

Stein had started work on this novel in 1903 and completed it in October 1911.[14] In its final 925-page form, *The Making of Americans: Being the History of a Family's Progress,* published in 1925 by Robert McAlmon in Paris, describes the individuals in two families, the Dehnings from Maryland and the Hershlands from California, both of which have their roots in branches of Stein's own family. Gertrude Stein considered this novel to be her most significant achievement, an opinion Mabel Dodge certainly shared. Dodge was one of the earliest readers to recognize in Stein a particular kind of genius.〜

[CIRCA APRIL 1911] VILLA CURONIA

Dear Miss Stein—

You must have been expecting to hear from me because you have been so much in my mind of late. When I left you in Paris I had to go & cheer up my mother in Nice after the death of my stepfather Admiral Reeder—then in arriving here I was ill with neuralgia & toothache, so that only these last days have I been able to plunge into your MSS. To me it is one of the most remarkable things I have ever read. There are things hammered out of consciousness into black & white that have never been expressed before—so far as I know. States of being put into words the "noumenon"* captured—as few have done it. To name a thing is practically to create it & this is what your work is—real creation. It is almost frightening to come up against reality in language in this way. I always get—as I told you—the shivers when I read your things. And your palete is such a simple one—the primary colors in word painting & you express every shade known & unknown with them. It is as new & strange & big as the post-impressionists in their way &, I am perfectly convinced, it is the forerunner of a whole epoch of new form & expression. It is very morally constructive for I feel it will alter reality as we have known it—& help us to get at Truth instead [of] away from it as "literature" so sadly often does.

One cannot read you & still go on cherishing the consistent illusions one has built up about oneself & others..—

Well—anyway—all that I may say of it is inadequate. I feel awfully strongly about it. I've not yet quite finished it. May I keep it a few days & then send it? I will be so glad to see you when you come. Let me know when you are here. Bring some more of it with you—will you?

> Always sincerely yours—with the greatest admiration.—
>
> *Mabel Dodge*

---

*According to *Webster's Dictionary,* "An object or concept which according to Kant can be known to exist but cannot be experienced and to which no properties can be intelligibly ascribed."

[POSTMARK: 27 APRIL 1911] [FLORENCE]

[TO MISS STEIN]

PLEASE BE SURE AND BRING THE SECOND INSTALLMENT OF YOUR
BOOK WITH YOU

MABEL DODGE

~Gertrude Stein arrived in Florence to rent the Casa Ricci in
Fiesole for the summer with Leo Stein and Alice B. Toklas. Since
April, Mabel Dodge had been living at the Villa Curonia outside
Florence, a house built by the Medici family in the fifteenth cen-
tury as a residence for one of its physicians.[15] When Mabel and
Edwin Dodge purchased the villa around 1903, they retained the
name the previous owners, who were Russian, had given it: the
Villa Curonia, using the Italian word for the Russian province of
Kurland, where their family originated.[16] The villa was reached by
a long and steep driveway that switched direction quickly in the
middle. Situated on top of a hill with views in every direction of
the surrounding hills and the city of Florence, the house had a
commanding presence. Brunelleschi's dome, the Arno River, the
Apennines, San Miniato—all were visible. Built during the Italian
Renaissance, the plaster exterior of the villa was embellished spar-
ingly with rows of arches, simple Tuscan order columns, embrasured
windows, and terra cotta urns at the corners of the curving roof.
Mabel Dodge had searched hard for the right home, where her
vision of herself could materialize:

> I knew quite well the kind of queen I wanted to be and the type
> of royal residence in which I would immolate myself. It must
> be very spacious, with the nobility and the dignity of ample
> spaces, but it must also have the poetic and tender charms of
> unexpected corners and adaptations to small, shy moods,
> twilight moods. It would allow one to be both majestic and
> careless, spontaneous and picturesque, and yet always framed
> and supported by a secure and beautiful authenticity of
> background.[17]

Mabel and Edwin Dodge set about reconstructing the villa in an
extremely ambitious and expensive manner, using Edwin's own
money and funds from Mabel's mother (between forty and fifty

thousand dollars, Mabel reports[18]). Edwin was trained as an architect, having recently graduated from the École des Beaux Arts in Paris, and thus was director of the renovations.[19] Mabel was in charge of the interior furnishings. As she put it, "He was to make the shell; I to line it."[20] She employs this same metaphor in a strikingly different state of mind when she describes her sense of feeling trapped by the villa at the end of the long period of its renovation: "Some part of me leaped—pressing against the barriers, yearning outwards towards the world, crying 'Let's go!' but another part sank deeper into feathers . . . decreeing I should stay in my beautiful shell. So to protect and comfort ourselves do we build our prisons."[21]

During the years of restoration and landscaping, windows were enlarged, large cypresses were transplanted along the border of the driveway, massive iron-studded wooden doors were installed at the entrance, jasmine and gardenias were planted, a ninety-foot music room was added with a loggia overlooking a formal garden, and an imposing statue of Atlas with the world on his shoulders was hauled up to mark the point of the driveway where it abruptly turned. Perhaps the most exciting point in the renovation process was when Edwin discovered underneath the plaster of the plain entrance hall a magnificent two-storied courtyard in the style of Brunelleschi, with Corinthian capitals on the columns and pleasing proportions. The Dodges added a glass roof over the entrance court and from the stone columns hung colorful banners from the Palio in Siena.[22]

Inside the villa, Mabel Dodge threw herself with endless energy into creating rooms with wildly different moods. Her longtime close friend Carl Van Vechten describes the breathless quality of this process in his novel *Peter Whiffle*, in which Edith Dale is based on Mabel Dodge:

> Then, with her superlatively excellent taste at her elbow, Edith rushed about Italy in her motor, ravishing prie-Dieu, old pictures, fans, china dogs, tapestries, majolica, and Capo di Monte porcelains, carved and gilded renaissance boxes, fantastic Venetian glass girandoles, refectory tables, divans, and divers bibelots, until the villa became a perfect expression of her mood.[23]

In *European Experiences*, Mabel Dodge takes the reader on a richly detailed tour of the villa, chronicling her completed designs for and responses to each room. The entrance court was "cold . . . and somber" with its stone staircase, non-functional stone fireplace, and minimal decoration. Dodge explains:

> I always had to hurry through spaces like these, though I created them with some feeling for the need of places to be other than merely encouraging, gay, distracting, or a consolation to the heart, and I have sometimes made spots in environments that were knife-thrusts to myself, yet had their true, authentic life and seemed to exist by themselves.[24]

The North Salon was "as aloof as it is possible to make a room in a dwelling house,"[25] with its vaulted ceiling, absence of direct sunlight, and a decorative wooden door frame, carved and painted, that was removed from its former context and hung with embroidered fabric. Dodge observes: "This door was a very fair symbol of myself at that time, for it led nowhere."[26] The music room, referred to as the *Gran' Salone* by the servants, was "warm and sumptuous and. . . . reassuring and bolstered one up."[27] This long, generous room with tall French windows and golden red damask covering its walls was filled with rich fabrics and tapestries, tall oil lamps, carved wooden figures including one of Buddha, and the smell of flowers from the formal gardens. A piano, mentioned only in passing, occupied the space near an imposing, and functional, fourteenth-century stone fireplace. When the art historian Bernard Berenson visited the *Gran' Salone*, he responded, "'Ah! No one can build rooms like this any more!'"[28] Mabel Dodge's essential experience of this room was as being "so embracing, and so alive like a womb."[29] In direct contrast to the *Gran' Salone*, the library was a place where "no one ever lingered."[30] It was dominated by a "stodgy" bookshelf filled with drably colored bound sets of books by famous authors. The formal dining room was Renaissance in theme, appointed with heavy furniture and fabrics of deep purple red colors.

The Yellow Salon was Mabel Dodge's sitting room and "the most comfortable, the most intimate room in the villa. It had a cheerful, smiling, reassuring air; and it was always crowded with fantastic, feminine oddments."[31] She decorated this room in pale French eighteenth-century fashion and filled it with her collections of ivory skulls and dogs, more temporary collections of found objects from excursions, and her favorite books, never too serious, including the latest Henry James. It was in this Yellow Salon that Dodge wrote most of her letters—the others were written lying in bed following breakfast. She describes her individualized, whimsical stationery: "Thick, white paper with a violet monogram inside a silver circle around which Whitman's words pursued each other: 'Do I contradict myself? Very well, then, I contradict myself.'"[32] These lines from Walt Whitman's "Song of Myself" (1855) are followed by another line that Dodge left out of her motto but that could be read as applying aptly to her expansive embracing of others and her ambition to take them into her own life to fill up her emptiness: "(I am large, I contain multitudes.)"[33]

Mabel Dodge's bedroom "drew one into a soft medieval hush"[34] with its gold vaulted ceiling studded with blue stars, and its massive green and gold bed attended on all four posts by carved lion heads and covered in midnight blue brocade. The room included a fanciful touch—a silk ladder coming from a trap door in the ceiling, intended for impulsive romantic visits from Edwin, whose room was directly above. "But," Mabel bemoans, "Edwin never hastened down it except once to see if it would work, and it did, perfectly."[35] Above the center windows of the bay was a bas-relief that Edwin had commissioned for Mabel in Paris. It depicted a man and a woman together with lines from a poem by Robert Browning that Mabel particularly liked:

> Oh, world as God has made it, all is beauty!
> And knowing this is love and love is duty;
> What further may be sought for
> Or declared?[36]

Mabel was later offended upon discovering that the bas-relief cleverly disguised the woman's hand holding the man's penis.

It was in her bedroom that Mabel Dodge dressed each morning, trying on dozens of outfits until satisfied with the look she had created. A gold cupboard contained her lingerie, collars, and hats. Behind blue curtains hung white silk dresses, Renaissance brocaded coats, velvet outfits, Parisian finery, and apparel for teas. This room was a source of deep regret for Mabel, as her expectations for how she would experience its mood were never met:

> But why can I never dwell in secret here in the blue and golden dream? . . . I can never, never tarry here in lazy contemplation. . . . I fancied myself hours on end in that room, alone, at rest. Free to sink into it and gather up the life of it. But never. Never, any more than Edwin hastened down the silken ladder, did I linger and look and listen and flow into it

all. Driven out. Always driven away, my heart seemed to beat me out from the place that it could not open to enjoy.[37]

Although she labeled it "one of the most attractive rooms in the house,"[38] Dodge reportedly entered the kitchen only once. Furnished in New England colonial style and hung with copper pots and blue and white dishes, this kitchen generated the lavish meals for the hundreds of visitors that the Dodges entertained during their years in Florence. When the weather turned warm enough to eat outside, meals were served on the loggia off the *Gran' Salone*—breakfast at a small table under the rose-covered arbor (female guests had their breakfast trays in bed), dinner at a long table covered with flowers, bottles of wine, and individual loaves of bread. Among those who came to enjoy the generous surroundings and feasts were Carl Van Vechten, the pianist Arthur Rubinstein, the novelist André Gide, the actress Eleanora Duse, and the artists Jacques-Émile Blanche and Janet Scudder. Mabel Dodge remembers:

> Sometimes Gertrude Stein is there, spreading through the openings in her chair, and always seeming to be dressed in brown corduroy; and Alice is with her. And other times Leo is there, the moon shining on his bald spot and he chewing absently with a swift rotating motion like a goat's, as he peers down the table seeing nothing but his own thoughts.[39]

At the beginning of their friendship, Mabel Dodge extended a rapid series of invitations to Gertrude Stein for lunch at the Villa Curonia, first to Gertrude and Leo, then to Gertrude and Alice.

[Postcard: Villa Curonia, Arcetri]

[POSTMARK: FIRENZE, 6 JULY 1911]

Dear Miss Stein

I am so glad to hear from Mrs. [Lucy] Perkins* that you & Mr. [Leo] Stein will come to lunch—could you come on Thursday at one? How you must dislike this cold weather in July. Hoping surely to see you.

Very sincerely yours,
Mabel Dodge

*Lucy Perkins, Bernard Berenson's secretary from 1909 to 1910 who then became an art dealer. I am grateful to Leon Katz for information on Lucy Perkins's identity.

Dear Miss Stein—

I am so sorry you got my card so late! I sent it on Monday! I meant last Thursday but it doesn't matter. Can't you both come on Monday or Tuesday instead? Let me know which day you prefer. The tram from the Duomo to the Viale dei Colli & Via San Leonardo leaves you with a ten minutes climb up to us. You see our facade from the Via San Leonardo something like this [drawing of curved façade appears here in original letter]—tho' not much! Hoping surely to see you.

I am very sincerely yours

Mabel Dodge

I'm leaving on Thursday.

[Villa Curonia stationery with address part torn off]

Dear Miss Stein—

I have decided to go up to Paris with friends on Wed. instead of Sunday—so can't you & your friend* come & lunch tomorrow instead of Thursday? I would like to see you so much before I go— tho' I will only be gone ten days. Do come if you can. I could send the motor to Giacosa's† to meet you at 12.30. Telephone me yes or no—If you can't I'll look you up as soon as I come back.

Ever yours sincerely—

Mabel Dodge

*Alice B. Toklas.

†Giacosa's was a popular café and bar on via Tornabuoni in Florence where in the 1920s Count Negroni invented a drink called the Negroni, a mixture of campari, vermouth, and gin. The café still exists and still serves Negronis.

～Mabel Dodge recalls that on occasion both Gertrude and Leo Stein walked down the hill from Fiesole into Florence and then up another hill to the Villa Curonia, a distance of approximately five miles by foot. Dodge describes Gertrude Stein's impressive appearance after such a journey:

> She used to wear a sort of kimono made of brown corduroy in the hot Tuscan summertime, and arrive just sweating, her face parboiled. And when she sat down, fanning herself with her broad-brimmed hat with its wilted, dark brown ribbon, she exhaled a vivid steam all around her. When she got up she frankly used to pull her clothes off from where they stuck to her great legs. Yet with all this she was not at all repulsive. On the contrary, she was positively, richly attractive in her grand *ampleur.* She always seemed to like her own fat anyway and that usually helps other people to accept it. She had none of the funny embarrassment Anglo-Saxons have about flesh. She gloried in hers.[40]

The pattern of Mabel Dodge's invitations—first to Gertrude and Leo, then to Gertrude and Alice—parallels the beginning of the deterioration of the relationship between the two siblings whose lives had been so closely connected for years. Most accounts credit the introduction of Alice B. Toklas into the household as the reason for the rift. Mabel Dodge observes: "Alice . . . began by being so self-obliterating that no one considered her very much beyond thinking her a silent, picturesque object in the background, but lo and behold, she pushed Leo out quite soon—no one knew how exactly . . ."[41]

After she returned from her trip to Paris, Mabel Dodge invited Gertrude Stein and Alice B. Toklas to the Villa Curonia for lunch, first by themselves and next to meet Julia Constance Fletcher, the American-born author of plays and novels, most notably *Kismet* (1878), who used the pseudonym George Fleming and lived most of her life in Venice. It could have been at lunch or over the telephone that Dodge asked Alice B. Toklas to meet Constance Fletcher's train, as Toklas recalls: "You will know her, said Mabel, because she is deaf and will be wearing a purple robe. When I got to the railroad station Miss Fletcher came up to me. She was wearing not a purple robe but a bright green one, she was not deaf but nearly blind and peered through her lorgnons."[42] This would not be the only time that Dodge would ask Toklas to run an errand for her, as later letters indicate. Dodge had also asked Gertrude Stein to bring along some of her recent work to read, which likely included a number of her word portraits of friends and acquaintances. In these usually short pieces, Gertrude Stein described individuals and groups of people, initially more narratively with the repeating sentences she used in *The Making of Americans*, and later more abstractly and imagistically as her style increasingly reflected the current Cubist tendencies in art.[43] In "Portraits and Repetition," a lecture she gave on her trip to the United States in 1934–35, Gertrude Stein explained, in her characteristic way, the driving force behind her experiments in portraiture:

> I had to find out what was inside any one, and by any one I mean every one I had to find out inside every one what was in them that was intrinsically exciting and I had to find out not by what they said not by what they did not by how much or how little they resembled any other one but I had to find it out by the intensity of movement that there was inside in any one of them.[44]

∼

[CIRCA JULY 1911] VILLA CURONIA
VIA DELLE PIAZZOLE
ARCETRI

Dear Miss Stein—

Will you both come over here & lunch on Friday? I could meet you at French Lemon's* at 12.30 in the motor. I nearly stopped to see you last night after dining at Castit di Paggio† but decided that it was too late & you'd probably all be in bed. I have been back some days from Paris but "all mixed up" over several occurences. Now I am longing to hear those short things of yours. Could you bring some along?

Miss [Constance] Fletcher is coming here next week. She will insist upon seeing you as soon as she arrives! To her you are a prophetess!

---

* Banca French-Lemon was a bank in Florence where Mabel and Edwin Dodge had their accounts.
† Unidentified restaurant.

Telephone me yes or no about Friday—you & Miss Taclos [i.e., Toklas].*

Sincerely yrs—

Mabel Dodge

———

[CIRCA JULY 1911] VILLA CURONIA
VIA DELLE PIAZZOLE
ARCETRI

Dear Miss Stein,

Won't you come & lunch—you & your friend†—on Friday? I will send the motor to meet you at the French Lemon Bank. We go away on Sunday motoring in the Abruzzi‡ for a week—& we want to see you before we go. Miss [Constance] Fletcher is here & is longing to hear some of your new short things so please bring some and read them to us. I do hope you can come.

Ever yrs—

Mabel Dodge

⌇After the lunch with Constance Fletcher, Mabel Dodge sent Gertrude Stein an enthusiastic letter of admiration in which she expressed her continued support of Stein's writing. Dodge remembers her earlier response to *The Making of Americans* and anticipates being jolted again by Stein's next book, which may refer to one of the following three works collected in *Matisse Picasso and Gertrude Stein with Two Shorter Stories* (1909–12; 1933): "G.M.P."

---

*As Edward Burns explains, many who corresponded with Gertrude Stein had difficulty with the correct spelling of Alice B. Toklas's name. Carl Van Vechten spelled it "Taklos" and others attempted with "Toklus" or "Tocklass." Burns quotes Henry McBride's way of dealing with this dilemma in a 1913 letter to Stein: "and kindest regards to your charming friend whose name I can't spell" (Edward Burns, ed., *The Letters of Gertrude Stein and Carl Van Vechten, 1913–1946*, 21 [hereafter cited as *GS/ CVV*]; Donald Gallup, ed., *The Flowers of Friendship: Letters Written to Gertrude Stein*, 83 [hereafter cited as *FF*]).

†Alice B. Toklas.

‡A region in central Italy that borders on the Adriatic coast and contains the highest mountains in the Apennine range.

["Matisse Picasso and Gertrude Stein"]; "A Long Gay Book"; and "Many Many Women." These works are considered transitional ones from Stein's focus on psychological analysis of character in both *The Making of Americans* and the word portraits toward the more humorous and playful use of language that began with *Tender Buttons* (1912; 1914).[45] ∼

[CIRCA JULY 1911] VILLA CURONIA
VIA DELLE PIAZZOLE
ARCETRI

Dear Miss Stein—

I want to send a few words to tell you how much you were appreciated the other day. <u>Why</u> are there not more <u>real</u> people like you in the world? Or are there & one doesn't attract them? Miss [Constance] Fletcher & I both felt as though we had been drinking champagne all the afternoon & what with that & all the cigarettes I smoked while we were talking I had a frightful reaction afterwords. You said so many significant things that everything everyone else said sounded trivial & insincere! I am <u>so</u> sorry that I am going away so that we can't have more talks together, but please don't forget me & let me see you sometimes in Paris.

I am <u>longing</u> for your book to get born! It will probably be a moral earthquake to me, as the other was quite a shock.

I hope you'l have a nice summer—

Sincerely yours,

Mabel Dodge

∼It seems that the appreciation was mutual with respect to influence, as both Mabel Dodge and Constance Fletcher later appeared as subjects of Gertrude Stein's word portraits. "Portrait of Mabel Dodge at the Villa Curonia" was written in 1912 and published in *Portraits and Prayers* (1909–31; 1934). "Portrait of Constance Fletcher" was written around the same time and appeared in *Geography and Plays* (1908–20; 1922).

Upon returning home from her trip to the Abruzzi, Mabel Dodge renewed her contact with Gertrude and Leo Stein and Alice B. Toklas and planned an excursion with them. Her travels seemed to have stimulated an interest in hearing Leo's aesthetic theories, ideas that he later collected in *The ABC of Aesthetics* (1927).⌁

[CIRCA JULY 1911] VILLA CURONIA
VIA DELLE PIAZZOLE
ARCETRI

Dear Miss Stein—

We are back! And <u>all</u> the colour of the Piot [?]* frescoes! He might have done us!

We will come to tea on Thursday—D.V.† at about 5.30 or six so don't wait tea for us!

We want a talk with your brother about aesthetics (!) So I hope he will be there. Miss [Constance] Fletcher is dying to ask him some questions.

Goodby—Greetings to you all—

Mabel Dodge

[Whitman motto]

[CIRCA JULY 1911] [ARCETRI]

Dear Miss Stein

I am <u>so</u> disappointed!! Last night Miss [Constance] Fletcher fell down & strained her foot & this morning she can't put it to the ground! And we can't go because I don't like to leave her alone in the house! And three cold chickens staring me in the face! I hope it won't upset <u>yr</u> domestic arrangements & that you'l all go instead on Tuesday. Will you? Because I don't want to miss this—I think

---

* It is likely that Mabel Dodge is referring to Piero della Francesca, a fifteenth-century Italian Renaissance painter, who is often called simply "Piero." Mabel Dodge was not always an accurate speller, particularly with proper names. On her trip south-east to the Abruzzi, she would most likely have passed through Umbria and may have stopped in Sansepolcro, Piero's birthplace, or Arezzo to see his famous frescoes.

† Deo volente, or God willing.

we'd have a lovely time. If I <u>don't hear</u> to the contrary we'l call on Tuesday at 10. I'm so-o-o-o-o- disappointed about today & so is she.

Goodby—yrs
Mabel D.

———

[CIRCA JULY 1911] VILLA CURONIA
VIA DELLE PIAZZOLE
ARCETRI

Dear Miss Stein

We are calling for you at 2, o'clock tomorrow after lunch if it doesn't rain. I do hope no mistake will occurr.

Mabel Dodge

———

[Italian Telegram]

[POSTMARK: 1 AUGUST 1911] [ARCETRI]

JUST LEARNED MOTOR IS BROKEN TOO! BUT IF MENDED AFTER LUNCH WILL CALL FOR YOU ALL TO TAKE A GIRO* IF NO RAIN.

MABEL

∽Other plans included visiting Florence Blood, an American philanthropist who was a friend of Gertrude Stein's and lived in the Villa Gamberaia in Settignano, a village on a hill above Florence. During World War I, Blood founded and directed a hospital for soldiers.∽

———

* Drive or tour.

41

Dear Miss Stein

I'm so sorry but a note from Miss [Florence] Blood says she's laid up & can't have us tomorrow so we won't be able to go tomorrow.

Affectionate greetings,

Mabel Dodge

———

[Note scribbled in pencil on scrap of torn paper]

[CIRCA AUGUST 1911] [FIESOLE]

Dear Miss Stein—

We are just passing in the motor—I am coming to see you this P.M.—earlyish unless you telephone me to the contrary—Forgive paper & pencil!

In haste—

Mabel Dodge

⮑Gertrude Stein's *Three Lives*, written in 1905–6, had finally been published, at Stein's own expense, by Grafton Press in New York in the summer of 1909. These three stories are psychological portraits of two German female servants, "The Good Anna" and "The Gentle Lena," and a black woman, "Melanctha." Most daring in content and form is Stein's "Melanctha," the story of a love affair between a black woman and a black physician that also contains suggestions of a lesbian relationship between Melanctha and another woman. In "A Transatlantic Interview" (1946), Gertrude Stein later explained the influences on her writing of *Three Lives:*

> Everything I have done has been influenced by Flaubert and Cézanne, and this gave me a new feeling about composition. Up to that time composition had consisted of a central idea, to which everything else was an accompaniment and separate but was not an end in itself, and Cézanne conceived the idea that in composition one thing was as important as another thing. Each part is as important as the whole, and that impressed me

enormously, and it impressed me so much that I began to write *Three Lives* under this influence . . . I was obsessed by this idea of composition, and the Negro story was a quintessence of it.[46]

Gertrude Stein very much wanted *Three Lives* to be published in England and in 1909 began sending copies to English friends and publishers, without success.

In 1911, Gertrude Stein continued to contact publishers in England and apparently asked Mabel Dodge about the *English Review*, a journal founded in 1908 by authors such as Joseph Conrad, Ford Madox Ford, and H. G. Wells and dedicated to, in Ford's words, "giving imaginative literature a chance in England."[47] The portrait Dodge refers to in the following letter may be one of several that the French painter Jacques-Émile Blanche was commissioned by her to do in the spring and summer of 1911. At least two of these paintings depict Dodge as a Renaissance woman, with voluminous gowns and period turbans.~

[circa August 1911] Villa Curonia
Via delle Piazzole
Arcetri

Dear Miss Stein—

That address is "English Review"
11 Henrietta Street
Covent Garden
London
Expect us at about 10 on Sunday morning. So glad I don't have to hang myself over that portrait!

Ever yrs—

Mabel Dodge

~Letters from August 1911 between the *English Review* and Gertrude Stein indicate that Stein sent three works to the journal for consideration: "studies of Henri Matisse, of Pablo Picasso[,] of someone's reaction to the new art movement."[48] The *English Review* responded courteously: "I return herewith your articles on Picasso, Matisse and 'You and Me,' as I cannot find an opportunity of using them."[49]

In the early fall of 1911, Mabel Dodge traveled to Maloja, a city in the Engadine area of Switzerland near the Italian border. The following letter from Dodge to Stein, written the day before she left on her trip, contains the first of a number of references to "Zuleika," or "Zulicka" as the name is spelled in later letters. This appellation appears to be a nickname for Alice B. Toklas that was used by Mabel Dodge. Its placement in the letters is where Dodge would naturally tend to refer to Toklas, and a closing passage in an October 1912 letter makes an association between "Zulicka" and polishing nails. Dodge remarked in her memoirs on what she believed to be the central importance for Alice B. Toklas of her manicured nails: "I couldn't understand Alice. Her life seemed to me so featureless. Gertrude had her writing and I had my struggle with my body and its continual 'Sturm und Drang'; it was my tension. But Alice seemed to me to have only her polished, painted nails."[50] Dodge again describes what she sees as Toklas's exclusive focus, outside of Stein: "She was forever manicuring her nails. Her hands were small and fine and with the almond-shaped, painted, glistening nails they looked like the hands of a courtesan. Every morning, for an hour, Alice polished her nails—they had become a fetish with her. She loved her hands."[51]

The origin of this apparent nickname for Alice B. Toklas is not clear, although there are four possible sources. The name could refer to Johann Wolfgang von Goethe's poem "Book of Zuleika" from *West-eastern Divan* (1819). Or, in the Muslim tradition, Zuleika was the name of the wife of Potiphar, an important official of the Pharaoh's. Zuleika was also the name of the heroine of Lord Byron's *The Bride of Abydos* (1813). The most likely source given its date of publication is Max Beerbohm's 1911 novel, *Zuleika Dobson*, but a reading of the book does not reveal any striking similarities between its central character, Zuleika, and Alice B. Toklas. It seems very likely that the story behind this apparent nickname for Toklas may remain a mystery, as do the elusive origins of many such appellations that often arise out of a chance association or encounter.~

Dear Miss Stein—

I am off tomorrow to the Maloja to join my family & I am sending you back yr books—I have been very upset about a sick baby—of a friend of mine*—that's why you haven't heard from me lately.—I will see you all in Paris rather soon—I think. Greetings to Zuleika! And affectionate rememberances to yourself.

Ever yrs—

Mabel Dodge

⮑While in Maloja, Mabel Dodge wrote to Gertrude Stein to recount a chance meeting in St. Moritz between Bernard Berenson, or B. B. as he was often called, and the art critic and collector Charles Loeser. This encounter had all the makings for an explosion, as Berenson had hired Loeser years before to landscape the gardens at his villa I Tatti in Settignano outside of Florence and the two men had argued vehemently over the final result. In her memoirs, Mabel Dodge identifies Berenson as Loeser's "bitter enemy" and describes Loeser's treatment of the garden: "He 'did over' the garden of I Tatti and killed it—having in the place of its poetic, irregular intimacy nothing but a graveyard. Somebody should restrain these art critics."[52] In an August 1912 letter to Gertrude, Leo Stein reports on visiting the garden at I Tatti: "Today Miss Blood took me to see the Berensons' garden. She takes a wicked delight in showing it to people, and it certainly is the most vulgar beastly horror that can be imagined. Everything's bad in design and carried out with an utter lack of taste & sensitiveness."[53] ⮐

Dear Miss Stein—

I suppose you are back again in Paris & hard at work—are you? I cannot resist sending you a "line" to tell you of the remarkable

---

* Unidentified.

dénouement at which I assisted yesterday! We had driven over to St. Moritz for lunch in company with [Charles] Loeser*—& as we drove thro' the town whom should we see but "B. B." [Bernard Berenson]† who saw <u>us</u> but didn't catch sight of our companion! He hailed us & ran after the carriage so Edwin & I tried to stop it & hop out in time to speak to him before he caught up to it & so avoid an unpleasant encounter! But the carriage was slow in stopping & B. B. swift in arriving & presently there he was at our carriage step directly in front of Loeser whom he <u>only</u> then noticed. I shivered for what would happen! To my amazement he pulled off his hat & put out his hand & said "How are you Loeser"—& they <u>shook hands</u>! Then we had some talk together—he all trembling & <u>quite</u> pale—& then drove off. "The first time in fifteen years" said Loeser meditatively! It was a meeting of the east & the west in art criticism as Dr. Martin‡ the Persian person was with us. Hope to see you soon—Greetings to the Universalities [?]§ & to Zuleika!

Aff. yrs.

Mabel D.

◁At the end of September 1911, Mabel Dodge returned to the United States to spend the winter at her family home in Buffalo. John was to be enrolled in the Morristown School in Morristown, New Jersey. At this time, she began to address Gertrude Stein as "Gertrude" rather than the more formal "Miss Stein" of the previous letters.▷

---

* It was at Loeser's villa in Florence that Mabel Dodge first saw the work of Cézanne. Dodge described Loeser's appearance as "like a terrier, with one ear up and the other down, so cocked was one eyebrow and so snapping his red-brown canine eyes. Head on one side, his long face creased into deep lines, he often laughed spasmodically and satirically with rarely a genial laughter" (*EE*, 388).

† Berenson was an influential advisor to prominent collectors and was instrumental in stimulating Leo Stein's interest in modern art, as he first introduced him to the paintings of Cézanne.

‡ Unidentified.

§Unidentified.

46

SAT. [CIRCA LATE SEPTEMBER 1911]* VILLA CURONIA
VIA DELLE PIAZZOLE
ARCETRI

Dear Gertrude

I am sailing for America with John to put him in school for the winter—leaving on the Majestic from Cherbourg on Wed. E.[dwin] will join me later. Whats this about the Phillipines? May I dine with you my one night in Paris—Tuesday? Sent me a line to Hotel de l'Empire Rue Daunon which I will get Tuesday P.M. when I arrive—will you? Letting me know if I may dine with you.

Aff. yrs.

Mabel Dodge

[Whitman motto]

[CIRCA OCTOBER 1911] 695 DELAWARE AVENUE
BUFFALO, N.Y.

Dear Gertrude

I am sending you two books that perhaps you will like. Let me know what you think of them. If you <u>can</u> read Henry James—read his new one "The Outcry"†—about picture buying & selling. An amusing situation with an americain who <u>can't afford</u> to buy a picture for <u>less</u> than a hundred thousand because it would lower his prestige etc & an english lord who <u>won't</u> take such a sum for one of his pictures! Quite well done the whole thing.

I suppose you are as well & blooming as ever. I am not—not having any particular emotion to be <u>out</u> of relation with! In these intervals I die.

Ever yours—

Mabel D.

---

* A review of the daily "Shipping and Mails" column in the *New York Times* from September through December 1911 yields only one date that the Majestic arrived in New York. The ship left Southampton on 27 September 1911 and docked in New York on 4 October 1911. Cherbourg is a port city in northwest France directly across the English Channel from Southampton and it is likely the ship stopped there to pick up passengers.

† *The Outcry* was first published in 1911.

~Gertrude Stein's first extant piece of correspondence to Mabel Dodge is intimate in its salutation and announces the completion of *The Making of Americans*. Stein makes her first of many requests to Dodge for assistance in publishing her writing. Stein had already sent copies of her manuscript to Grant Richards, a publisher in England, and to New York friends who might be able to engage a publisher for her.[54]~

[Postcard: Cézanne landscape]

[POSTMARK: PARIS, 2 NOVEMBER 1911] [27 RUE DE FLEURUS]
My dear Mabel.

The long book is finished. I am sending it to America to see what it can do. If you meet any one who wants to publish it let me know. Your books have come I will write you a letter soon

Yours

Gertrude.

~

1912

Mabel Dodge's first letter to Gertrude Stein in 1912 is an early example of the kind of communication that characterized their correspondence when it was at its most intimate and conversational. Dodge's letters from this time include references to their friendship, assumptions of understanding between them, gossip-filled and sometimes lengthy anecdotes, news briefs on mutual acquaintances, and encouragement about Stein's writing and chances of publishing. This letter seems to be in response to a non-extant letter from Stein to Dodge that described Stein's experiences with trying to get *The Making of Americans* published and included news about several mutual friends, among them the English artist and author Stephen Haweis, who was married to the English poet Mina Loy. As Stein writes in *The Autobiography of Alice B. Toklas*, Haweis was

> among the very earliest to be interested in the work of Gertrude Stein. Haweis had been fascinated with what he had read in manuscript of The Making of Americans. He did however plead for commas. Gertrude Stein said commas were unnecessary, the sense should be intrinsic and not have to be explained by commas and otherwise commas were only a sign that one should pause and take breath but one should know of oneself when one wanted to pause and take breath. However, as she liked Haweis very much and he had given her a delightful painting for a fan, she gave him two commas. It must however be added that on rereading the manuscript she took the commas out.[1]

~

[EARLY 1912] BUFFALO

Dearest Gertrude,

I am still here & have been having an awfully good time—or, at least, of course, only thinking I have been having a good time, as my good & bad times, according to you, are largely illusions without relation to facts!

Anyway—I've been sleighriding & dancing & ski-ing & playing generally with old playfellows—& it has <u>seemed</u> very pleasant! But just the same I am longing for you all. I shall be along presently—the first of June I think. Will you be in Paris then? I want to be there when you are there.

I believe we'l be winters altogether over here now. John is in school near N.Y.—Edwin is actively architecting—got a rather good garden to do—& so I fancy New York will see us next winter. Why don't you come over in the autumn? We're going to be all summer & every summer in Florence anyway. For heaven's sake don't get discouraged yet over yr book! It's <u>too good</u> to get immediate attention. Pubs. will be afraid of it at first. If someone would die (& someone may any minute) & leave me a fortune I'd make you let me publish it—I'd <u>adore</u> to! I believe it's the biggest thing of our time. I knew Mrs. Watts* in Florence! I've heard <u>nothing</u> of Constance [Fletcher]—! How are you all? I'm glad Stephen Haweis is succeeding at last. Write again—I want to know <u>when</u> you leave for Florence.

Yrs—

Mabel

∼Gertrude Stein responded to Mabel Dodge's encouragement by letting her know the status of her four current writing projects. Stein reports that she is working on: "a long gay book" and "many portraits of women," both of which appeared in *Matisse Picasso and Gertrude Stein with Two Shorter Stories* as "A Long Gay Book" and "Many Many Women"; "a study of two a man and woman," which was published as the title piece of *Two: Gertrude Stein and Her Brother and Other Early Portraits* (1908–12; 1951); and "a family of five," which also appears in the collection *Two* as "Jenny, Helen, Hannah, Paul and Peter."

---

* Unidentified.

In this letter, Stein also reports on the first Italian Futurist exhibition in Paris, which was held 5–12 February 1912 at Galerie Bernheim-Jeune. Filippo Marinetti, the poet and writer who was the founder of this new art movement that depicted machines, objects, and people in motion, declared in 1909 in *Le Figaro* that "a roaring motorcar, which runs like a machine-gun, is more beautiful than the Winged Victory of Samothrace."[2] The public's response to the Bernheim exhibition was shock, outrage, and excitement. The controversial show traveled to London, Berlin, Brussels, The Hague, Amsterdam, and Munich.

Gertrude Stein and Alice B. Toklas did not spend the summer in Florence in 1912, as had become their habit for several years, but traveled together to Spain, leaving Paris by train on 1 May and journeying southward. They spent almost two weeks in Avila instead of the two days allotted because Alice was intensely captivated by the town: "I immediately lost my heart to Avila, I must stay in Avila forever I insisted. Gertrude Stein was very upset, Avila was alright but, she insisted, she needed Paris. I felt that I needed nothing but Avila. We were both very violent about it."[3] They arrived in Madrid at the beginning of June and then went on to Toledo, Cordova, Seville, Gibraltar, Tangier, Ronda, and Grenada. ⌇

[CIRCA MARCH 1912] 27 RUE DE FLEURUS

My dear Mabel.

Your letter was a great comfort to me. I was kind of low in my mind about the publication end and even Wagner's* letters were ceasing to be a comfort to me. I have been trying some English publishers with collections of the shorter and longer things those you saw and the ones I did this summer and when I first came back but there is nothing doing. I am working on four books now. One is a long gay book and has lots and lots of everything in it and goes on. It will be quite long. I have written about 120 pages of it. Another is a study of two a man and woman having the same means of xpression and the same emotional and spiritual xperiences with different quality of intellect. That is going very well and slowly. Then I am doing one that will be finished in a couple of months that consists of many portraits of women. Then I am doing another which is a description of a family of five who are all peculiar

*Unidentified.

and are in a peculiar relation each one to every other one of the five of them. This one is just fairly begun.

I am still sending the volumes of the short and longer things about but they come back, quite promptley and with very polite hand written and sometimes regretful refusals. The long book is in America. I have not heard anything of it for a long time. You can understand how much I appreciated your letter.

This afternoon when we were out walking we met the Johnstons* for the first time. Its strange that we have not run across them before they live so near. He was very pleasant but she was querulous. Perhaps spring does not agree with her. It has been wonderfully spring here for two weeks now. Also the futurists are in town. You know [Filippo] Marinetti and his crowd. He brought a bunch of painters who paint houses and people and streets and wagons and scaffoldings and bottles and fruits all moving and where they are not moving there are cubes to fill in. They have a catalogue that has a fiery introduction demolishing the old salons and they are xhibiting at Bernheims and everybody goes. Marinetti has given several conferences and at the last he attacked the art of the Greeks and [Elie] Nadelman† who was present called him a bad name and Marinetti hit Nadelman and they were separated.

I am afraid we won't see you until the fall. We are going to Spain this year instead of Italy. We leave the first of May and will go slowly down to Granada getting there in July and spending July and August between there and Tangiers. Surely we will meet here in the fall. I am delighted that Edwin has gotten something nice to do. Remember me to him. I have heard nothing of or from Miss [Constance] Fletcher. Miss [Florence] Blood is still here but getting pretty tired. She is still taking the Watts‡ course and has had a very good time here this winter. She has gone about a great deal. [Jacques-Émile] Blanche§ has been here and I have met him at shows. He is worried to death there is so much doing in funny

---

* This reference is likely to Dawson Johnston and his wife, whom Stein identifies in *The Autobiography of Alice B. Toklas* as "the librarian of the American Library" (236).

† Elie Nadelman, Polish-born sculptor who lived in Paris until 1914, when he moved to the United States. In 1911 Stein wrote a word portrait of him, "Nadelman," that is included in *Portraits and Prayers* (hereafter cited as *P&P*).

‡ Unidentified.

§ Jacques-Émile Blanche, French painter and author who painted a number of portraits of Mabel Dodge and also portrayed her as the fictional character Gisell Links in his novel *Aymeris*. In his autobiography, Blanche describes Dodge as "an irresistible person" who "confounded me in argument" (Blanche, *Portraits of a Lifetime*, 271). Dodge saw him as "subtle, feminine, malicious, and amusing" (EE, 407).

kinds of art these days. He does not know what bothers him the most. He was almost xhausted entirely by a picture that Picasso calls a portrait of Buffalo Bill.* Miss Blood goes back to Florence the end of the month.

Much love to you always

Gertrude.

⤳While Gertrude Stein and Alice B. Toklas were in Spain, Mabel Dodge wrote from Florence about the antics of the ghost who haunted the Villa Curonia. When Dodge moved in, she had asked Marguerite, the previous owner's live-in companion and tutor for the children, to stay on. Marguerite grew intensely attached to Dodge and was ferociously jealous of all those who visited the villa. When Marguerite became so ill that she had to move to a nursing home in Florence (where she soon died), she warned, "I am going now, . . . but I love this house very much and I will come back to it no matter what happens."[4] Marguerite's vacated room then became the guest room, and many visitors passed fitful nights of sleep there. The American sculptor Janet Scudder felt "'a long, cold foot pushing against me, as though trying to force me out of the bed.'"[5] Constance Fletcher was the only visitor to have a joyous experience with the ghost of Marguerite, claiming to have spent "'the most marvelous night of my life'"[6] when she heard Marguerite's voice. Constance had awoken feeling very happy and felt her room filling with light. She suspected that it was the presence of Marguerite and called out to her. Constance heard Marguerite's voice answer, "Si—sono Io," and implored her to wait until she could get Dodge to come to the room. But Marguerite did not want to disturb Dodge, saying, "Non, non, Mabella dorme, dorme cosi bene! Mene vado—mene vado—m-e-n-e v-a-d-o!"[7] Rather than being frightened by the presence of a ghost, Mabel Dodge found herself feeling "exultant" and having "a curious, secret elation."[8] She seemed to take enormous, even cruel, pleasure from the fearful responses of her guests.

---

* Pablo Picasso's *Buffalo Bill* (1911) is a painting from his analytical Cubist period. Mabel Dodge had tried to convince Blanche to consider the exciting advances that Picasso and Matisse were making in art: "'They are going to teach the world to *see*,' I reiterated over and over. But he was up against middle-age, past his zenith, past the growing period. Sadly obdurate, puzzled, and discomfited, he continued his portrait, shaking his head" (*EE*, 323).

In the incident described in the following letter, the guests included the American sculptor Jo Davidson and his wife Yvonne who was an actress,[9] the American actress Florence Bradley, the American portrait painter Mary Foote, and Paul Ayrault, the Columbia University student whom Mabel soon fell in love with and who had been hired to teach her son John. In Jo Davidson's autobiography, *Between Sittings* (1951), he related his experiences at the Villa Curonia and the role he believed Dodge played in the spooky incidents:

> There were all sorts of quasi-supernatural pranks going on, much to Mabel's amusement. She would glide into the room; her eyes were everywhere, like a trainer in a lion's cage—never relaxing, always alert. But she was a patient woman. She knew something would happen—it always did, she saw to that.
>
> One night, about three in the morning, I was awakened by Yvonne.
>
> "Did you hear that?"
>
> "No," I replied. "Never mind, I am here."
>
> But she insisted that there was some presence in the room stronger than myself. . . .
>
> I did a bust of Mabel Dodge. I would watch for that enigmatic smile of expectancy and wonder, "What is she plotting now?"[10]

Dodge's longtime friend Hutchins Hapgood claimed that she "'haunted houses'. . . making actually visible and audible, to sensitive people, forms and sounds of abysmal woe."[11]⁓

[Whitman motto]

24 JUNE [1912] FLORENCE

Dear Gertrude

I am missing you very much. How much nicer it would be if you were here. We are having an exceptional time just now—& you would love it. We have been having a <u>great</u> <u>deal</u> of "spook." The Jo Davidsons are here—Florence Bradley* an americain ac-

---

* Dodge met Florence Bradley on board a ship returning to the United States from Italy. Each was drawn to the other, and Dodge described Bradley as having "something special about her that marked her out from the rest of the passengers. . . .This girl had a distinctly different atmosphere about her. She was flashing. Her bright brown eyes flashed and her white teeth flashed in wide smiles....I liked her and we became friends.

tress—Mary Foote* a portrait painter & a tutor—(football player of 22). All these people have been haunted by our ghost and I not at all. I almost believe I have hypnotised the whole lot of them. It has been screamingly funny. They have seen, heard & felt all sorts of things. They have been driven from one room to another & finally from the loggia downstairs to <u>my</u> upper terrace always—at night—persued by the spook who moans, clatters & jiggles their beds—pulls off the bedclothes & punches them in the back. They—from real lack of sleep have grown more & more hysterical. Davidson has nearly gone mad! Before sleeping the other night they all saw—in the hall—a large brass platter reel from side to side on the table & make an awful clatter. I had to read the <u>Bible</u> to them all to quiet them down. We wanted to read the Sermon on the Mount & no one knew where to find it—Jo Davidson opened it to read a chapter on hazard—& of course it was all about persecution of the jews & he was still more frightened & thought the spook was in that too. The chapter ended up by a description of adultery which was <u>really</u> irrelevant. Then they went to bed—two Davidsons & the tutor—in beds they had pulled on to my terrace. I was waked up in an hour—in my room just inside—by screams & weeping & I heard Davidson saying, "My God! My God! I can't stand this." I got up & went out & found that really their bed had been lifted up & down under them—while their candle was still lighted & he was reading & another clattering of metal like the brass platter made sounding just by the bed. I've <u>never</u> seen people so petrified! He was nearly out of his head. He said he <u>had</u> to get out of the house—& yet he dared not go to his room & dress! I said we'd all go with him! I felt he had to be saved! I had tried making them all three (the tutor was just as scared!) do deep breathing exercises out there but it did no good. So we all solemnly marched into his room (the knob of his door came off in his hand which only added more terror!) & the tutor held up a large bath towel & Mr. D. hastily clothed himself behind it. Then <u>he</u> accompanied the tutor while <u>he</u> dressed & they went out, Davidson having kissed his wife passionately goodby & left her behind with the spook & me & Miss Bradley. These two <u>both</u> got into my bed & we three lay like saints on tombs perfectly straight out there was so little room, until morning—no one sleeping a wink. The next day I had a priest come & spend a

She made me feel more feminine in my dependence, she gave me a right to be helpless by her swift seizure of the dominant rôle" (*EE*, 429). Bradley first introduced Jo and Yvonne Davidson to Dodge in New York (Davidson, *Between Sittings*, 81).

 * Mary Foote studied painting in Paris and was close friends with Mark Twain, Henry James, and John Singer Sargent.

night in the "haunted room" to see what <u>he</u> would do. He read prayers till four & saw nothing but said he thought he'd better perform the service of exorcism the next night—So he came with a porridge bowl of Holy Water & an olive branch & we made a pageant thru' all the rooms while he exorcised & blessed all over. Miss Bradley laughed with nerves during it which scared her so she said she was going to sleep down on the loggia. Friendship & all that were quite forgotten! With all those newly blessed beds to sleep in no one offered to accompany her. We all went to bed—but at 2, she came hastily up—for the spook, driven out of the upstairs rooms had gone down to the loggia & groaned twice <u>just</u> <u>beside</u> her! No more sleep that night for anyone except <u>me</u> who had locked my door! At dinner last night Mrs. Davidson suddenly left the table & dashed into the garden—We paid no attention but she came back soon & had hysterics saying someone behind her chair had pushed her out of the room. A general panic ensued—which resulted in the two Davidsons & Miss Bradley leaving in hot haste <u>for</u> <u>Rome</u> on the 11.20 last eve. So there we are. Thats what happens when you come to the Villa Curonia for a good rest & vacation!

Of Florence the news is slight. Our friend Mr. [Pen] Browning* is very low—we hear dying—poor [Herbert] Horne† is also very low—& dying. [Charles] Loeser is laid up—in his villa—with varicose veins & a blond young second cousin who plays Beethoven magnificently. Herbert Vaughn‡ the friend of the english clergy, Brocklebanks & Miss Mansfield§ was arrested in the cortile of the Palazzo Vecchio for indulging there in the classic vice. Miss [Constance] Fletcher is in Venice, the [Paul and Muriel] Drapers¶ are

---

* Robert Wiedemann Barrett Browning, called Pen, an artist and the only child born to the English poets Robert Browning and Elizabeth Barrett Browning.

† Herbert Horne, English art historian and art collector who had been friends with Bernard and Mary Berenson for years. He eventually died on 13 April 1916, according to Mary Berenson (Barbara Strachey and Jayne Samuels, eds., *Mary Berenson: A Self-Portrait from her Letters and Diaries,* 208). Harold Acton included this description of Horne in his *Memoirs of an Aesthete:* "But I can only remember that he was supposed to have a double row of teeth, and as he rarely opened his blood-red lips, I scrutinized him in vain" (16). I am grateful to Leon Katz for providing information on Horne's identity and for drawing my attention to the passage from Acton.

‡ Unidentified.

§Both unidentified.

¶ Paul Draper, acclaimed American tenor and his American wife Muriel Draper, a popular salon hostess in London. In one of her early experiments in trying to become a powerful inspiration to an artist, Dodge had lured Paul Draper to her in Florence: "I don't know how it began but Paul thought he fell in love with me. I suppose I must admit I tried to attract his attention for it was a compulsion with me in those days" (*EE,* 257). Dodge believed that she briefly succeeded in her goal: "He was well installed in the magical hollow dream I used to create around people, and in which they drew

in London, [Lord] Acton* is as Actonish as ever & Mrs. [Lady] Acton has grown rather fat & has a queer look in her eyes & keeps asking me to dinner which makes me think she must take drugs because we are not supposed to be friends. I took all my party to Miss [Florence] Blood's last Sunday which rather flustered her. She cannot easily handle large masses of mixed humans. She gave us tea & said "Now do go & see all the garden & then come back & say goodby!" Mrs. [Lucy] Perkins arrives soon & the [Bernard and Mary] Berensons have left. I am well & happy & can't get enough sun. Write yr news.

Love,

Mabel

⌒When they returned to Paris, Gertrude Stein and Alice B. Toklas found several telegrams and letters from Mabel Dodge urging them to come to Florence.[12] Although the telegrams are not extant, the following two letters contain Dodge's appeals to Stein.⌒

[CIRCA SEPTEMBER 1912] VILLA CURONIA
VIA DELLE PIAZZOLE
ARCETRI

Dear Gertrude

Now please listen to reason. Won't you & Miss Taclos [i.e., Toklas] come down here where it is hot & the sun magnificent at once & spend a fortnight or a month with me? Please do—I suppose you hate moving once you get there but you know you are longing for real sunshine & for Italy & we'd talk & talk! Won't you? I'm all alone till Oct. 1st. Then Constance Fletcher is coming—please wire at once that you'd be a sport & come—Florence is at its bestest best—never better & the figs magnificent. We'l sit in the sun all day—Do come—

Ever yrs—

Mabel

---

delighted breath for a little while" (*EE*, 257–58). Dodge described Muriel Draper as "like a hard, slender, polished ivory figure carved from an elephant's tusk" and "so fair, without a darkness anywhere about her" (*EE*, 255). Stein included Draper in her triple word portrait, "And So. To Change So. Muriel Draper Yvonne Davidson Beatrice Locher," published in *Portraits and Prayers*.

* Lord and Lady Acton, important English figures in the international community in Florence. Their son, Sir Harold Acton, visited the Villa Curonia as a child and met Mabel Dodge and Gertrude Stein there. He later frequently visited Stein and Toklas at 27 rue de Fleurus (*GSC*, 138).

Dear Gertrude—

Well—are you coming? I am still waiting to hear. I enclose you a friend's letter which speaks of yr articles—a very intelligent young actress—so that you can see how immediately you are read you affect people. Your writing is destined to <u>count</u>. Please send me those articles—you said you would & didn't—I'm going to send Florence Bradley* to see you—please be nice to her.

Always yrs—

Mabel

⌁The articles referred to by Mabel Dodge in the previous letter are Gertrude Stein's word portraits of Picasso and Matisse, both written in 1909, that appeared in the Special Number August 1912 issue of *Camera Work,* the journal published by Alfred Stieglitz. His gallery at 291 Fifth Avenue was by this time an established center for the avant-garde in art and literature with its exhibitions of work by American modernists such as Arthur Dove, Marsden Hartley, and John Marin. The inclusion of her portraits in *Camera Work* marked Gertrude Stein's first publication in an American periodical.[13] A letter from Stieglitz to Stein on 26 February 1912 relates his response and commitment to her word portraits:

> They interest me hugely and I feel as if I would like to publish them. I am not in business, and therefore cannot afford to pay for the privilege, should you be willing to extend it to me. My idea would be to have a few Picasso's and a few Matisse's reproduced as illustrations to accompany your text. . . . You have undoubtedly succeeded in expressing Matisse and Picasso in words, for me at least. It is for that reason that I am desirous of sharing my pleasure with others.[14]

Gertrude Stein agreed to the publication plans that led to her work being featured in *Camera Work.* Stieglitz's editorial introduced her writing to his readers:

> These articles bear, to current interpretative criticism, a relation exactly analogous to that born by the work of the men

---

* It seems likely that Florence Bradley is the "very intelligent young actress."

of whom they treat to the painting and sculpture of the older schools. So close, indeed, is this analogy that they will doubtless be regarded by many as no less absurd, unintelligible, radical or revolutionary than the so-called vagaries of the painters whom they seek to interpret. . . . We wish you the pleasure of a hearty laugh at them upon a first reading. Yet we confidently commend them to your subsequent and critical attention.[15]

The Special Number issue was devoted exclusively to Stein's word portraits. "Henri Matisse" was accompanied by seven reproductions of Matisse's work, including *Joy of Life* (1905–6), *The Blue Nude* (1907), *Woman Combing Her Hair* (1907), and two bronze sculptures of female nudes. "Pablo Picasso" was also illustrated with seven images, among them *The Reservoir of Horta de Ebro* (1909), *Portrait of M. Kahnweiler* (1910), and two views of the bronze sculpture *Head of Fernande Olivier* (1909). A number of the reproduced works, including Matisse's *The Blue Nude* and Picasso's *The Reservoir*, were in the collection of Gertrude and Leo Stein at that time. "Henri Matisse" begins:

> One was quite certain that for a long part of his being one being living he had been trying to be certain that he was wrong in doing what he was doing and then when he could not come to be certain that he had been wrong in doing what he had been doing, when he had completely convinced himself that he would not come to be certain that he had been wrong in doing what he had been doing he was really certain then that he was a great one and he certainly was a great one. Certainly every one could be certain of this thing that this one is a great one.[16]

"Pablo Picasso" begins like this:

> One whom some were certainly following was one who was completely charming. One whom some were certainly following was one who was charming. One whom some were following was one who was completely charming. One whom some were following was one who was certainly completely charming.[17]

The word portraits caused quite a commotion in America and Europe. Bernard Berenson wrote to Stein on 23 November 1912:

My cordial thanks for the pamphlet full of extraordinarily fine reproductions of Matisse's & Picasso's. In a moment of perfect peace when I feel my best I shall try again to see whether I can puzzle out the intention of some of Picasso's designs.

As for your own prose I find it vastly more obscure still. It beats me hollow, & makes me dizzy to boot. So do some of the Picasso's by the way. But I'll try try again.[18]

In a letter to Stein on 22 December 1912, Constance Fletcher reported on the response to the portraits in Venice:

I must tell you, dear Gertrude, about your book. Incidentally, I, too, can *see* the Picassos. Some of them are more Egyptian than Egypt. A dozen cubes—& the result is something august. . . . But Matisse—. No. I'm not in that game yet. But I must tell you of how you have revolutionized a solemn sitting of the Professors of the Belle Arti![19] One of them asked & asked until I, reluctantly, lent you for a day. Then you were carried off & read aloud at a "seduta"[20] & fought over, & ramped over, & stormed over, & considered as something between a prophet & a bombshell. Several of them know English: the others, I am told, clamored for a translation. At all events, the whole sitting was devoted to you. They did 'no other work that day.' It must have been a scene. I wish we could have witnessed it.[21]

Gertrude Stein's longtime friend Mabel Weeks, a Radcliffe graduate who served as an assistant to the dean of social affairs at Barnard College for thirty-two years, wrote from New York on 12 December 1912, questioning Stieglitz's genuine commitment to the avant-garde cause:

To get my precious copy of your Matisse and Picasso, I had to have an interview with Stieglitz. . . . I suspect him of something of a pose in his interest in the new things, because he is so pitifully eager to shock people with them. When he found that I knew the work of Matisse & of you, at least to the extent of not being in the least shocked, his face fell ludicrously and he lost all interest. What he dotes on is a chance to harangue some astounded soul . . .[22]

Gertrude Stein and Alice B. Toklas responded to Mabel Dodge's invitations and visited the Villa Curonia in the fall of 1912. The following note was left for them during their stay and includes plans for a dinner party with the French novelist André Gide.

Dear Gertrude

We have just got the idea of motoring to Arezzo to put Paul [Ayrault] & John on the train there—The chauffeur said we must go light to do it as the motor is so sick so I don't get you up for it. I'l be back for dinner—I have told Margurite* to order <u>Mario</u> the cabby of Arcetri for you & Alice if you want to go in town—So we're off—for a farewell spin—

Yrs,

Mabel

I leave this note to Miss Blood with you & when [André] Gide answers Margurite will bring it to you to read <u>so</u> <u>if</u> he says he is coming <u>you</u> send this to Miss B. & have boy wait for answer & tell Margurite how many then there will be for dinner—See? I hope the motor will get us there all right!

The dinner party with Gide was not considered a success in Gertrude Stein's eyes: "André Gide turned up while we were at the Villa Curonia. It was rather a dull evening."[23] Alice B. Toklas recalls the same event in her memoirs, *What is Remembered* (1963):

> Mabel had met and invited André Gide for dinner at the villa. When the dinner hour was approaching, Mabel sent word to me saying, If you are dressed, go down at once. If not, hurry and do so to receive André Gide who is due now. Which I did, making conversation with him until Mabel appeared. After dinner Mabel, stretched out on one of the long sofas, was talking in a low voice to Monsieur Gide who, sitting opposite, was leaning over her.[24]

While Gertrude Stein was visiting the Villa Curonia in the fall of 1912, she wrote "Portrait of Mabel Dodge at the Villa Curonia," originally titled "Mabel little Mabel with her face against the pane,"

---

* Margurite, the maid at the Villa Curonia, also called Margherita, to be distinguished from Marguerite, the inherited live-in companion and tutor, who had died by this time and reportedly returned to haunt her old room at the villa (*EE*, 281).

a comparatively accessible word portrait describing in both concrete and abstract language Stein's experiences of the villa and her hostess.[25] Muriel Draper, who was also a guest at the time, attributes Stein's creative output to the following stimulus: "There had been an incident of a slow donkey cart expertly avoided by Mabel in a fast motor on a narrow hill road that day, that had sent Gertrude Stein into a subconscious fury (or was it conscious?) that demanded expression."[26] However, it seems that even without the near accident, there was intrigue and adventure enough at the villa to provide Stein with stimulation for her writing. In her memoirs, Mabel Dodge supplies the background details for the portrait, thus conveying her own understanding of what she believed was the inspiration for Stein's portrayal of her. During her visit, Stein slept in Edwin's room, which was adjacent to Mabel's bedroom, and Toklas stayed in a small room next to Stein's. At that time, Edwin was away from the villa and Mabel's attention was much drawn toward Paul Ayrault, the young tutor for John, who, according to Mabel, "was in love with me just as a matter of course, and his blond, fresh, blue-eyed youthfulness had a great allure for me. Merely of the flesh it was—but so it was."[27] On at least one occasion, Paul quietly snuck down the hall to the door of Mabel's bedroom, whispered her name, and was welcomed into her room.[28] Dodge was keenly aware of Stein's habit of writing at night after everyone had gone to sleep and thus was acutely conscious of having a possible audience in the adjoining room:

> The walls between Gertrude and me were thick but the doors were just ordinary ones. . . . He and I clung together in the moonlight with no whispers. We grew tired standing together and swayed towards the wide, white-hung bed—until we were lying, arms about each other. . . . My natural desire for him was so strong that it passed over me in deep waves . . . yet I only clung to him and began to babble: "I can't—I can't—I can't . . ." And so we remained, for heaven knows how long— while Gertrude wrote on the other side of the wall, sitting in candle-light like a great Sibyl dim against the red and gold damask that hung loosely on the walls.[29]

In the retelling of her long and passionate embrace, Mabel Dodge certainly casts Gertrude Stein in an important role.

"Portrait of Mabel Dodge at the Villa Curonia" begins: "The days are wonderful and the nights are wonderful and the life is pleasant." It is filled with images and statements joined together by no apparent logic but with rhythm and linguistic play, as in, "Looking is not vanishing. Laughing is not evaporating. There can be the climax. There can be the same dress. . . . Abandon a garden and the house is bigger. This is not smiling." The portrait ends with Stein's apparent explanation about the inevitable incompleteness of any experience: "There is not all of any visit."[30] Mabel Dodge was thrilled with her portrait and immediately arranged to have three hundred copies of it printed and covered in Florentine wallpaper.[31]

It was during or soon after this visit to the Villa Curonia in 1912 that Gertrude Stein most likely wrote the final two sections of her word portrait of Constance Fletcher, the first having been written at the time of their initial meeting the summer before.[32] This portrait, with its three stylistically distinct sections, is considered by Stein scholars to be an important transitional work clearly marking the differences between the styles of the early and late portraits. The first part contains long sentences with similar repeating phrases, the second signals a rapid shift in style with its introduction of more varied images and less repetition, and the third section alternates between long and very short, often one- or two-word, paragraphs.[33] The portrait begins: "When she was quite a young one she knew she had been in a family living and that that family living was one that any one could be one not have been having if they were to be one being one not thinking about being one having been having family living." And ends: "All houses are open that is to say a door and a window and a table and the waiter make the shadow smaller and the shadow which is larger is not flickering."[34]

It was at the time of this visit to the Villa Curonia that the beginning strains in the friendship between Mabel Dodge and Gertrude Stein were felt. According to Dodge, Alice B. Toklas was jealous of her intense connection with Stein and worked to dissolve it. Dodge tells the story in her memoirs:

> As Gertrude went on with the "Portrait of Mabel Dodge," writing her unconscious lines, she seemed to grow warmer to me, to which I responded in a sort of flirtatious way though I didn't feel anything for her now because my fire was drawn to another. . . .

But one day at lunch, Gertrude, sitting opposite me in Edwin's chair, sent me such a strong look over the table that it seemed to cut across the air to me in a band of electrified steel—a smile traveling across on it—powerful—Heavens! I remember it *now* so keenly!

At that Alice arose hastily and ran out of the room onto the terrace. Gertrude gave a surprised, noticing glance after her and, as she didn't return, got up and followed after. . . .

Pretty soon Gertrude came back but without Alice and said, "She doesn't want to come to lunch. She feels the heat today."

From that time on Alice began to separate Gertrude and me—*poco-poco*—but the real break came later on when I wrote the first thing that was ever published in America about her writing.[35]

Gertrude Stein and Alice B. Toklas returned to Paris, and Mabel Dodge continued to receive guests at the villa that fall. Constance Fletcher stayed on during the visit of Emily Cary and Alice Thursby. Emily Cary was the wife of Seward Cary, Dodge's treasured and adventurous childhood companion in Buffalo, and the first bride that Dodge had ever seen.[36] Alice Thursby was the sister-in-law of Emily and Seward's daughter, Phoebe Cary. Phoebe had married Arthur Brisbane, Alice Thursby's brother, who was a prominent newspaper editor and publisher and a longtime acquaintance of Mabel Dodge's from Buffalo.

If "Zulicka" refers to Alice B. Toklas, as discussed earlier, then it appears in the second of the following letters that Mabel Dodge is feeding Gertrude Stein material to make her jealous. She reports that Constance Fletcher felt that "Zulicka had a passion for her" and noticed that Zulicka was particularly attentive to her. It could be that after the incident at the lunch table where Dodge and Stein connected so palpably, thus resulting in Toklas's leaving the scene, Dodge now wants to get back at Toklas for the wedge she was beginning to place between Dodge and Stein.〰

[Whitman motto]

[CIRCA OCTOBER 1912] [ARCETRI]

I wish you'd let me know if George Field* still loves me or if he has a young man curiosity.

* Unidentified.

Dearest Gertrude

I miss you <u>awfully</u>. When are you coming back?

Emily [Cary] arrives Sunday with Alice Thursby.

Do see George Field soon & as often as you can & see if you can get him out of the ethical prison house. Also he & Leo would get on, I think.

Then write me what you think. Bad weather.

Best love,

Mabel

[CIRCA OCTOBER 1912] VILLA CURONIA
VIA DELLE PIAZZOLE
ARCETRI

Dearest Gertrude

A note from Florence Bradley says she is settled at 25 Rue Humboldt & tho' she wants like everything to see you she says she's timid & seems inclined to wait until I come & take her to you. This is silly. She is timid because there is something about her that makes most people feel she is different from them tho' they don't know why—& they don't like her & this makes her sensitive. But you'd like her all right. Would you send her a note & ask her to come & let me know what you think it is that scares people off in her?

Constance [Fletcher] confided to me that she <u>knew</u> last year that Zulicka had a passion for her & that this year she was really quite embarrassed by Zulicka's little attentions—etc!!! I enclose a letter from an old friend of <u>hers</u> to Edwin about her & I have written to ask for the answer to the mystery about the income.

She says she thinks you should have touched (!) on my "Vie Passionée" in your portrait & <u>not</u> have left it quite out! Emily [Cary] & Alice Thursby arrive tomorrow. Have you see[n] George Field yet? <u>What's</u> going to happen? I miss you both. Tell Zulicka we do our nails every morning.

Best love to you both,

M.

⌇When Gertrude Stein was a guest at the Villa Curonia in the fall of 1912, Mabel Dodge had confided to her about her increasingly passionate attachment to the tutor Paul Ayrault and the ways

65

that this involvement threatened her marriage to Edwin. In a rapid succession of letters written to Stein after her return to Paris, Dodge pleads with her to come back to Florence, expenses paid for her and Toklas, to help out with this crisis of Dodge's heart. Or, if Stein cannot return to Italy, Mabel asks, meet Edwin in Paris and intercept him before he travels on to the Villa Curonia. Dodge appeals urgently to Stein, insisting that no other person can help and practically giving her a script and directions on how to speak with Edwin. The relationship between the two women at this time seems to be one of real need on Dodge's part, accompanied by her enthusiastic outpourings of emotion and turmoil, and an attentiveness on Stein's part, as evidenced by references to a number of non-extant telegrams that she sent. However, Stein would not continue for long in her reaching out to Dodge in this way.

At the same time that Mabel Dodge was dealing with her situation with Edwin and Paul, it appeared that Emily Cary was distressed over her daughter Phoebe's marriage to Arthur Brisbane and tormented both the bride and groom with her behavior. And the tensions in the relationship between Gertrude Stein and her brother Leo, which had begun around the time that Alice B. Toklas moved into 27 rue de Fleurus, seemed to have increased, as indicated by Dodge's reference to "won't you brave Leo & come back?"〜

FRIDAY [CIRCA OCTOBER 1912] VILLA CURONIA
VIA DELLE PIAZZOLE
ARCETRI

Dearest Gertrude

There isn't the slightest reason for you to be anxious over my dip[htheria]. I'm much better & besides as you know I have the constitution of a dray horse—worse luck—I'm told the second part of the malady will arrive in a week—very painful. But won't you please come back? Someone has got to help out in this thing of E.[dwin] & me. I shrink like anything from hurting him. Who wouldn't after that wire? I wish he weren't coming. It will be awful. Now please come back! If you positively can't will you meet his train (from Havre) on the 31st I believe & tell him you've got to see him & talk before he leaves Paris. If he leaves at once you can talk at once. You can tell him you were with me thro' this business & that I talked openly to you. He will be apalled & outraged that I should have talked about it to anyone for he is so reserved himself, however you can explain I'd have got nutty if I hadn't—& how much good it did me to—(You can delicately hint of the inestimable benefit you were to me if you want to.) Then please proceed to the advice that for Gawd's Sake he leave me— nay—encourage me to stay over here this winter & work it out. I can't face a winter with him—not seeing Paul having promised I wouldn't—seeing Paul having [(](of course) broken my promise) confessing all over again—promising all over again—making E. frantic—interrupting his work—turning him into a spy—myself into a criminal—in fact all you yourself can forsee in such a pros- pect. Do make him leave me here or in Paris. He is so generous & magnaminous to wire me like that—that of course I'd go with him if he wants me to but for heaven's sake make him see it otherwise.

The way I feel about Paul is queer. Not wild impatient longing but sustained-resigned-to-the-fact-it-will-be-so knowledge that in the spring the real trouble will begin. A kind of sad sure feeling that he is going to be determined about this—that he is going to make me choose between E. & him & that it will be awful—be- cause I will by instinct want him and yet feel it impossible to go if it will hurt E. I simply couldn't. To me the sin against the Holy Ghost is the sin against love—& I should feel it wrong to do that to E. if he continues to love me. He can count on my doing right—in a crisis but not in every day life. I certainly will do wrong if I go back to N.Y. Now can you tell him all this? Can't you make him stay over in Paris too? I wouldn't mind that so much. You will see him—won't you? If he tries to freeze you silent by his reserve— don't you care—go right on for his own good. Theres no one else can help in this thing but you.

Emily [Cary] & Alice [Thursby] only staid 3 days & left. Emily was afraid of dip. She was drunk off & on all the time. One day she drank a quart of whiskey—the next morning woked too sweet & blooming. She only alluded to the marriage once—she said—"I've lost 30 pounds in 6 weeks. What broke me down was that I've known this for two years. When Phoebe [Cary] came & told me she liked Arthur [Brisbane] I said 'Dam the world'["]—She means to stay over here all winter in Paris so you will see her. I have decided it is a pure case of double personality. She is a devil when she drinks. Alice got nervous & confidential & told Constance [Fletcher] the whole story. She said "She [Emily] has nearly killed my brother [Arthur Brisbane] & now she will kill her daughter [Phoebe]." Constance asked her how & she said—"Only a short time after the marriage she [Emily] tooke her daughter's place in my brother's bed & it nearly killed the girl."

Its all terrible & tragic. Alice told me that the aim of her life is to postpone a tradgedy & that this has been her aim for years but that it will come yet. She says she brought Emily away now so as not to let her kill her daughter.

Does George F.[ield] love me or a young man? <u>Please</u> come back. I've seen no one—[Lord] Acton or otherwise.

Best love to both

M.

———

[OCTOBER 1912] VILLA CURONIA
VIA DELLE PIAZZOLE
ARCETRI

Gertrude—

if you love me you'l come back. I can't do without you—especially now <u>won't</u> you come & help E.[dwin] & me out? I'l send you & Alice nice round trip tickets for it's not fair otherwise—but first this once won't you brave Leo & come back?

<u>Dam</u> everything.

M.

You see I still <u>do</u> care for P.[aul.] I know thats more than meets the eye.

Pleaaaaaase say yes.

If <u>absolutely</u> not you've got to catch E. on the boat train from Savoie S.S. as he arrives to talk to him & tell him he's <u>got</u> to leave me alone over here to decide this & <u>not</u> to tear me to pieces with his magnaminity. Please.

———

THURSDAY [CIRCA LATE OCTOBER 1912] VILLA CURONIA
VIA DELLE PIAZZOLE
ARCETRI

Dearest Gertrude

I am much better but was awfully sick—that serum did wonders. In a week I shall suffer from that I suppose. I am in a confused state of delight & despair & don't know <u>what</u> to make of myself or things or <u>what</u> I want. Two cables on my breakfast tray this morning—one from Edwin says "Sailing on Savoie tomorrow for I love you"—the other from Paul in answer to a letter I wrote him same time as E. wondering if I'd better come back this winter & if he still cared or thought he would or I would—& asking him to cable me.

It says "Yes! Yes! Yes!—Paul" Very certain—decided & steady.
What am I to do? Edwin seems such a <u>dear</u>—so steadfast—so commending himself to my "respect" (((and yet I couldn't help a slight feeling of disappointment at his coming))) this last <u>very</u> confidential because I'm so ashamed of it & hate to feel so disloyal to such a generous soul. But really not <u>many</u> men would have taken that letter so—would they? Oh dam !!!!!!!!!!! And Gertrude if Paul had wired he was coming I'd just be jumping on the roof! Oh! I wish God <u>would</u> pay attention sometimes & look after his business. Everything's so slovenly & slipshod—one thing begins before another's finished. Did you get our answer to yr wire* last night? Were you anxious? I suppose you knew it seemed a good way out to me but I'm a[s] tough as a hickory nut. I shall wire E. to see you in Paris & I want you to talk heart to heart to him about me—plunge in thro' his reserve & lack of understanding & tell him I've talked to you & that he's <u>got</u> to leave me over here a year under your "supervision(!)" to find out what I'm to do—<u>Will you</u>? For Gawd's Sake do! I <u>can't</u> go back—& yet I'l seem so <u>ungrateful</u> if I don't. <u>Please</u>. <u>Dam</u>.

Best love,

M.

[CIRCA NOVEMBER 1912] VILLA CURONIA
VIA DELLE PIAZZOLE
ARCETRI

Dearest Gertrude

Am still in bed weak as a rat & can't imagine ever getting up again so I can't possibly come up to Paris this week. Can't you come down here? If not you'l see E.[dwin]—won't you? Do you know it's so awful the way I feel about him—seeing him. Such reluctance—such a distaste for it all. I know I'l feel a pig more than ever when I do see him for this disloyalty after his generous answer to my letter & his coming all this way—If only he <u>wouldn't</u>. I can't see things ahead—at all—Sometimes I think that no matter what I do he'l always be there—unhappy—reprochful & uncomprehending but still hanging on! A sort of New England blueness comes down on me as I think of him—a feeling he often gives me when he makes me see myself as <u>he</u> sees me. What <u>is</u> to be done?

---

* This telegram from Stein to Dodge and Dodge's reply are not extant.

I am thro' with the white spots & now beginning the malady the serum brings on. At least I begin to feel queerish no other ways now.

Mrs. Taylor* is very ill & tho' she has peritonitis & was operated yesterday for appendicitis. Haven't heard today. Arthur Brisbane wrote me that the house where my N.Y. flat is—is going to be sold over the owner's head so I probably won't have <u>that</u> anyway. He is trying to recover the money I've paid out on it already.

How I wish you were here! Constance [Fletcher] <u>such</u> a good nurse.

Best love—

Mabel

EXTRA!
Special edition!
Constance has been the most charming devoted nurse—cooking my food deliciously—doing <u>every</u> thing charmingly & transforming herself to a <u>loved</u> one.

⌁When Mabel Dodge was laid up with diphtheria, she received a gift from Alice B. Toklas and wrote to thank her and to continue to plead for her return to Florence with Gertrude Stein. At the end of the letter, Dodge wrote "(Zahdah!)" after her name, a possible reference to herself that might correspond to "Zulicka" and "Zuleika," possible nicknames that Dodge used for Toklas. The origin and meaning of both apparent appellations are not clear.⌁

FRIDAY [NOVEMBER 1912] VILLA CURONIA
VIA DELLE PIAZZOLE
ARCETRI

Dear Alice

Two adorable bottles are sitting by my bed—they came today & make <u>such</u> a difference. I smell them all the time. Thank you, dear, for sending them. You know, they almost persuade me life is just like that—sweet & not very serious. Am much better but the dip. weakens one in the heart—won't be up for some time. Was <u>terribly</u> pleased & flattered at Gertrude's wires! But am <u>still</u> waiting for the "<u>important</u> letter" which will change "everything."†

* Unidentified.
† Neither the letter nor the wires are among the existing correspondence.

Constance [Fletcher] is a treasure—a born nurse!!! When she is felt she is needed by anyone it makes her adore them. Tell Gertrude Irma, the cook & Margherita's husband all had tonsilitis but I had the dip.! How you will all adore Emily [Cary] when you see her! She looks younger than ever. Like a child now. I didn't find out why Arthur [Brisbane] married Phoebe [Cary]—but she hates it & A. & she still care for each other. Its all so queer.

Please you & Gertrude come back as soon as you get my letters—will you?

Best love—

Mabel. (Zahdah!)

◦Mabel Dodge's torment over her affair with Paul Ayrault continued, and she sent Stein letters she had received from him now that he had returned to New York where he was an undergraduate at Columbia University. In these letters, dated 23 October and 24 October 1912, he repeatedly expresses his love for Dodge and his distress at their being apart. He writes:

> It was like you, you dear honest soul, to tell E.[dwin] about yourself and I can only love you the more for it since I know you do care for me, even to the extent of putting yourself into a terrible mess. Do let me know at once what he says about the thing. Gertrude was very kind in her summing up of the matter. . . . Please write me all about what Gertrude said and what made her suspect.[37]

Paul also writes about his visit with Mary Foote, the painter who had visited at the Villa Curonia that summer and had painted portraits of both Paul and Mabel:

> I called on Mary Foote this afternoon and she confessed that she knew that we love each other. . . . I told Mary exactly how things stood and none of it seemed to be very much like news to her. She advised waiting awhile longer but said we had her blessing if we went ahead now. . . . We had tea and a long talk and smoke and she brought out my portrait and also the one she started from the loggia with you in one of those chairs.[38]

In one of the following letters, Mabel Dodge refers to her possible infatuation with Gertrude Stein, an idea purportedly introduced by Edwin Dodge but considered by Mabel as she struggled to find some clarity in her confused and complicated emotions.◦

Dear Gertrude—

Todays mail.*
Please burn.

Yours—

Mabel

<u>Everything</u> unsettled.
One enclosed from Mary Foote†

MONDAY [CIRCA NOVEMBER 1912] VILLA CURONIA
VIA DELLE PIAZZOLE
ARCETRI

Dear Gertrude—

Everything is in darkest confidence here. E.[dwin] arrived Saturday in a mood to laugh at & make light of this "last episode" & surprised to find me pulled down & ill from the situation. Then he grew gradually more serious as he learned it is not "over" yet—that I want to stay in Paris etc. I "<u>must</u> get over it" & not be "silly", etc. He will talk to Paul & I will "never see him again." All this sounds simple. E. goes from one misunderstanding to another—out of it all he evolves a theory that I—infatuated by <u>you</u>—because I have succeeded in getting your attention wish to remain in Paris on account of you—that my letter to him about Paul was <u>written</u> on account of <u>this</u> rather than on account of him or Paul. That I am a coward anyway <u>not</u> to have lived with P. & that he's not the only one who thinks me one. That your portrait of me could have been said in much simpler language, that he has him-

---

* Enclosed were two extant letters from Paul Ayrault to Mabel Dodge.

†"One enclosed from Mary Foote" may be Dodge's reference to "one" imitation of Stein's portrait of Mabel Dodge that Mary Foote wrote in September 1912. Foote's "Portrait of Mabel Dodge" begins: "Luminous days & lurid nights & a saffron uplift" and ends: "A bell does not ring for somebody so there must be other open windows. As a lamb has fleece there will be a way to change it before." A final comment by Foote appears after this last verse: "To be continued any time you like as life unrolls itself" (MDLC).

self begun "a portrait of anyone at any place at any time," that if I stay over in Paris it is the end forever between him & me & that if I go to America I will make it impossible for him. And mixed in with all this a great deal of conversation about cement brick, what will or will not grow in America, & such like.

Today he intercepted & opened & read a letter of mine to Paul— which surprised me in him very much. He said I was despicable, & trying to hold them both. In the letter I had told Paul I was trying to find out the right thing to do & wanted to spend the winter in Paris to test the thing. He says he doesn't care for my friends & that he is made for the world. I am in a state of confusion worse confounded. He seems to me very inefficient & completely un-comprehending—at least of me. He says he understands me per-fectly & is the <u>only</u> one who does. I cling to my idea of his general "niceness" & goodness (vide his coming over in answer to my let-ter & illness) which get a rude shaking when he gets hold of my letters & reads them. I tell him if his feeling for me makes him do these things it's better I left him—"despicable" is the only term he has in answer. I told him I should go to Paris tomorrow, he says if I do before he does I shall never see him again—a veiled threat of suicide added to the other in felicity! He understands some & most he doesn't which makes conversation impossible. He gives me no credit for any unselfish motive <u>any</u>where & makes me doubt my-self! Almost I believe I am infatuated with you! Am I? I feel just the same towards P. as he also does—a wire from him yesterday (which E. opened & handed to me) saying "Just received word of your illness. So sorry. Write full details. <u>I</u> <u>still</u> <u>do.</u> Yours Paul." If he walked in here now there would be little hesitancy except that E. seems so weak and helpless. I wonder if he is. I also seem so. I wonder if I am.

I am just up this last day or two & weak yet. Brain goes round & round on this. If I go to N.Y. it will precipitate things. E. says I am in the same condition as a man who goes to whores. I hope I'm not. I suppose I seem feeble to you. Things are too complicated for me. I don't see them clear. Don't write, he reads all my letters & mis-understands them.

Yours,

M.

Dearest Gertrude—

I may be spending the winter in Paris—it looks like that now—
to try six months separate from E.[dwin] & also from P.[aul] without communicating with either! So I was wondering about appts.
I'd like to find a small one with <u>some</u> sun—furnished. If you hear
of one make a note of it. Perhaps Mike [Stein]* will hear of one.
We will be coming up in the course of a week. I am getting calmer
tho' I cried all day yesterday which maddens me. I must say
Constance [Fletcher] is behaving well. Both E. & I have talked to
her about him & me—(not about P.) but about how little we get on
tho' we are so fond of each other & she is very wise on this subject.
She suggested this separation as we've never tried it before. Of
course no one else is to know we aren't communicating but are to
think I'm just spending the winter over here so don't tell anyone.
Things seem to be slowly shaping themselves.

Best love to you & Alice—

Mabel

I got the books & will bring them when I come. Am reading them.

◦In the midst of her turmoil over her marriage and her love for
Paul Ayrault, Mabel Dodge was able to compose a letter to Gertrude
Stein praising her for writing such an accurate and inspired word
portrait in her "Portrait of Mabel Dodge at the Villa Curonia." In
this letter, Dodge highlights an aspect of her own presence—"I
keep still & let people talk"—that was to be repeated in both fictional and biographical accounts of her in the years to come.

Mabel Dodge delights in the uproar over her portrait. In her
letter to Stein, she includes quotations from both named and unnamed sources, including Florence Bradley—whose quoted letter
dated 1 November 1912 finishes with a jab at Dodge's former guests
Emily Cary and Alice Thursby ("In spite of Mrs. Cary and—that
insanely annoying person with her you <u>must</u> come to Paris

---

* Michael Stein, the eldest brother of Gertrude and Leo, who lived with his wife
Sarah at 58 rue Madame in Paris. Michael and Sarah Stein were art collectors themselves and important patrons of Henri Matisse.

soon.")³⁹—and Mrs. Napier, an English woman living in India whom Dodge describes in her memoirs as

> that little woman with crinkly hair parted in the middle, who always had two famous superlatives quoted about her (Sergeant [i.e., John Singer Sargent?] had said of her that she had the bluest eyes in England, while [Rudyard] Kipling had called her in his preface to "Plain Tales from the Hills" [1888] "the wittiest woman in India.")⁴⁰

∾

[CIRCA NOVEMBER 1912] VILLA CURONIA
VIA DELLE PIAZZOLE
ARCETRI

Dearest Gertrude—

I must snatch a lucid moment when "argument is clear" to tell you that I consider the "Portrait" to be a masterpiece of success from my (& your) point of view <u>as</u> a portrait of <u>me</u> as I am to others! When I repeat to you some of the comments you will see that their application to <u>me</u> is absolutely perfect. I keep still & let people talk. What they see in <u>it</u> is what, I consider, they see in me. No more no less. Florence Bradley (<u>at 25 Rue Humboldt</u>) writes "my head aches with the throb of it, the portrait, shall I ever be able to swing in line with it? You see I cannot think while it goes on but I feel a lot & I shall be at it until—do I please you when I say—until I feel it more <u>wholly</u>." In fact I enclose <u>all</u> <u>her</u> letter to you.*

My english friend Mrs. Napier† (to whom [Rudyard] Kipling dedicated "Plain Tales from the Hills" to as "The wittiest woman in India"[)] writes "it is bold effrontery to do this sort of thing" (<u>If</u> she <u>knew</u> me!!!) Others say (as they would of me! they know <u>so</u> little they <u>are</u> saying it of me!) "there is no beauty in it." Someone else says "would not one of the only five or six (literary) forms done to express this in?" Edwin says "If it is a portrait then it is the portrait of anyone anywhere at any time." Muriel [Draper] who is here & who makes me feel more like <u>mush</u> & seems to me more

---

* Florence Bradley to Dodge, 1 November 1912, MDLC.

† Mrs. Napier is mentioned only once in Charles Carrington's *Rudyard Kipling, His Life and Work*, in a brief description: "A gossiping, over-dressed lady who believed herself to be in the Viceroy's confidence" (113).

like a dogbiscuit herself than ever says "Ducie Haweis* & I wanted to wire from London 'We understand the cover (!) We know that'"—Someone else says "it is all a confusion—things do not seem to follow each other out of each other." [Jacques-Émile] Blanche writes "I shall strain my brain more to try & understand"—someone reads it aloud with des regards louches†—implying horror all through—someone else reads it aloud reverently with an evedent desire to please tho' understanding nothing & not even seeing horrors! Someone said mockingly "Mabel brought it me & I read it carefully determined to find some good in the little book." Someone writes me "I cannot see anything in it"—everyone is mystified as you say most are about me—No one (but me!) can remember a line in it to quote without referring to it! In fact it is so faithful a portrait as, I think, to produce about the same effects as myself were the truth always said! I think it better & better as time goes on & they say more & more things. Some days I don't understand it, but some days I don't understand things in myself, past or about to come! When I tell people that my "precious coherence" is in it they roar never having perceived any in me! When I say it seems to me "middleclass, confused, & rather sound," Edwin laughs with contempt at my daring to even mention the word "sound" in connection with myself not to mention it!

Good by—best love—

Mabel

◠These responses to Gertrude Stein's "Portrait of Mabel Dodge at the Villa Curonia" were only the beginning. In the following months, Mabel Dodge was to hear and read numerous reactions to

---

*Ducie is a nickname for Mina Loy Haweis, an English poet and artist married to the English artist Stephen Haweis. Mabel Dodge owned a painting by Mina Loy, *The Wooden Madonna*, that she made the night her daughter died. It depicts a mother with her baby who is blessing another mother whose baby lies dead beside her on the ground (*EE*, 340–41). Mina Loy wrote a poem about Gertrude Stein that reads in full:

Curie
of the laboratory
she crushed
the tonnage
of consciousness
congealed to phrases
to extract
a radium of the word (*GSC*, 114)

† Shady, suspicious, or equivocal glances.

the portrait, and both she and Gertrude Stein were to be the subjects of parodies and imitations. There were also many comments that they were not to hear directly. Mary Berenson, the wife of Bernard Berenson, wrote to her family on 21 November 1912 from Florence:

> I am sending along Gertrude Stein's latest amazing (and horrid) production. . . . When you have hated it enough, send it to Grace to keep. *We have another* sent by herself to B. B. What can he say? And many people take it seriously as a new worthwhile "departure." It isn't even funny, only horrible. I should like to see Logan's face when he opens it.[41]

The American poet Edwin Arlington Robinson asked in a letter to Mabel Dodge, "How do you know that it is a portrait of you, after all?"[42] In her memoirs, Dodge recalls that Robinson's comment constituted "the first setback in my enthusiasm for Gertrude's 'Portrait.' He never stopped joking about that, always bringing it up."[43] Leo Stein called the portrait "damned nonsense" and observed that it was "directly inspired by Picasso's latest form,"[44] synthetic Cubism. Leo wrote his own "Portrait of Mabel Dodge" that begins:

> Mabel Dodge
> Hodge Podge
> What is up,
> What is down,
> What's a smile,
> What's a frown,
> What is passion,
> What is pose.
> What is guessing,
> What is nose. . . .

And ends:

> Burning ice and freezing flame,
> Half is brisk and half is lame,
> Some is wild and some is tame.
> Whistle and creek,
> Florid and bleak
> Hodge Podge
> Mabel Dodge.[45]

Leo Stein's was not the only parody written of Stein's portrait of Mabel Dodge. Grant Watson, an author and new acquaintance of Dodge's in Florence, also produced a parody of "it." ✺

Dearest Gertrude

Our new friend Mr. Grant Watson has written a critical parody of "it."* He says when he began to read it he thought his leg was being pulled but he soon saw there was something in it & finally pored over it until three in the morning—which is as well aplied to me as to it too? Here it is. Keep it till I come please.

M.

———

[1912 ?] Villa Curonia
Via delle Piazzole
Arcetri

Dear Gertrude—

This is to introduce to you Mr. Grant Watson who evedently has some feeling for the fourth dimension as he has been one of the few who has caught on to "it"!

Ever yrs—

Mabel Dodge

⌒Mabel Dodge remained uncertain and tortured about how or whether to choose between her husband Edwin and her young lover Paul. For a time, she occupied herself with the affairs of the Swami and Isidor and Lily Braggiotti. During a visit to Boston to meet Edwin's relatives in the early summer of 1912, Mabel Dodge had met the Swami at her hotel. In *European Experiences*, she describes her first contact with him and its effects on her troubled state of mind:

> The Swami stood before us in his apricot-colored robe, a turban on his head. Tall and slim, he looked about twenty-six or -eight years old. . . . He was intoning a monotonous refrain over and over again in a high, almost female voice and his dark eyes were on us all, and I seemed to swim in a warm, slightly sticky element of some kind. . . . He was conjuring up some state of being that had its manifest place there in that room, and into which we could all swim along with him. So we all

———

* Not located.

drifted out into the alleviating flood of warm existence issuing from the Swami—and we *felt* perfume, sound, heat, oils, and unguents in our souls. My heart ceased aching and I felt the most exquisite relief and happiness, all in the twinkling of an eye.[46]

The Swami was a follower of the Hindu mystic Vivekananda, who was a teacher of the Vedanta religion, a branch of Indian philosophy. In her characteristic manner of immediately responding to a figure who captured her interest, Mabel Dodge invited the Swami to Florence for the rest of the summer.

Isidor and Lily Braggiotti lived in a villa in Florence, where they gave voice lessons. Isidor was a blend of Turkish and Bostonian roots: "[He] used to enjoy saying that his aunts on his father's side were selling peanuts in Constantinople, while his aunts on his mother's side were Cabots of Boston."[47] In Paris he met the composer Sebastian Schlesinger and married his daughter Lily. Mabel Dodge describes her:

> Lily Braggiotti was marvelous. She was the rarest, last flower of Jewish fineness and beauty, of loveliness and elegance. . . . She couldn't sing true. Braggiotti at the piano played with ease, his eyes on hers, trying to fix her gaze, to catch her eyes, and with his tip-tilted face, to raise her a pitch. But she looked over beyond him and sang sweetly on, quite off the key, making a beautiful picture.[48]

The Braggiottis were immediately interested in meeting the Swami once he arrived in Florence, "for," Dodge explained, "they were far gone in Theosophy and were always having psychic things happen in their house."[49]

As was also Mabel Dodge's characteristic pattern, as soon as the Swami appeared in Florence, she was no longer entranced by his presence: "I saw now the Swami was not very impressive. He looked very dark and slim in his civilian clothes. His face looked too short."[50] Now in a different frame of mind than the turmoil she had been experiencing in Boston, Dodge found herself inwardly mocking and resisting the Swami: "When he excused himself and went up to his room a succession of '*my dear's*' broke out of all of us: that acute, heart-bounding, Aryan protest at everything a little other."[51] Mabel Dodge hastened to introduce the Swami to the Braggiottis and schemed to entice them to invite him to live at their home. After a lengthy Indian dinner prepared by the Swami at the Villa Curonia, Dodge got her wish, and he moved to the Braggiottis' villa, where he remained until the fall.[52]

Dearest Gertrude—

Still nothing decided yet. Strange, isn't it? The excitement here
is all over the [Isidor and Lily] Braggiottis. He, suddenly, is leaving
for America for the winter, indefinitely. This follows on the Swami's
departure last Tuesday. Lily is <u>radiant</u> at the idea of his going. He is
a broken & suffering wreck of a man at present! Lily is two months
along with a baby!

<u>What</u> does it all mean? I see three possibilities. Either Lily &
the Swami determined to present a "master" to the world and made
Braggiotti allow it & now he can't stand it, or the Swami has persuaded <u>both</u> of them to come to America & settle in Boston or he
has woven a spell & has "suggestione"* Lily to "suggestione" Mr.
Braggiotti to go, by making the latter so miserable, & thus he will
<u>go</u> to Boston, find a place for them, & they will all move over there—
but he, Braggiotti, doesn't know he is acting in accordance with
Swami's designs & is only leaving to se faire valoir† in his wife's
eyes & naturally goes to Boston where his friends & relations are.
Lily beams, hugs herself tightly as tho' she had a precious secret &
says "One must think of the future if one has children & America
would be so much better when they are older. <u>I</u> think it's a splendid
idea of Isidor to go & he will probably send for us all in the spring."
Braggiotti meanwhile is <u>dark</u> brown, shaky & tragic looking. A
friend of his to whom he has talked told me a little, as much as he
could, which was that Braggiotti felt that Swami had absolutely
swept him out of his place & to bring Lily to her senses he said he
was going away which instead of a shock was a joy apparently to
Lily. If he goes, instead of making his value increase in her eyes, <u>I</u>
think she'l simply forget him & they'l never get together again
the way they have been in the past which was for having children
etc. <u>I</u> think Braggiotti is up against the <u>real</u> impersonality of Lily
for the first time in his life. She's like a bowl of water.

He's terribly unhappy, this is a real tradgedy. People whisper to
me, (so differently from Lily's attitude towards it—you remember?) "Do you realize that you are responsible for all this," & I still
reply "Only an accident!" So E.[dwin] & he will probably sail together in a week. I wonder if I will go to[o]. If E. should seem to
want me very much I would, I suppose. Mr. B. is perfectly helpless.

* Hypnotize or influence.
† Assert oneself or show off.

He's never done without her. I don't believe he can. He said to this friend of his that she is a "little better" than she was, speaking as tho' she were ill or insane. I wonder if she is and then there is that baby coming! What of that? Perhaps she thinks it is Swami's spiritual child. Of course no ordinary husband would care for that as an idea, no matter if it is uplifted! I have been there these last two days & B. looks at her as tho' she were a woman he didn't know, & his hands shake. He is less the male bird than before & his plumage is not gay at all, while she has a glorious radiant steady smile & hugs a secret. She has got a little careless in her clothes since Swami left, & is very thin & beautiful. She never had hysteria when any other child was coming so she's not to be accounted for that way. So you tell me when I see you what you make out of it all.

Lucy Perkins has turned up, very shining & lovely & looks as tho' she were going to be married. She won't deny it. [Charles] Loeser & his wife are in separate cures, I hear! I have succeeded in putting [Lord] Acton completely in the wrong, by having had diptheria for he doesn't know there was an interrim between the night they were coming to dine & my having it. He thinks I went right home to bed with it that day! So the first time I saw him when I was out I looked as pathetic as I could, & cut him. He came rushing after me & begged & begged me to forgive him, that when he'd heard I really had diptheria he'd been broken hearted over the way he'd acted & had thought of it for days & days, & finally he'd been ill himself & was just out & would I forgive him, that he should have known me better but that people did do such nasty things all the time, but that no! no! of course I didn't ever, & that he should have known that, & remembered how different I am to all those others & would I forgive him, really forgive & tell him so?? So I finally, very sweetly & generously, did & said E. & C.[onstance Fletcher] & I would all lunch with him next day to prove I was friends, & tonight he's coming here. So that's that.

I saw B. B. [Bernard Berenson] & Mrs. B. B. at Miss [Florence] Blood's yesterday. He looked well & was quite sweet & she was lusty. Miss Blood begged a copy of the portrait which I have sent with this translation of A.[ndré] Gide's from [Rainer Maria] Rilke— in the front of it. "Le temps, de l'autre explication va venir ou chaque signification se défera comme un nuage et s'eculera comme de l'eau."*

---

* "The time for other explanation will come when each meaning will dissipate like a cloud and fall down like water." The source of this quotation from Rilke has not been located. I am grateful to Tom O'Connor for assistance in translating this passage.

By this time you have seen Florence Bradley. I wonder if you like her?

Constance left here this p.m. threatening suicide—etc—as her things are all to be seized (?) by a bank (?) as she cannot pay interest (?) on a loan (?). She was marvellously dramatic when she left— saying "I shall probably never come back here again Mabel dear—for I would not come back as Margurite (the ghost) comes back!"

She is a most curious mixture of wisdom & folly. She nearly exterminated E. trying to get $400 out of him which he can't afford to give her just now—& at the last brought suicide as a powerful lever. This is a long gay letter—so goodby now.

Love,

M.

⮑Mabel Dodge continued her support of Gertrude Stein's writing and offered herself as an informal agent to publishers in the United States. In this role, she had contacted Mitchell Kennerley, a New York publisher at that time of the journals *Papyrus: A Magazine of Individuality* and *Forum*, both of which featured literature and poetry as well as political and social commentary. As she is preparing to return to the United States for the winter, Mabel Dodge writes to Gertrude Stein and presents herself as an enthusiastic and assertive coach in her appeals and questions.⮑

[AFTER 22 NOVEMBER 1912] VILLA CURONIA
VIA DELLE PIAZZOLE
ARCETRI

Dearest Gertrude—

We have had our usual fall diptheria & the two patients are now convalescing. I begin to think there is a bad drain or something around here—couldn't write you before because the doctors were rabid this year about centagrin* & said I'd certainly send germs if I sent letters out of the house. We've all been fumigated & disinfected now however. It delayed our sailing—we leave three weeks late next Monday—from Naples. I wish like <u>anything</u> you'd both come over this winter—I also wish you'd give me some directions about what you want me to do for you there. Do you want [Mitchell] Kennerl[e]y to publish those <u>six</u> <u>short</u> things which I have—(which I got back from him) & consequently take on in connection with

* Unidentified.

that "Three Lives" to sell? Or do you want an agent? Or do you want to send direct to some other publishers? I think you should make <u>some</u> move this fall—& the best would be to come over. People are all ready for you. You have already influenced people with the small amt. of stuff of yours they have seen. Two or three people have sent me MMS [i.e., MSS] this summer to show how they had adopted yr way—one, a story by a very known woman writer of short stories named Edna Kenton* & a poet† whose book of sonnets comes out this fall with the enclosed one—after you—in it. And of course all the ones I haven't even heard of—who have been caught up by it. There should be more of yours forthcoming at once. Write me to the Moltke—Naples—Sailing 29th—<u>what</u> <u>I'm</u> to do.

Best love to you & Alice. <u>Please</u> <u>pose</u> for [Arnold] Rönnebeck.‡ He wants to.

M. D.

⌇It appears that Mabel Dodge changed her sailing plans and traveled to Paris on her way back to the United States for the winter. While in Paris, in a miserable state over her love affairs, she visited Gertrude Stein. As she did at least once before, Dodge asked Alice B. Toklas to run an errand for her.⌇

[CIRCA NOVEMBER 1912] VILLA CURONIA
VIA DELLE PIAZZOLE
ARCETRI

Dearest Gertrude—

I am going with Edwin (& [Isidor] Braggiotti!) on Sunday. It somehow seems the thing to do. We will arrive on Sat. in Paris & will come to see you that evening.

Best love—

Mabel

---

* Edna Kenton, American author of novels, short stories, and articles who was close friends with Carl Van Vechten. Like Mabel Dodge, Kenton was a member of Heterodoxy, an organization of emancipated women in Greenwich Village.

† This may refer to Donald Evans, an American poet whose book of sonnets, *Discords*, was issued in 1912. Two years later, Evans wrote "Portrait of Mabel Dodge—Chiaroscuro," also titled "Her Smile," a poem that appears to have been modeled after Stein's style of portrait writing.

‡ Arnold Rönnebeck, a German sculptor who had been introduced to Gertrude Stein in the fall of 1912 by his close friend Marsden Hartley.

Dear Alice

I forgot today was going to be Sunday & left two important errands till this morning so of course here I am asking you to do them! There is a horrid one. And you needn't do either till you happen to pass the places—no hurry at all. One is to get my monogram stamp at Magnet's [?] on the Rue de la Paix & post it to 23 Fifth Aven so I can have some paper stamped & the other is to leave this bracelet at Iecla's [?] (imitation stones) for me—saying the reason I didn't send them a cheque was because I wanted them to take it back, as I only wore it a few times & all the stones fell out as they all turned out to be loose. And give them my address so they can row with me if they want to. I was in sort of a hazy dream last night with fever & everything—still feeling very queer & brainish. You don't mind my bothering you with these things—do you? I hope you & Gertrude will write soon & often.

Best love

Mabel—

Please for yr own sake send the Picasso-Matisse portraits* at once to F. Grant Watson,† 2 Lung'Arno Acci.‡ in Florence.

Dearest Gertrude—

I wonder what you thought of me last Saturday night. I was near the breaking point, whatever that is, & just why I don't know yet. Since I got on this boat I haven't left my cabin but once & I

------

* Gertrude Stein's word portraits of Picasso and Matisse were published in *Camera Work* in August 1912.

† Although Dodge refers here to F. Grant Watson, Muriel Draper calls him E. Grant Watson in *Music at Midnight* (154, 230).

‡ Acci. may be an abbreviation for "acciottolato," meaning cobbled paving of a street.

have relaxed to the large crocodile tears* that hour after hour pour down my face. I am too near myself to know what is the matter with me. I wish it were a baby, but anything less than a miracle . . .†

I want to see Paul. E.[dwin] in his dear good role of forgiving husband threatens "choose then" etc., & I feel myself in a vague way hastening slowly on to my doom, whatever that is. I want to see Paul but E. in the usual manly way, will not be a "mari complaisant."‡ I grow thinner & thinner & he remains the same. Paul, I suppose, is as hearty as ever. Does the woman always do it all, I wonder, feel it all, see it all & hear it all?

E. has just been in. He surmises that our ways shall part at the dock. These phrases make me laugh while I sob. I am so tired of it all.

I can't see 2 hours ahead, everything goes round & round in my brain. Of what earthly use is <u>resistance</u> if it <u>weakens</u> me like this. I wish you were here. I think I'm all in.

Mabel

~Upon arriving in the United States, Mabel Dodge placed herself in the hands of a doctor near her home town of Buffalo. She had already secured an apartment at 23 Fifth Avenue in New York where she would soon live.~

[CIRCA DECEMBER 1912] CLIFTON PLACE
NIAGARA FALLS CENTRE
WELLAND CO., ONT.

Dearest Gertrude

I am now in the clutch of an americain doctor who has wrung my trouble from me & who is on the point of suggesting a rest cure which is what they always advise over here when the one & only remedy is out of the question. They call my disease nervous breakdown & I certainly am gibbering. Paul—I hear from Mary Foote—is in the same state—& is neglecting his college career ex-

---

* Mabel Dodge seems to have misused this term, as she is not suggesting that her tears are false or affected.

† Dodge seems to be suggesting here that she would welcome the news that she was pregnant, but that it would be unlikely news. Notes taken by her analyst Dr. Smith Ely Jelliffe during the course of her analysis with him in 1916 suggest that there were medical reasons possibly making it difficult for her to get pregnant again, including an operation following the birth of her son for some sort of prolapse, and the removal of one ovary. (Jelliffe notes, 11 January 1916, MDLC).

‡ Complacent husband.

cept for the Italian course or class in which he is most diligent.* He writes me he is a wreck & that he will soon be in a "nut house" if things don't go right for us. E.[dwin] continues to be more than good & generous & offers me everything—my choice—etc—but not both. He makes me shudder when he looks into the future at my ruin if I have him however. I also dimly see his disintegration if I do. All this is nothing compared to my own present collapse which is certainly a complete one.

[Isidor] Braggiotti & I cried all the way over—& he is now in Boston while I weep alone. E. continues cheerful for the most part, & works at his work. I am not allowed by the medical man to go to fix up that appartment yet. So I don't know what's going to happen next. Never was anyone so hypnotized & taken possession of by anything as I am by Paul. He is the only one who can cure me. I will send your "Constances"† back soon with a note about them. They are great stuff all of them. You can show her the last because she would never understand it. Noone here understands my portrait. [illegible]

Yrs,

Mabel

Write to 23 Fifth Ave. it will be sent on if I'm not there but remember if E's about he opens my letters—Best love to you all— M.

---

* Mary Foote wrote to Mabel Dodge: "Paul came tearing down here today—poor child— apparently with the idea that if he didn't speak to somebody he would burst. . . . He looked rather pasty & ill still. . . . I was awfully glad to see him but I did hate to have him in such a mess—& I hate to have you too." She continues on to question Mabel's judgment: "I am so sorry for everybody—Lord what a world. Why did you do it? I should think you'd better keep away from N.Y." (Mary Foote to Dodge, c. 1912, MDLC.) It seems that Paul Ayrault did not graduate from Columbia University, as an inquiry at the alumni office yielded no mention of him in the graduating classes from this time. It is possible that he was so distraught over his relationship with Mabel Dodge that he had to abandon his studies.

† This reference to "Constances" indicates the three stylistically distinct sections of Stein's portrait of Constance Fletcher, as it appears in its published version in 1922. According to Ulla Dydo, Stein wrote the three parts at different times and in different notebooks. Dydo notes that the original typescript of the portrait includes spaces between the three sections (Stein, *A Stein Reader*, 260-61). Although Stein recalls in *The Autobiography of Alice B. Toklas* that she wrote the portraits of Mabel Dodge and Constance Fletcher during the summer of 1912 while visiting the Villa Curonia where she first met Fletcher (130), the correspondence between Dodge and Stein indicates that it was the summer of 1911 when they first met. It is uncertain whether Stein and Fletcher saw each other again in 1912.

⁓As she had done with the Villa Curonia, Mabel Dodge dramatically transformed her apartment at 23 Fifth Avenue to suit her emotional needs. Located on the second floor of a four-story brownstone near the northern border of Greenwich Village, Dodge's apartment was ideally situated to become the home for her famous salons, although those gatherings were not yet a thought. Immersing herself in decorating, Dodge had all the woodwork in the apartment painted over with white paint and the walls covered with white wallpaper. There was a mantelpiece in white marble and a Venetian chandelier of white porcelain. Dodge used white linen and white silk for curtains and hung white silk on all four sides of her canopy bed. As she admitted in her memoirs, "It seemed to me I couldn't get enough white into that apartment. I suppose it was a repudiation of grimy New York. I even sent to the Villa for the big, white bearskin rug and laid it in front of the white marble fireplace in the front room."[53] For furniture, Dodge had the pale-colored French chairs and couches from the Villa Curonia. Dodge described her feeling near the time of completion of her apartment:

> I have always known how to make rooms that had power in them. Whatever the need at any time I have been able to make for myself a refuge from the world, so I know that even if I had nothing I could somehow create an *ambiente* to creep into where I could breathe as I want to breathe. . . . If I don't know anything else, and sometimes I am convinced I don't, I do know how to assemble things and make them do their work.[54]

At first, she believed that the apartment worked for her, as it provided a striking alternative to the dirt and commotion of New York. However, soon Dodge became restless for company to populate her carefully decorated rooms.

In her next letter, Gertrude Stein provides Dodge with a lengthy quotation from one response to the Mabel Dodge portrait, written by her college friend and former lover May Bookstaver, now married to Charles Knoblauch, who is one of characters in the love triangle in Stein's *Q.E.D.*⁓

[CIRCA DECEMBER 1912] 27 RUE DE FLEURUS

My dear Mabel,

Are you alright. Its too soon to hear from you yet but I hope to when its time. I got a wonderful letter from Constance [Fletcher] so she is not dead yet. Apparently she did not know that you were not wintering in Paris. I have been getting some replies to the Portrait, most of them not very much but one which should please you. She* writes, "Many thanks for Mabel Dodge. I am not sure that I should recognise her if I were to meet her but that I suppose is the merit of the portrait. Who is William. Is he a romance or a cross between the garden and the armchair. Charlie (thats her husband) says Mabel Dodge sounds like the bottle of old Lacrima Christi I induced him to drink all by himself upon the occasion of our arrival in Venice. I was very anxious that Italy should make a great hit with him from the very start as he had not wanted to come there at all and so at the conclusion of our first day's run on Italian soil I consulted at great length with the head waiter at the Hotel in Venice so as to have a wonderful dinner. The wine bothered me awfully as my palate knows no distinction, but the waiter said no man can resist del Lacrima Christi, you see Madame it is sixteen dollars a quart. Charlie had to drink it all and he has never fully recovered from it. He thought it so siropy and he found it so different. For nearly two hours after he had finished dinner he sat immobile, looking at the canal and murmuring, this is paradise, the air is filled with music, that great church across the way is coming nearer, I can't move my legs. I I am afraid I never shall come to, perhaps a zephyr will waft me to bed. I certainly never shall understand it." And so on. As he is usually an xceedingly lucid mortal you can see what his confusion meant.

I got a very sweet letter from [Lord] Acton thanking me for the M.[atisse] & Picasso, and a very friendly and unconvinced one from [Bernard] Berenson. By the way what is Andre Gide's address. [Stephen] Haweis writes that he is thinking of lecture on Modern Art in Australia but you probably know all about that. I have been laying off work for the last two weeks. I found I was very tired. I am much rested now. I have finished the Two.†

Lets hear from you soon Respects to Edwin

Always yours

Gertrude.

---

* Gertrude Stein's next letter to Dodge, from late December 1912, reveals that this passage is from a letter written by May Bookstaver.

† "Two: Gertrude Stein and Her Brother" was written as Gertrude Stein was becoming more distant from Leo and more attached to Alice B. Toklas. It is included in *Two*.

~Always finding intrigue in the scandalous activities of others, even when immersed herself in emotional turmoil, Mabel Dodge became more deeply involved in the ongoing saga of the Swami and the Braggiottis. Apparently lifted from the tearful paralysis she experienced on the trip to the United States and during her first days after landing, Dodge now energetically pursued her contacts with others and continued her tendency to assemble various combinations of people.~

DEC. 11 [1912] 23 FIFTH AVENUE

Dearest Gertrude—

I am in the most exciting situation with [Isidor] Braggiotti and as you already know so much of the story I will tell you about it but please don't talk of it to anyone but Alice because it is all, for obvious reasons, secret. As you would imagine from Braggiotti's personality, the minute one gets intimate with him one is drawn into a current of astronomers, alienists, secret meetings for consultations in out of the way place & a whirl of intrigue & melodrama! As he calls it "this is a game of souls with <u>God</u> as a rival!" He had become very confidential with me & told me the whole thing since I approached him on the subject one day. It appears Lily [Braggiotti] went even farther than we thought, completely estranging herself from Isidor from the time the Swami entered her house, & putting up a shrine to him there, washing His Feet daily & drying them with her hair, etc., considering him the Divine Incarnation, & her forthcoming child the Messiah, born of <u>their</u> thought. Braggiotti got out because he couldn't stand it any more. Here he has consulted a wonderful person, Miss Evangeline Adams,* an astronomer who has worked the whole thing out of his & Lily's horoscope & who had advised his whole plan of action. It was she who decided, after seeing me & talking with me, that <u>I</u> am to be the one to save the situation <u>if</u> it can be done peaceably— if not—"the most prominent lawyer in Boston" will take up the matter! It was she who directed Braggiotti to "the most prominent alienist"† in New York to whom he told the whole thing. This latter man told him that Lily has got to be freed <u>at</u> <u>once</u> from the

---

* Evangeline Smith Adams, an American astrologer whose later radio broadcasts drew an average of four thousand letters a day.

† Unidentified. "Alienist" was a term at that time for a specialist in mental disorders, specifically a psychiatrist.

hypnotic spell of the Swami or she will go irrevocably mad. (Miss Adams finds softening of the brain in Lily's horoscope but it need not be until old age if she can be tided over this.) The alienist then sent for me & directed me to go to the Swami in Boston & simply relate to him the gossip I have heard about his stay in the Braggiotti family, how it seperated husband & wife, threw her into an exalted & overbalanced state which is dangerous in pregnancy, & appealing to him in the grounds of his public career, get him to write her that now she has gone far enough with <u>him</u>, that she must go the rest of the way alone since he has put her on the path, at least until the baby is born, etc., & I am to <u>see</u> if possible his letter telling her this. Saturday Braggiotti & I have a meeting with Miss Adams to plan the details & Monday I go to Boston! It is all terrific & scary! The Swami may try to do away with me as Vivekananda did Mrs. Oley [?] Bull* if he suspects me! The alienist as well as Miss Adams says it is fearfully serious & that Lily will go mad for good unless it is stopped. Braggiotti says he will hesitate at nothing. The things that went on at his house were beyond belief. Lily would go to the Swami's room at half past one & finally emerge at eight, Brag[giotti] pacing the floor in the meantime. Then she would appear in the doorway of his room & her eyes shining, say "Isidor you are wonderful, the way you understand," & he would reply, "No, I am not wonderful but I have two qualities. I love & I trust." The Swami nearly drove <u>him</u> mad as well as Lily! Sometimes it <u>wasn't</u> peaceful & controlled—Isidor would break out of his restraint & sob & howl about his love, & losing Lily, etc., & then the Swami would tell him that love on earth was only a morbid symptom & complete detachment was the only thing to want. Isidor can't risk having Lily know he's fighting the Swami for that would estrange her still more. He read me some of her letters. She says such things as the following: "There is now no reality for me but the love of God" (Swami) "No life but in God" (Swami) "And I hope that you will receive the conviction of this as I have! All I care for now is to come nearer & nearer to Him" (Swami) leaving all else & caring not if all the world forsake & defile me for it, but if I should believe that it is for yr happiness that I stay with you I should try & do it even tho' it cost me the peace of my soul. Already you have come so far on the Path, from physical & moral cowardice, gross materialism & ill feeling you have progressed so that the Divine One (Swami) feels that you are <u>almost</u> ready to be taken to His Heart. I

---

* Unidentified person and event.

pray that you may never lose sight of the Spiritual Life."

Braggiotti says she wants to become a nun—either "of the Household" or take Swami's veil. It is all extroidenary! There is much more to write but it takes so long. I will let you know results.

The situation in the Seward Cary family* here is bizarre indeed. Arthur Brisbane & his little Phoebe are wonderfully happy. Seward is being pushed out by all of them, by the Brisbanes & by his other daughter Elenor [i.e., Eleanor Cary Smith] who is married to a henchman of Arthur's. Seward complains to me now that everything makes him mad. That it makes him mad to see Emily's nice embroidered sheets on Phoebe's bed! I said I thought he could stand that alright. He said that Emily had only given her consent to the marriage on condition that Phoebe would promise to always live with her as (Seward said so naively!) Emily says that Arthur is so inconsiderate that he will forget Phoebe isn't strong & will rush her to death. Phoebe is to have a baby next April!

Emily is now in Paris at the Hotel Ste. Anne, Rue Ste. Anne with Arthur's son Jack & Arthur's sister.† You must know her—if you go around with enclosed note she may see you tho' they have seen absolutely no one as yet. Seward sails in Saturday with his halfwitted son, to join her, do get to know them, wonderful types all of them. Make an effort for it's worth it. I am leading a hectic life, can't get this appartment settled. Promised not to see P.[aul] & haven't but dying to—most miserable & run down, & on the verge of nervous collapse but not in a Rest Cure. Please make me know Mabel Weekes [i.e., Weeks],‡ & Hutchins Hapgood.§ I will try & connect the latter with [Henri] Bergson¶ when he comes as he

* Seward Cary, Mabel Dodge's childhood friend from Buffalo, who was married to Emily Cary and had two daughters, Eleanor and Phoebe.

† Alice Thursby.

‡ Mabel Foote Weeks had been a member of the group of liberated women in Baltimore with whom Stein met regularly during her later years at Johns Hopkins University School of Medicine. Weeks corresponded frequently with both Gertrude and Leo and was a confidante for each of them. Despite their long friendship, when Gertrude Stein made her 1934 American lecture tour, she did not see Weeks. As Alice B. Toklas explained in *What is Remembered*, she sat next to Weeks during one of Stein's lectures at Columbia University and Weeks asked Toklas when she could see Stein. Toklas replied that she did not know, recalling, "Miss Weeks was one of her [Gertrude Stein's] old friends whom she was not intending to see" (*WIR*, 145).

§ Hutchins Hapgood, celebrated author, journalist, and social critic who was married to the writer Neith Boyce.

¶ Henri Bergson, French philosopher.

wants to know him. Janet Scudder* turned up yesterday, very full of business. Do you ever see George Field or Florence Bradley? Send me <u>any</u> one of my kind that you know here. I will send Constance [Fletcher]'s portraits back if you have not copies. Otherwise would rather keep them. They are marvellous, each one from its different angle. I had a frantic wire from her to see if I had news of her play—& saying "Situation here impossible"—I have nothing but bad news as Brisbane said when he read it that he wouldn't send it to [David] Belasco† because the characters are not real people, etc. I enclose his letter—please return it. Let me know if you meet young Grant Watson who did the parody of the Portrait. Constance's things will all be seized on the 1st Jan, & then I don't know what will happen to her. She will then be without furniture, appartment or money, an awful situation. Don't forget to arrange with the Picassos to come with you to Curonia next summer. Do write me a decent letter & give me some news—don't talk of P. as E.[dwin] will read it.

Best love to you & Alice—

Mabel

Mary Foote sees P. who is worse off than I am, doesn't eat or sleep or study. It has hit him harder than we thought. E. is also a wreck but is very fine over it all.

[Enclosed letter to Emily Cary]

[CIRCA 11 DECEMBER 1912] 23 FIFTH AVENUE

Dearest Emily,

    I am going to ask you to make an exception in not seeing people in Paris & <u>see</u> & <u>know</u> my great friend Gertrude Stein. She is wonderful & just the person for you. I promise you you will like her & like to talk to her. You & she are the two wisest women I know. <u>Please</u> see her—You won't regret it. But you must talk to her & then you will get to know her.

Best love,

Mabel.

---

* Janet Scudder, American sculptor who moved to Paris to study art and lived there for forty-five years. Her studio was a popular gathering place for American and European artists.

† David Belasco, American playwright and producer, owner and manager of the Belasco Theater in New York.

⌒Mabel Dodge had asked Gertrude Stein for an introduction to the author and journalist Hutchins Hapgood, who would soon become one of her closest companions in New York and a regular at her weekly salons. Hapgood had first met Leo Stein in the fall of 1895 on a ship bound for Japan, a trip during which they "argued the livelong days."[55] He met Gertrude Stein the following year in Heidelberg when she joined her brother at the end of his year of travel. Hapgood had been impressed by "her singular devotion to Leo" and her physical presence: "powerful, a beautiful head, a sense of something granite."[56] Although Mellow claims that Stein introduced Dodge to Hapgood, both Dodge and Hapgood recall in their memoirs that it was the sculptor Jo Davidson who provided the opportunity for their first meeting. Dodge described Hapgood as "so sympathetic! Always ready to have a tear in his eye!" and as having "deep, faithful-looking blue eyes whose lids drooped at the outer corners, and he had the massive arched nose of an eminent man. But he was not just an eminent man. He was an old bloodhound on a leash—with full, generous lips and melancholy jowls."[57] Hapgood proved to be a loyal confidant and soon introduced Dodge to many of the avant-garde members of the political, literary, and art worlds, including the anarchist Emma Goldman, the birth control advocate Margaret Sanger, and the author and editor Max Eastman.

Hapgood had already written an article about Gertrude Stein, entitled "A New Form of Literature," which appeared in the *New York Globe* on 26 September 1912 and was reprinted in the October 1912 issue of *Camera Work*. In this article, he presents his understanding of the art of Picasso and Matisse as it relates to his grasp of Stein's writing: "They [Picasso and Matisse] are artistically strenuous persons who are passionately attempting to find a way to express more intimately and intensely the emotional-mood-subjective life of all of us than the historical forms in painting and art have been able to do." He believes that Stein is "the only American living who is trying to do in writing what Picasso and Matisse and others are trying to do in plastic art." Hapgood continues on to discuss Stein's word portraits of Picasso and Matisse:

> She does not mention their work or their ideas, what they are aiming at, or how they are doing it. All she does is to try to do in words what they are trying to do in painting; or, rather, not what they are trying to do in painting, but what their

moods and deeper dreaming consciousness is which leads them to do what they are trying to do in painting.

In this last paragraph, by the way, I have unconsciously, to a slight degree, imitated a fragment of her style, as far as it involves repetition.

Hapgood describes the state that he arrived at after reading Stein's *Three Lives*, thereby providing for the American public an evocative introduction to her work: "I began to see that, somehow, the picture of life was attained in this mass of repetition, simplicity, and apparent inanity. . . . This book of Miss Stein's makes us dream about the fundamental mood-realities of our existence."[58]

In her next letter, Gertrude Stein supplies Mabel Dodge with other introductions and names of people she considers worth knowing in New York.⮀

[CIRCA LATE DECEMBER 1912] 27 RUE DE FLEURUS
My dear Mabel,

Thanks for the letter of introduction to Miss [Emily] Cary, I will present it next week. I was very much interested in [Arthur] Brisbane's letter, its got a lot of quality in it and very robust in its spacing.* I would like to know more of him. I hope you have not been translated by the Swami. Say that was an awfully quick performance. I have just received another letter from Constance [Fletcher]. I enjoy my correspondence with her immensely. Keep the copy of her that I sent you by all means. I have written to Hutch [Hapgood] telling him about you and giving him your address. He can be reached at the Harvard Club in New York. I have also written to Mabel Weeks about you. Her address is Brooks Hall, Barnard College. She thinks I am departing from my best manner in your portrait, and she does not understand it.† I don't know any one else to recommend to you in New York. There is a man by the name of Paul Chalfin‡ that I like very much and think interesting.

---

* Not located.

† Mabel Weeks wrote to Gertrude Stein on 12 December 1912: "The Portrait I am very glad to own though I should be disingenuous if I said I either understand or enjoy it. It puzzles me because in it you seem to have gone back on the principles that have guided you in your other writing and that were bringing you to such a point of success. . . . and I feel rather sad because it evidently marks your taking of a path in which I can't follow you" (Included in *FF*, 67).

‡ Paul Chalfin, American painter and subject of Gertrude Stein's word portrait "Chalfin," included in *Two*.

He is I think in New York now but I don't know his address. There must be some one you know who would know it and him as he is fairly well-known in the art crowd. Then there is a fellow by the name of Arthur Lee* who was rather pleasant over here but may not be so pleasant over there. His address is Society of Beaux Art Architects 159 E. 48 St. Then there is a Mrs. Charles Knoblauch, she is the one whose letter I quoted to you about your portrait. She is a Bryn Mawr woman and a friend of Georgiana King† etc. Her address is The Wyoming, 7th Ave & 55 St. I won't write to her about you so you can let her know or not about meeting her. She has my long book at present. She is awfully good about helping me to place my things. She was the one who thought of [Alfred] Stieglitz.‡ I think I told you about her. Don't be surprised Mabel but I may be going over to England to see if I can find a publisher. I don't know very well what I am to do when I get there but everybody tells me that I should go,§ that it is important to see the people ones self and so I am almost thinking that I will. If you know any one who knows a publisher and can tell me how to meet him will you let me know. We have been busy very much as usual. I have a couple of new Picassos. We see a great deal of them. They live in this quarter and we are very chummy. The new Mme.¶ is a very pleasant Mistress [?] and quite a cheerful person. The late lamented is gone forever. I don't know anything about her. Pablo is very happy. They are at Barcelona for Christmas, she is to be introduced to his parents as a legitime** which I think she is although nothing is said. There has recently been an American millionaire from

* Arthur Lee, American sculptor who was represented by four pieces in the Armory Show.

† Georgiana Goddard King, art history professor at Bryn Mawr, authority on Spanish art, and author.

‡ Stieglitz had responded enthusiastically to Stein's word portraits of Picasso and Matisse and published them in *Camera Work*.

§ It seems that one of the "everybody" was Myra Edgerly, a miniaturist, who strongly believed in Gertrude Stein's writing and advised her to go to London to look for a publisher. Edgerly was acquainted with the publisher John Lane. She agreed to write several letters herself to publishers in England and provided instructions to Alice B. Toklas on how to write such letters of introduction (*AABT*, 126–27).

¶ Picasso's new partner was Eva Gouel, also known as Marcelle Humbert. His relationship with Fernande Olivier, which had begun in 1905, had started to deteriorate in 1911 and ended when Fernande left with another artist (Mary Mathews Gedo, *Picasso: Art as Autobiography*, 97). Although Stein refers to her as "the new Mme.," Eva and Picasso were not married. His first marriage was to Olga Koklova in 1918.

** Legitimate or lawful.

Philaddelphia* who would have rejoiced Constance. He did literally wave his chequebook in the air. He came over to buy the Rouard
[?] collection at least a piece of it and he was perfectly flabber-
gasted at the prices Europeans were prepared to pay and did pay
for the pictures. He was the real thing in Constance's Americans.†
We have not seen much of the [Robert and Sonia] Delaunays‡ lately.
There is a feud on. He wanted to wean Guillaume Appolinaire [i.e.,
Apollinaire]§ and me from liking Picassos and there was a great
deal of amusing intrigue. Guillaume Appolinaire was wonderful.
He was moving just then and it was convenient to stay with the
Delaunays and he did and he paid just enough to cover his board.
He did an article on cubism and he spoke beautifully of Delaunay
as having "dans la silence crut something or other of the couleur
pur."¶ Now Delaunay does conceive himself as a great solitaire
and as a matter of fact he is an incessant talker will tell all about
himself and his work at any hour of the day or night to anybody,
and so he was delighted and so were his friends. Appolinaire does
that sort of thing wonderfully. He is so suave you can never tell

*The millionaire may be Albert C. Barnes. He was in Paris in 1912 and visited
Gertrude and Leo Stein at 27 rue de Fleurus (William Schack, *Art and Argyrol: The
Life and Career of Dr. Albert C. Barnes*, 80–81).

† This reference may be to an unlocated work by Constance Fletcher.

‡ Robert Delaunay, French painter whose colorful form of Cubism was labeled
"Orphism" by Apollinaire in 1912. His wife, Sonia Delaunay, was a Russian artist.

§ Guillaume Apollinaire, French poet, author, and art critic. One of the first supporters of Cubism, Apollinaire ardently embraced new movements in art and literature and is credited with being the creator of the terms "Orphism" and "Surrealism."
Gertrude Stein admired Apollinaire for his engaging and brilliant discourse and his
flamboyant character. Although they shared similar approaches to writing, including a
disregard of punctuation, it appears that the two writers did not converse about their
work (*GSC*, 144). Stein wrote a four-line word portrait of Apollinaire in 1913: "Give
known or pin ware. / Fancy teeth, gas strips. / Elbow elect, sour stout pore, pore caesar,
pour state at. / Leave eye lessons I. Leave I. Lessons. I. Leave I lessons, I" (*P&P*, 26).
Apollinaire's writings include *Les Peintres Cubistes: Méditations Esthétiques* (1913), a
collection of his art criticism, and *Alcools, Poèmes 1898–1913* (1913). Apollinaire en-
listed in World War I and suffered a head wound, the treatment for which left him
weakened and susceptible to influenza. He died two days before the Armistice was
signed. Stein recalls: "The death of Guillaume Apollinaire at this time made a very
serious difference to all his friends apart from their sorrow at his death. It was the
moment just after the war when many things had changed and people naturally fell
apart. Guillaume would have been a bond of union, he always had a quality of keeping
people together, and now that he was gone everybody ceased to be friends" (*AABT*,
60).

¶ "Silently invented an art of pure color," as translated by Leroy C. Breunig, ed.
and trans., in Guillaume Apollinaire, *Apollinaire on Art: Essays and Reviews,
1902–1918*, 261. This article by Apollinaire was entitled "Art and Curiosity: The Be-
ginnings of Cubism" and appeared in *Le Temps*, 14 October 1912.

what he is doing. He is going to do a portrait of me for the Mercure.* I am not always entirely happy when I think of it. I have not seen Florence Bradley since you left. She is coming to dinner Saturday. There was an awful row about your portrait the other day at the Cafe du Dome.† Some one had given a copy to Isadora [Duncan]‡ and Isadora had given it to a man named Skeene§ and he had read it at the Dome and there was an awful row. [Harry Phelan] Gibb¶ who was there gave a very amusing description of it. He said everybody remembered all their grievances against any member of the family and let loose. A few were earnest inquirers and a few were vigorous defenders. Mabel Weeks doesn't care about my last manner. You will have to convert her. Mildred [Aldrich]** just read

---

* *Le Mercure de France* was a bimonthly French literary magazine for which Apollinaire wrote a kind of gossip column called "La Vie anecdotique." The article on Gertrude Stein does not seem to have appeared. However, Apollinaire had written a portrait of Gertrude and Leo in 1907 that was published in *Je Dis Tout,* a reportedly scandalous publication for a restricted audience. Apollinaire wrote a review of six paintings by Felix Vallotton, one of which depicted Gertrude Stein:

> That American lady who with her brother and a group of her relatives constitutes the most unexpected patronage of the arts in our time.

> *Leurs pieds nus sont chaussés de sandales delphiques,*
> *Ils lèvent vers le ciel des fronts scientifiques.*

> (Their bare feet shod in sandals Delphic,
> They raise toward heaven their brows scientific.)

> Those sandals have sometimes done them harm. Caterers and soft-drink vendors are especially averse to them.

> Often when these millionaires want to relax on the terrace of a café on one of the boulevards, the waiters refuse to serve them and politely inform them that the drinks at that café are too expensive for people in sandals.

> But they could not care less about the ways of waiters and calmly pursue their aesthetic experiments. (Apollinaire, *Apollinaire on Art,* 29)

† Le Dôme was a popular restaurant, café, and gathering place in Montparnasse.

‡ Isadora Duncan, American dancer who was a neighbor of the Steins' in Oakland, California and who made the brown corduroy suits worn frequently by Gertrude and Leo Stein. Stein wrote a word portrait of Duncan, "Orta or One Dancing," that is included in *Two.*

§ Unidentified.

¶ Harry Phelan Gibb, an English painter who was the subject of Gertrude Stein's "A Portrait of One. Harry Phelan Gibb," included in *Geography and Plays.*

** Mildred Aldrich, an American writer who lived in France and was close friends with Stein and Toklas. Stein described her as "a stout vigorous woman with a George Washington face, white hair and admirably clean fresh clothes and gloves. . . . She made one very satisfied with one's country, which had produced her" (*AABT,* 120). Stein wrote two word portraits of Aldrich, both from the 1920s. The first one, "Mildred's Thoughts," is included in *Reflection on the Atomic Bomb* (1913–46; 1973) and the second portrait, "Mildred Aldrich Saturday," is included in *Portraits and Prayers.*

it and said she had no idea you were so energetic and comfortable. I guess thats all. If I go to London it will be toward the end of January. Love to you and respects to Edwin

Yours

Gertrude.

⮑Mabel Dodge descended again into a confused and anxious state of mind over her indecision about Edwin and Paul. In her characteristic enthusiasm for the new, she tried alternative approaches to curing her ills and embraced astrology as the new science. At this time, she also wrote to Alice B. Toklas to ask her for another favor.⮑

Dec. 18 [1912] [23 Fifth Avenue]

Dearest Gertrude—

I cannot express to you in what a condition of nervous prostration & hysteria I seem to have fallen. I am <u>gibbering</u> as never before in my life & poor E.[dwin] seems to increase the condition every time he enters the room, reducing me to tears & violent depression or else an irritable antagonism. I haven't seen P.[aul] & daily want to see him more & more. I have had a horoscope done which faithfully cites the whole condition & gives correct dates to an extriodenary degree—saying that 10 years ago I was in the same condition induced by a man whose personality, tastes, etc., were the same as in the present instance—a man entirely <u>personal</u> as is P. & as was the other of whom I told you. It also appears these occurrences are due to the planet Herschel* who is trying to break up man made laws & conventions & who is antagonistic to marriage laws & the purely domestic relation. I feel that I am being forced to drive E. away from me against my (worldly) reason & judgement. The horoscope notes that under such conditions I am a subject for hysteria & that under such influences I should go in for cures outside the "regular" profession such as osteopathy & suggestion—hence I am now having osteopathic treatment daily, & have this afternoon my first appointment with a doctor [John] Quackenbas [i.e., Quackenbos]† (unfortunate name!) for hypnotic treatment to see if he can calm the nerves & induce a more harmo-

---

* Uranus.

† John Duncan Quackenbos, American physician specializing in mental diseases who was the author of *Hypnotic Therapeutics* (1908), *Body and Spirit* (1916), and *Rational Mind Cure* (1925).

nious state of mind. We are simply frantic, E. & I. It's fearful & I don't see how it's all going to end. I can take no interest in anything or anyone & am a terror to live with, I confess. How I wish you were here. Perhaps I should never have come but perhaps things are working out somehow. The curious planet Uranus is dominant in the horoscope, & this star makes for unexpected & unaccountable changes & happenings all thro' life. I wish you would please write me <u>at</u> <u>once</u> your <u>hour</u> (approximately) day & year of birth for I want to see what <u>your</u> horoscope shows, for this woman, Evangeline Adams is really wonderfully & has the support of all the scientists here. She is absolutely scientific herself. Please send this at once to me—won't you?

Do speak of something besides myself. I am sending the Swami a wonderful letter full of alarms to be followed up by an excursion by Miss Adams & me to his shrine to see if we can turn him off Mrs. B. She writes that they think of moving the whole Vedanta Centre to Florence. [Isidor] Braggiotti will never go back until he has been eradicated from the atmosphere down to the last photograph. (Mrs. B. has six in a row on the altar of the chapel before which she kneels & sobs in exstacy. What <u>do</u> you think is going to happen to us all? Miss Adams says that with my horoscope (& Paul's) that I would be just as badly off if I married him as Herschel won't have marriage a success in my life but that an "alliance" of long or short duration is indicated & would be helpful & harmonious. This is impossible as long as I am with E. The horoscope says also that any man intimately in relation with me will always be removed suddenly from my life either by an accident or circumstances—(as you know my first husband was shot* & the other man I was really in love with sent me away finally† & I stopped caring from one day to another.) It now remains to see if E. won't up & leave me some fine day. Its all a perfect hell & I'm not enjoying it a bit.

Ever yours—

Mabel D.

---

* Mabel Dodge's first marriage was to Karl Evans in Buffalo in 1900. He was accidentally and fatally shot by a friend while they were hunting together in February 1903.

† Here Mabel Dodge is most likely referring to her long affair with her physician in Buffalo, Dr. Parmenter. In "Doctors: Fifty Years of Experience," Dodge explains that he "became the motivation and the cause for living" (17). She also describes finding him in the sexual act with her own mother at the time that she and the doctor were also having an affair (19). The relationship ended when Mrs. Parmenter warned that she would expose the situation in court.

DEC. 29. [1912] 23 FIFTH AVENUE

Dearest Alice—

Here I am after you to ask another favor. Its really for Paul Draper's sister* who by the way <u>has</u> the genius Paul <u>just</u> hasn't got. You know she has helped her family for years doing monologues professionally—<u>very</u> well—but the obvious thing to please publics. Well, here last night she did one in her <u>own</u> way, & the exciting thing about it is it is as post-impressionistic as Picasso or Gertrude & thrilling. She takes <u>sound</u> to express <u>emotion</u> & she makes up as she goes along a kind of <u>queer</u> <u>language</u> which perfectly expresses her emotion—in its most complex nuance—the <u>situation</u>, the characters of those to whom she is speaking & the whole law of life! She called it—to put us off—a scene after dinner in a servian [?] house. First her husband & herself—& <u>all</u> their relation is exposed—then after a fearful climax he puts on his hat & goes out—then her lover comes, another fearful scene with infinite variety—then he leaves, she rings for the servant & tells her she can put out the lights & go to bed. Now she did this in <u>gibberish</u>—she let her tongue loose in her head to express herself & we understood <u>every</u> <u>word</u> she spoke—even to a few words of a poem she quoted to her lover. It was the most <u>subjective</u> <u>performance</u> I have ever seen done. I was alone with one other man—a friend of us both—& we were so overcome that we couldn't say anything at first. It seems to me she has realized that language originally was sound expressing feelings & she has cut right <u>back</u> to this—& got at a method of expressing emotion <u>pure</u> & <u>direct</u>. It was great! And she said she had never done that monologue for anyone because she was afraid they wouldn't understand—& yet here she has got hold of a <u>great</u> idea—& deserves to stand by Gertrude & the others who are doing the same thing in other forms. Don't tell people of this—someone else, if they got the idea—could do <u>wonders</u> with it—she must be <u>made</u> to herself. I think I see in her just the quality Paul lacks. Well, she wants a plaster copy of the drowned girl that they sell in all the art shops in the quarter. Could you send me one C.O.D. if its not too much bother—one day when you're going by one of these shops—& thank you <u>so</u> much for doing those other things.

Best love—

Mabel.

* Ruth Draper, famous American monologuist.

PHOTOGRAPHS

೪ৱ

All photographs are courtesy of the Beinecke Rare Book and Manuscript Library, Yale University, unless otherwise indicated. All photographs listed as property of the New York Public Library are from the Carl Van Vechten Papers, Rare Books and Manuscript Division, New York Public Library, Astor, Lenox, and Tilden Foundations.

Mabel Dodge's first extant letter to Gertrude Stein, circa early spring 1911. It was written on Dodge's personalized stationery with her monogram "MD" surrounded by a circle containing a quotation from Walt Whitman's "Song of Myself": "Do I contradict myself? Very well, then, I contradict myself."

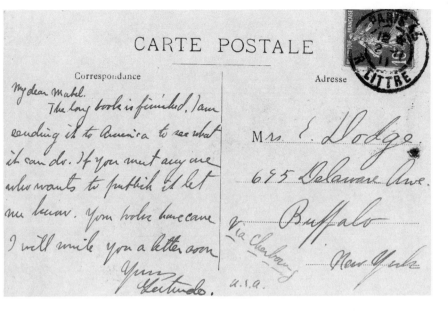

CARTE POSTALE

Correspondance   Adresse

My dear Mabel.
The long book is finished. I am
sending it to America to see what
it can do. If you meet any one
who wants to publish it let
me know. Your books have came
I will write you a letter soon
Yours
Gertrude.

Mrs. E. Dodge.
695 Delaware Ave.
Buffalo
New York
Via Cherbourg
U.S.A.

Gertrude Stein's first extant piece of correspondence to Mabel Dodge, postmarked 2 November 1911. The postcard featured a black-and-white reproduction of a Cézanne landscape.

Mabel Dodge with second husband Edwin Dodge and three-year-old son
John Evans, 1905. This photograph was taken within a year of Mabel
Evans's marriage to Edwin Dodge in October 1904. Her first husband,
Karl Evans, had died in 1903, the victim of a hunting accident. Mabel
Evans met Dodge in July 1904 on a ship bound for France and was per-
sistently pursued by him until she agreed to marriage.

Mabel Dodge and fourteen-year-old John Evans in Buffalo, 1916. By this date, Mabel Dodge was separated from her husband Edwin—their divorce was finalized around June 1916—and romantically involved with the artist Maurice Sterne.

Villa Curonia, Arcetri, 1904. In *European Experiences,* Dodge described the loggia and the descent from it into the formal gardens:

> One could sit on the stone ledge. . .and gaze at the semicircle of misty hills dipping over and over again beyond the fluted horizon. . . . At each end of the brick-paved loggia, stone stairs led down to the terraces half way below, and these had wide, shallow steps that turned abruptly downwards to the paved space at the base of the villa. Under the villa three high archways opened upon a place for tools and things, and made the round, black, shadowed openings one loves in the light façades of Italy.*

It was on this loggia facing the gardens that Dodge entertained guests such as Bernard Berenson, Gertrude Stein, and André Gide.

---

* *EE,* 149–50.

(Facing page:) Villa Curonia, 1992. These photographs show the villa as it currently appears, with its lush gardens and abundant vines, overgrown considerably since Mabel Dodge's occupancy. The original carved stone signs, though chipped, still proclaim "Villa Curonia" at the bottom gate (now electric). The villa has gone through a number of ownership changes since the Dodges vacated it. In most recent times, it housed

a restaurant and now is subdivided into apartments. (I am grateful to
the unidentified man staying as a guest at the Villa Curonia in 1992
who understood my Italian enough to let me into the courtyard and
allow me to climb up on the wall around the garden and take pictures.)
Photographs by the author.

Photograph of Mabel Dodge at the Villa Curonia by Jacques-Émile Blanche, 1911. At one of the Paris salons in the spring of 1911, Dodge had been particularly taken with a portrait of the Russian dancer Nijinsky painted by Blanche. She immediately arranged for an appointment with the painter at his studio in Passy and invited him to come to Florence to paint her portrait that summer. As Blanche describes in his autobiography, when he arrived to begin his work, Dodge met him wearing a "Paul Poiret gown in the Bakst style" and announced: "'This is my present fancy. . . . You can do other studies of me; I can be a Manet or a Berthe Morisot—anything you like except an American for Mr. Sargent'."* Blanche sometimes worked from photographs for his paintings, as the close resemblance between this picture and the finished portrait reveals. Photograph courtesy of Bruce Kellner.

———

* Blanche, *Portraits of a Lifetime,* 271.

Portrait of Mabel Dodge by Jacques-Émile Blanche, 1911. On the verso of this photograph, Dodge wrote "Painted in studio of Jacques E-Blanche Paris. France." In *European Experiences,* Dodge describes this painting: "He did a portrait of me sitting in a high, blue Renaissance chair with my hands on the arms, and an orange gown full and sumptuous, and with the everlasting turban wound on my head."*

---

* *EE,* 407.

Photograph of Mabel Dodge and John Evans at the Villa Curonia by Jacques-Émile Blanche, 1911. On the back of this photograph, Dodge noted that it was taken by Blanche "to determine poses." On the verso of a similar photograph that also featured a dachshund in the scene, Dodge wrote:

> Posed in music room—the scene of the portrait—background is enriched by presiding deity, a Kwannon of the Han period, 7 century B.C.
> Attention mostly on "Amiel," the melancholy Swiss dachsund named for the philosopher— & wearing a collar on which is engraved "Que vivre est difficile! Oh! Mon couer fatigué!"
> Color scheme—dark red & pinks in background—gold alterpiece & gold pedestal—vermillion sweater—apricot dress—tiger skin— & sunshine. Very exciting.

In his autobiography, Blanche remembers that "John was crouching on a lion's skin at his mother's feet. Bored with sitting, the boy in knickers and a pullover wanted to go back into the garden with his dogs."* The dachshund was not included in the final painting.

---

* Blanche, *Portraits of a Lifetime*, 272.

Portrait of Mrs. Mabel Dodge and Son by Jacques-Émile Blanche, circa 1911. In *European Experiences*, Dodge describes this double portrait of herself and John Evans: "his large canvas of me, sitting to face the somewhat malicious morning light and shimmering in apricot and orange silk, with the long string of amber beads like frozen honey, John kneeling beside me on the tiger in a dark blue sweater and an expression both deprecating and impatient on his irregular face."* Although Dodge reported that Blanche held onto his portraits of her after painting them, this is the only one whose location is known. Albright-Knox Art Gallery, Buffalo, New York; Gift of Mabel Dodge Luhan, 1924.

---

* *EE,* 152–53.

Photograph of Mabel Dodge at the Villa Curonia by Jacques-Émile Blanche, 1911. Dodge reported that Blanche did a portrait of her that was similar to this picture, showing her "standing, holding a gold mirror."* On the verso of this photograph, Dodge wrote: "Taken in blue bedroom—gold cupboard—apricot-colored gown—orange & white turban./The expression of artificial amiability is not particularly usual." The blue bedroom was Dodge's own room, featuring walls covered in blue damask, a bed with four curved corner posts topped by carved lion heads, and a trapdoor in the ceiling that was equipped with a silk ladder for Edwin to use on romantic descents from his own bedroom. However, as Mabel Dodge bemoaned, "This silken ladder was also for haste, lover's haste. But Edwin never hastened down it except once to see if it would work, and it did, perfectly."† The large gold cupboard was "painted all over in Persian colors with tiny Raphaelesque grotesques" and its shelves contained "piles of silk things and underclothes, of white stockings and blue and pink ones and thin black ones. . . .black and white spotted veils and chiffon veils, and lace collars and sashes and chiffon motor bonnets and lingerie, hats and ribbons."‡ Behind the curtains on each side of the cupboard hung Dodge's dresses, coats and Renaissance costumes. Gift of Gertrude Stein to the Beinecke Library.

---

* *EE*, 407.
† *EE*, 159.
‡ *EE*, 156.

Portrait of Mabel Dodge by Florence Bradley, 1910. Dodge recalls her first meeting with Bradley: "On one of my visits back to America in the last years of my life in Italy, I made a friend of Florence Bradley. She spoke to me first as we passed and repassed on the deck, for I have never spoken first to anyone in my life." Bradley ventured to Dodge: "'You were the only interesting-looking person on the boat,'" and Dodge "felt she too had something special about her that marked her out from the rest of the passengers."* Bradley may have painted this portrait of Dodge in either Italy or New York.

------

* *EE*, 429.

Portrait of Mabel Dodge by Mary Foote, circa 1915. This painting was likely the one included in an exhibition of Foote's portraits in May 1916 at M. Knoedler and Company in New York, the catalogue for which lists a portrait of "Mrs. Mabel Dodge." It is also possible that this painting is the one that Foote began during her visit to the Villa Curonia in the summer of 1912, when Dodge was tormented by her love affair with her son's tutor, Paul Ayrault. In a letter to Dodge, Ayrault refers to an afternoon spent with Foote in New York in the fall of 1912 during which "she confessed that she knew that we love each other" and "she brought out my portrait and also the one she started from the loggia with you in one of those chairs."* Around the same time, Mary Foote wrote to Dodge about Ayrault: "I was awfully glad to see him but I did hate to have him in such a mess—& hate to have you too. . . . I am so sorry for everybody—Lord what a world. <u>Why</u> did you do it? I should think you'd better keep away from N.Y."† After much turmoil and indecision concerning her marriage and her affair, Mabel Dodge returned to New York (not heeding Foote's advice), established herself at 23 Fifth Avenue, agreed not to see Paul, and soon banished Edwin to a nearby hotel. Mary Foote lived at 3 Washington Square, close to Dodge's apartment.

---

* Paul Ayrault to Dodge, 24 October 1912, MDLC.
† Mary Foote to Dodge, c. 1912, MDLC.

Portrait Bust of Mabel Dodge by Jo Davidson, circa 1912. In his autobiography, Davidson writes that during a visit to the Villa Curonia in 1912 he "did a bust of Mabel Dodge. I would watch for that enigmatic smile of expectancy and wonder, 'What is she plotting now?'"* Dodge remembers that Davidson "procured some clay and started a head of me that had that slightly mysterious smile with some secrecy in it, that has often annoyed people. If they knew what it meant they wouldn't mind. It simply means: 'I've got the most marvelous flow of life and happiness in me. I feel better than anyone else. I have a secret spring of pure being. Nothing else matters!'"†

---

* Davidson, *Between Sittings,* 82.
† *EE,* 435.

To Mabel Dodge No. 2 by Andrew Dasburg, 1913, as shown in the *New York World*, 8 February 1914. This painting is the only one of Dasburg's three abstract portraits of Dodge for which a reproduction exists. The critics pretended that they could not determine which was the top or bottom of the work, so it appeared in the newspaper upside down, right side up, and on either side, with the mocking comment next to each image, "Try it this way." The locations of all three Dasburg portraits are currently unknown. Photograph from microfilm at the New York Public Library.

118

The Purple Pup by Charles Demuth, circa 1918. Carl Van Vechten appears in this watercolor as one of the patrons of this popular new tearoom in Greenwich Village. Shown in profile with a sharply pointed nose and pale hair, Van Vechten sits at the table in the foreground. Demuth included Van Vechten in another drawing from this time, *Cabaret Interior with Carl Van Vechten* (circa 1918), showing him in a similar profile pose in the midst of an animated nightclub scene. Courtesy, Museum of Fine Arts, Boston, Charles Henry Hayden Fund.

(Opposite:) Carl Van Vechten/Co-ordinated Explosion, a Cubist Portrait by Andrew Dasburg, 1914. Van Vechten was the only person besides Dodge to whom Dasburg paid such homage in an abstract portrait. Exhibition records from the time and letters between Dasburg and Van Vechten strongly suggest that this painting is actually a renamed portrait of Mabel Dodge. The painting conforms to descriptions of Dasburg's early abstractions exhibited in November 1913 at the MacDowell Club and the following year at the National Arts Club in New York. Contemporary reviews and surviving photographs indicate that these early works contained curved and pointed abstract shapes that were colored and overlaid. The Regis Collection, Minneapolis, Minnesota. Photograph courtesy of Barbara Mathes Gallery, New York.

Gertrude Stein and Alice B. Toklas in Venice, 1908. Stein and Toklas
sit outside the cathedral in the Piazza San Marco in the company of
the ever-present pigeons. Stein wears her characteristically voluminous clothes, most likely with sandals underneath, and a brooch
pinned to her shirt. Her large straw hat is decorated lavishly with
artificial pansies. Toklas is shown in the dark batik dress that she
often wore on her travels with Stein.*

* *CC*, 156.

Gertrude Stein at 27 rue de Fleurus, 1913. This photograph was
taken by Alvin Langdon Coburn on 7 May 1913, according to his
typewritten note on her letter to him, postmarked 6 May 1913, that
offered two possible dates for him to take her picture. Coburn's
photography had been featured in a 1904 issue of Alfred Stieglitz's
Camera Work at the same time that he was at work on a book of
photographs of famous people in the arts, among them Henry James,
Ezra Pound, and George Bernard Shaw. Stein recalled in *The Autobiography of Alice B. Toklas* that Coburn was a "queer american" who
"was the first photographer to come and photograph her as a celebri-
ty and she was nicely gratified. He did make some very good photographs of her and gave them to her and then he disappeared. . . ."*

---

* *AABT,* 139, 140.

Gertrude Stein by Pablo Picasso, 1906. In *The Autobiography of Alice B. Toklas,* Stein gives her account of how Picasso came to paint his famous portrait of her:

> Picasso had never had anybody pose for him since he was sixteen years old, he was then twenty-four and Gertrude Stein had never thought of having her portrait painted, and they do not either of them know how it came about. Anyway it did and she posed to him for this portrait ninety times and a great deal happened during that time.*

Having gone to Italy for the summer while Picasso went to Spain, Stein returned to Paris in the fall to find her portrait finished:

> The day he returned from Spain Picasso sat down and out of his head painted the head in without having seen Gertrude Stein again. And when she saw it he and she were content. It is very strange but neither can remember at all what the head looked like when he painted it out.†

Stein also wrote about the painting in "Picasso" (1938): ". . . he gave me the picture and I was and I still am satisfied with my portrait; for me, it is I, and it is the only reproduction of me which is always I, for me."‡ The Metropolitan Museum of Art, Bequest of Gertrude Stein, 1946.

---

* *AABT,* 45–46.
† *AABT,* 57.
‡ Stein, *Gertrude Stein on Picasso,* 14.

The studio at 27 rue de Fleurus, 1913. This photograph shows Picasso's portrait of Gertrude Stein hanging in a focal corner of the studio, in addition to a number of his other paintings, including *Woman with a Fan* (1905), *Young Girl with a Basket of Flowers* (1905), *Two Women at a Bar* (1902), and *Young Acrobat on a Ball* (1905). Also visible on the crowded walls, which were covered with art from floor to ceiling, are Matisse's *Music (Study)* (1907), Auguste Renoir's *Brunette* (1890), Édouard Manet's *Ball Scene* (1873), and Cézanne's *Portrait of Mme Cézanne* (1879–82).

Gertrude Stein and Alice B. Toklas at 27 rue de Fleurus, 1922. Photograph by Man Ray. In *The Autobiography of Alice B. Toklas,* Stein recalls that when she first met Man Ray, he asked if he could come and photograph her at 27 rue de Fleurus: "He did and. . .we were very pleased with the result. He has at intervals taken pictures of Gertrude Stein and she is always fascinated with his way of using lights."[*] Stein is shown wearing sandals on her feet, a habit of both hers and her brother Leo's that always drew comments from others. Guillaume Apollinaire featured this quirk in their manner of dress in an exhibition review he wrote in 1907: "Those sandals have sometimes done them harm. Caterers and soft-drink vendors are especially averse to them. Often when these millionaires want to relax on the terrace of a café on one of the boulevards, the waiters refuse to serve them and politely inform them that the drinks at that café are too expensive for people in sandals."[†]This view of the studio, with its now less crowded walls, includes the following works: Picasso's *Head of a Boy* (1905), *Standing Nude* (1906), study for *Guitar on a Table* (1912–13), and *The Architect's Table* (1912), Cézanne's *Bathers* (circa 1895), and *Portrait of Mme Cézanne* (1879–82).

---

[*] *AABT,* 198.
[†] Apollinaire, *Apollinaire on Art,* 29.

Mabel Dodge at 23 Fifth Avenue, 1912. When this photograph was taken, Dodge had recently arrived in New York, having left Italy for good, and had not yet happened upon her roles as salon hostess and energetic promoter of the Armory Show. On board the ship that returned her and her family to the United States, Dodge "rebelled against the idea of starting all over again" as she "sat at the rear of the ship with my back turned to the bow, facing back, towards Europe, for that, at least, I knew." As the ship passed the Statue of Liberty, Dodge grabbed her son's hand and cried: "'Remember, it is *ugly* in America. . . .We have left everything worth while behind us. America is all machinery and money-making and factories—it is ugly, ugly, ugly! Never forget that!'" John looked at the city they were approaching and disagreed: "'*I* don't think it's so ugly.'"* After the frenzy of renovating, furnishing, and decorating her apartment at 23 Fifth Avenue, Dodge fell into a deep depression that was only relieved when she forced her husband to move to a nearby hotel and then became more involved with her friends, Carl Van Vechten and Hutchins Hapgood in particular, and with causes such as the controversial Armory Show and the promotion of Gertrude Stein's writing.

---

* *EE*, 452–53.

Mabel Dodge at 23 Fifth Avenue, 1915. Although this photograph of Dodge is not dated, one of her in the same setting and dress is dated 1915. The metal candlesticks on either side of her appear in the photograph of the interior of her apartment at 23 Fifth Avenue, on a chest of drawers at the back right. It is possible that Dodge donned this dress and turban for the occasion of one of her Evenings.

Interior of Mabel Dodge's apartment at 23 Fifth Avenue, 1916.
When she moved into this apartment, Dodge "had every single bit of
the woodwork painted white, and had all the walls papered with
thick, white paper." She observed: "It seemed to me I couldn't get
enough white into that apartment. I suppose it was a repudiation of
grimy New York." She furnished this front living room with many
of the chairs and couches from Italy and "many dim old carved and
gilded frames with new mirrors in them and these made the room
lively with glints and sparkles."* In addition to these mirrors, seen at
the left in this photograph, Dodge hung variously shaped branches
on the walls for decoration. It was in this apartment that Dodge
began hosting her famous Evenings in late January 1913, providing
the setting for the exchange of ideas among intellectuals and activists. In his novel, *Peter Whiffle*, a fictional portrayal of Mabel Dodge
and her circle, Carl Van Vechten describes the atmosphere at her
gatherings: "The crowds flocked to her place and she made them
comfortable. Pinchbottles and Curtis Cigarettes, poured by the hundreds from their neat pine boxes into white bowls, trays of Virginia
ham and white Gorgonzola sandwiches, pale Italian boys in aprons,
and a Knabe piano were added to the decorations. . . . Arguments and
discussions floated in the air, were caught and twisted and hauled
and tied, until the white salon itself was no longer static. There were
undercurrents of emotion and sex."†

* *M&S*, 4, 5.
† Van Vechten, *Peter Whiffle*, 122.

Leo Stein, circa 1913. This photograph shows Leo Stein with a pensive look that matches Dodge's description of him as a "thoughtful, ram-ish scholar"* who was ardent in his support of the new art of Cézanne, Matisse, and Picasso. He commented once that Dodge was "the most serious person he had ever known,"† an observation that she took as a great compliment in contrast to the views of some others who saw her as more frivolous and flighty. The friendship and correspondence between Mabel Dodge and Leo Stein long outlasted her relationship with Gertrude. Leo Stein visited Dodge in Provincetown and Taos, and their letters to each other often have an impassioned and serious quality as they mutually grappled with issues in areas such as aesthetics, philosophy, and psychoanalysis.

---

* *EE,* 321.
† *M&S,* 58.

Bernard Berenson at his villa I Tatti in Settignano, Italy, circa 1911.
Berenson stands in front of the fifteenth-century Italian painter
Domenico Veneziano's *Madonna and Child,* one of the most famous
paintings in his collection. When Mabel Dodge lived at the Villa
Curonia, she was friends with the celebrated art historian and his
wife Mary. In *European Experiences,* she reports on a popular activity that the Berensons hosted: "They played a guessing game that
consisted of spreading a lot of photographs of paintings on a table
and then, taking one, somebody would cover it with a piece of paper
out of which a little hole was cut, so that only a fold of a cloak, or a
part of a hand or face would be seen, and everybody would guess, by
the 'treatment' who had painted it. That was considered the way to
pass a really gay evening up at I Tatti!"*

---

* *EE,* 389.

Carl Van Vechten, circa 1917. As Mabel Dodge recalled, Van Vechten was "the first person who animated my lifeless rooms" at 23 Fifth Avenue. When she met him at a dinner party in the winter of 1913, Dodge described Van Vechten as "really queer-looking. . .his neck never seeming able to hold up his head, or his knees his body. When he laughed, little shrieks flew out between the slits in his big teeth."* Van Vechten quickly became one of Dodge's most intimate friends. They talked every morning on the telephone and he called her "Mike," a nickname with forgotten origins. Dodge was responsible for introducing Van Vechten to Gertrude Stein, a meeting that resulted in a lifelong friendship and Van Vechten's eventual role as Stein's literary executor. The New York Public Library.

---

* *M&S*, 16, 15.

Hutchins Hapgood, most likely in Provincetown, Massachusetts, circa 1916. Mabel Dodge considered "Hutch," as he was called, her "confidant of all my years in New York," and described him as having "deep, faithful-looking blue eyes whose lids drooped at the outer corners," "the massive arched nose of an eminent man," and "full, generous lips and melancholy jowls."* According to Dodge, they were first introduced by the sculptor Jo Davidson, although Dodge had also written to Gertrude Stein for an introduction. Hapgood was a regular presence at Dodge's Evenings at 23 Fifth Avenue and for several summers they both rented cottages in Provincetown at the same time.

* M&S, 17, 45.

Hutchins Hapgood and Neith Boyce in a production of *Enemies,* in Provincetown, 1916. In this play that Hapgood and his wife Boyce wrote together, they essentially put their relationship up on the stage. In keeping with the radical spirit of the time, the couple tried to uphold the goal of free love while still married to each other. Whereas Hapgood had many affairs but never felt an emotional bond with anyone other than his wife, Boyce had fewer involvements and did find a satisfying bond with one man, a development that caused Hapgood to accuse her of "spiritual infidelity" and demand that she focus more of her energies on him. In *Enemies,* the character of Hapgood admits, "'I've never been able to be essentially unfaithful, more's the pity.'"* The character of Boyce complains about her husband's efforts to subdue her: "'You, on account of your love for me, have tyrannized over me, bothered me, badgered me, nagged me, for fifteen years. You have interfered with me, taken my time and strength, and prevented me from accomplishing great works for the good of humanity. You have crushed my soul, which longs for serenity and peace, with your perpetual complaining.'"†

* Quoted in Watson, *Strange Bedfellows,* 158.
† Quoted in *1915,* 109.

Alfred Stieglitz at his gallery 291, located at 293 Fifth Avenue, New York, circa 1909. Dodge first met Stieglitz at 291 in the winter of 1913 when Hutchins Hapgood took her on her first trip to the innovative gallery with its exhibitions of photography and avant-garde art. She recalls that Stieglitz "stood talking there day after day" and "was the spirit of the place. It was one of the few places where I went. It was always stimulating to go and listen to him analyzing life and pictures and people—telling of his strange experiences, greatly magnifying them with the strong lenses of his mental vision."* Dodge was inspired by Stieglitz's belief in his artists and became an enthusiastic supporter and patron of modernist art, collecting works by Andrew Dasburg, Marsden Hartley, and Max Weber, among others.

---

* *M&S*, 71–72.

Marsden Hartley, circa 1915. Photograph by Alfred Stieglitz. As
Mabel Dodge recalls in *Movers and Shakers,* "I met Hartley there at
'291'—that gnarled New England spinster-man who came to New
York with his tragic paintings of New Hampshire and Maine landscape where the trees were fateful, and Hartley told me how Stieglitz kept him from starving. He sent Hartley to Germany soon after
I met him and supported him through the leanest years."* After his
first visit to 23 Fifth Avenue, Hartley wrote to Dodge: "I want to tell
you that I think we are going to have lots to say to each other and I
want just to tell you of it. I felt as if I were in such a large place last
night—a large place lighted with exceptionally good light. It had a
sense of home to me. . . . I do hope you don't go away for long while
I am in New York because I feel the need of unusual lights in dark
places and there seems so much of this there around you."† Gift of
Gertrude Stein to the Beinecke Library.

---

* *M&S,* 72.
† *M&S,* 95.

John Reed on the beach at Provincetown, circa 1914. Mabel Dodge first met Reed, the journalist and poet who was on the staff of the magazine the *Masses*, in the spring of 1913 at a gathering of radicals in Greenwich Village. It was at this meeting that the idea of the Paterson Strike Pageant was born, an event that drew Dodge and Reed together as they feverishly worked to organize the dramatization of the striking silk workers in Paterson, New Jersey, that was staged at Madison Square Garden in June 1913.

———

(Opposite) Mabel Dodge in Provincetown, circa 1914. In the summer of 1914, John Reed and Dodge rented a cottage in Provincetown, which at that time "was just a double line of small, white clapboarded cottages along a silent village street, between the bay and the open sea." This photograph shows Dodge dressed in her characteristic garb for that summer: "I wore Peter Thompson sailor suits with bloused tops and long skirts. I liked their coarse, dark blue flannel feeling. I didn't wear a lot of things under them as other women did—just a chemise seemed enough."* Dodge was wearing one of these flannel dresses when she and Reed went out rowing in a leaky boat that soon began sinking. As Dodge recalls, Reed had to force her to get out of the boat, as she did not know how to swim, and to remove her cumbersome clothing:

My blue flannel dress weighed me down terribly, and I could feel it drag the boat farther under the water. Reed was swimming actively and giving me directions that I couldn't understand and meanwhile the rescuers were approaching. I knew I was almost drowning and didn't really know what to do about it.

"Undo your skirt," shouted Reed as I came up to the surface. I felt his hand under my chin.

"I c-c-can't!" I choked.

"Well, *I* can," he replied and fumbled at my belt. I began to fight him, then. I didn't want him to take my skirt off.

"I'm not *going* to be rescued with my skirt off," I spluttered. An unattractive picture of myself being hauled into the rescuers' boat dressed in the upper part of a Peter Thompson sailor suit and practically *nothing* else, had appeared before me. Truly I preferred to drown than to be in such a foolish position.

Reed cursed and dragged at the skirt which came off and sank, leaving the lower part of me scantily draped in a shift and a pair of white stockings.†

Abandoned at the shore by Reed and the rescuers, as she refused to come out of the water to expose herself to further humiliation, Dodge waited until the beach was deserted and then walked home, where Reed met her with a blanket.

---

* *M&S*, 282, 283.
† *M&S*, 284.

Page from Carl Van Vechten's photograph album showing "Avery [Hopwood] at Atlantic City," "Mabel Dodge, Provincetown, 1914," and "Mabel Dodge" in Taos. The photograph of Dodge on the beach in Provincetown was taken by Van Vechten in June 1914. The other picture of Dodge, showing her with long braids and wrapped in an Indian blanket, was most likely taken in Taos shortly after her move there in 1917, since it was soon after her arrival that she cut off her long hair. Avery Hopwood was a well-known playwright who was close friends with Van Vechten. The New York Public Library.

Maurice Sterne, circa 1917–18. Mabel Dodge first met Sterne in 1915 at
a dance recital given by students from the Elizabeth Duncan School. She
was immediately drawn to him for his "handsome look of suffering"
and observed that he was "positively enveloped in a cloud of secrecy and
caution. The man might have been in a jungle, so watchful he was, so
studied every glance and motion. That interested me. I wondered what
it was all about."* Soon after their impulsive marriage in August 1917,
Dodge became weary of the relationship and sent Sterne to New Mexico
to paint. She joined him in December 1917, immediately disliked Santa
Fe and then decided upon Taos as her new home. Given Sterne's cowboy
boots and overall appearance, in addition to the mountains in the background, this photograph was likely taken in Taos in either 1917 or 1918.
Sterne returned to New York in August 1918 after Dodge became involved with the Pueblo Indian Antonio Luhan.

---

* *M&S,* 350.

1918
Tony Lujan – Taos, N. M.
John Evans – Cody – Wyo.

Antonio Luhan and John Evans at Niagara Falls, 1918. Mabel Dodge had met Luhan soon after her arrival in Taos. She immediately recognized him from a dream she had after Sterne had left for New Mexico: "[Luhan] looked at me for the first time, with a quick glance that penetrated to the depths with an instantaneous recognition, and I saw his was the face that had blotted out Maurice's in my dream—the same face, the same eyes, involuntarily intense, with the living fire in their depths."* At Dodge's invitation, Luhan came to visit her, making a strong and magical impression on her with his singing. They slowly began a relationship that eventually drove Sterne out. At the time this picture was taken, John Evans was living in Cody, Wyoming, at the home of Bob Rumsey, a family friend from Buffalo. As Dodge explained, Rumsey, "the hero of so many young hearts, married now to a woman his mother's age, had undertaken to console my son for a mother's inconsiderateness. He was tutoring John himself—preparing him for Yale, which he had influenced the boy to choose."†

This photograph shows Luhan during a trip that he made east with Julia, a friend of Dodge's whose last name is unknown. It was Julia's idea to have him accompany her so that she could show him New York City and possibly Washington, D.C., where he might meet the President. When they arrived in Chicago, Julia suddenly seemed embarrassed by Luhan's appearance, dressed as he was in a striped blanket with ribbon wound around his long braids. She took him to a department store and urged him to choose any outfit. As Julia related to Mabel Dodge: "'It was terrible, Mabel!. . . He picked out a kind of light green suit, and a blue shirt—and the hat! Well! The clerk took him off to put them on, and when he came back, I wouldn't have known him.'"‡ On their way to New York, Julia and Luhan stopped in Buffalo, most likely meeting up there with John Evans. This photograph shows Luhan in his new suit and hat.

---

* *ETD*, 94.
† *ETD*, 7.
‡ *ETD*, 211.

Mabel Dodge Sterne in New Mexico, circa 1917–18. This photograph
shows Dodge with her new haircut, a bob that she thought made her
look more Indian. Shortly after arriving in Taos, as she remembers in
Edge of Taos Desert, Dodge asked her son John to cut off her hair:

> "Just straight around—just below the ears. . . ."
> He clipped and clipped excitedly, and laid the long brown tresses
> in a pile.
> "I love doing this!" he murmured.
> Soon it was all off. Straight across my eyebrows, then down a few
> inches and hanging heavily over my ears in an angular bob. I had no
> precedent for this kind of hair-cut. No one I knew or ever saw wore
> short hair like this, but I remembered Maxfield Parrish illustrations
> and medieval pages.*

* *ETD*, 73.

Antonio Luhan, circa 1918. Mabel Dodge described Tony, as she called him, as having a face that "was like a noble bronze—rather full and ample, with a large nose and a generous mouth." It is possible that this photograph is the one Dodge refers to in *Edge of Taos Desert* when she reports that Luhan was taken to the studio of Jimmy Fraser in New York: "Jimmy photographed him in his blanket, looking very down in the mouth and ill, really. Julia sent me a copy of that picture. I have never seen him as they saw him there at that time."* Dodge and Luhan were married in April 1923 and remained together until Dodge's death in 1962.

---

* *ETD*, 102, 213.

Los Gallos, Taos, date unknown. This photograph shows the Big House where Mabel Dodge lived, from an angle that features the rooms in her following description: "The house grew slowly and it stretches on and on. At one end it piles up, for over the Big Room there is the bedroom where Tony sleeps, next to my room, and a big sleeping porch off of it; and from this room one climbs a steep little stairway up into a kind of lookout room, made of helioglass set in wooden columns on all four sides, where one has the views of all the valley. . . . There is nothing on this bare, blue-painted floor but some *serapes*, and up here under the sky, winter and summer, one can lie in the sunshine and bathe in it until 'untied are the knots in the heart,' for there is nothing like the sun for smoothing out all difficulties."* The second-floor bathroom windows were painted by D. H. Lawrence who was reportedly shocked by Dodge's lack of modesty in having clear panes of glass in such a room.

---

* *WIT,* 66.

Mabel Dodge Luhan House, 1992. These two recent photographs show the D. H. Lawrence windows more closely and, on the roof, the ceramic roosters that Dodge purchased in Mexico, for which the estate was given its name, Los Gallos. Now called Las Palomas de Taos, Dodge's home serves as a bed and breakfast and conference center. Photographs by the author.

Mabel Dodge Luhan in Taos, 1938. On the back of this photograph,
Dodge wrote: "Mabel Dodge Luhan on Jocko, her favorite horse, near
the dove-cotes in courtyard of the Big House, Los Gallos." She also
indicated that this photograph was taken by her psychoanalyst, Dr.
A. A. Brill, who visited her in Taos in the fall of 1937. Dodge began
analysis with Brill in the fall of 1916 and met regularly with him
until she moved to Taos at the end of 1917. They maintained both a
therapeutic and a personal relationship through often frequent letters until Brill's death in 1944.

Mabel Dodge Luhan and Carl Van Vechten, 12 April 1934. Photograph by Van Vechten. This picture was taken a year after Van Vechten had visited Dodge in Taos and a year before the two old friends
experienced the second major rift in their relationship (the first having been between 1914 and 1927, triggered by Dodge's refusal to
fully understand Van Vechten's reasons—he wanted to ask the Russian actress Fania Marinoff to marry him—for leaving Europe to
return to New York at the beginning of World War I). In 1935 Dodge
sent Van Vechten a copy of *Movers and Shakers,* an autobiographical
account of her New York years, and received no response. At her
urging, he finally replied and his frank criticism caused Dodge to
remain silent toward him for the next sixteen years. Van Vechten
had written: "It didn't seem very important to me to write to you
about the book because I don't like it and I didn't see any sense of
telling you that! You seem to belittle every character in it including
yourself."*

* Quoted in Kellner, *Carl Van Vechten and the Irreverent Decades,* 269.

(Opposite:) Gertrude Stein and Alice B. Toklas, 7 November 1934. Photograph by Van Vechten. This picture was taken shortly after Stein and Toklas arrived in the United States in October 1934 to begin Stein's celebrated lecture tour around the country that lasted until they returned to France in May 1935. After the critical and financial success of *The Autobiography of Alice B. Toklas* following its serialization in the *Atlantic Monthly* and its publication by Harcourt, Brace in 1933, both Van Vechten and the writer Sherwood Anderson had encouraged Stein to come to the United States for a lecture tour. On the back of this picture, Van Vechten wrote: "This photograph shows the beginning of Miss Stein's and Miss Toklas's first airplane voyage, when they flew to Chicago to hear a performance of 'Four Saints in Three Acts' at the Chicago Auditorium. I flew with them and made these pictures just before the start. The fetishes in their hands, presents from me, are little beaded men on bases of rabbits' feet, made by the Hopi Indians of the Southwest. This photograph was used on the jacket of 'Everybody's Autobiography.'"

Gertrude Stein, Carl Van Vechten, and Alice B. Toklas, 4 January 1935. Photograph by Van Vechten. This picture was also taken in the United States during Stein's lecture tour.

~

1913

Within weeks of returning to New York, Mabel Dodge became involved with the organizers of the famous Armory Show of 1913, which served to introduce the American public to the current trends in modern art in both the United States and Europe. Popularly known as the Armory Show because it was held in the Sixty-ninth Regiment Armory at Twenty-fifth Street and Lexington Avenue in New York, the International Exhibition of Modern Art was sponsored by the Association of American Painters and Sculptors, whose president was the painter Arthur B. Davies.

Dodge's material investment in the Armory Show consisted of enlisting her mother to donate five hundred dollars and contributing two hundred dollars of her own money toward decorations for the building.[1] Dodge reports that she lent her chauffeur and car for errands and helped arrange some loans of paintings in private collections. Although her involvement in promoting and working for the show began only about a month before its opening, Dodge characteristically claimed its ideas and spirit as her own and somewhat exaggerated her role:

> I felt as though the Exhibition were mine. I really did. It
> became, over night, my own little Revolution. *I* would upset
> America; *I* would, with fatal, irrevocable disaster to the old
> order of things. . . . *I* was going to dynamite New York and
> nothing would stop me. Well, nothing did. I moved forward in
> my rôle of Fate's chosen instrument, and the show certainly
> did gain by my propulsion.[2]

Dodge reports that she was elected vice-president of the Association of American Painters and Sculptors after her financial contributions and expressions of faith in the show.[3]

Gertrude Stein already knew about the upcoming Armory Show, as Arthur B. Davies and Walt Kuhn, a painter and fellow committee member, had visited 27 rue de Fleurus in November 1912 in search of loans for the exhibition. The Steins agreed to send Matisse's *The Blue Nude* (1907) and two Picasso still lifes, listed in the catalogue without dates as *Nature Morte No. 1* and *Nature Morte No. 2*. Davies and Kuhn also secured two Matisse loans from Michael and Sarah Stein, *Le Madras Rouge* (c. 1907–8) and *La Coiffeuse* (1907).〜

[CIRCA JANUARY 1913] [23 FIFTH AVENUE]

Dearest Gertrude—

I know "Hutch" [Hapgood] now. At a conversation one day here between him & Jo Davidson & me I explained about your literature. Then, as usual he made an article about all he'd heard!* As you observe, Jo talked more than I did! But it's good propaganda anyway. I have bad nervous pros.[tration] with a nurse & Edwin banished to a hotel by the doctor.† Still have an (intermittent) interest in ideas!

Yours—

Mabel

A wonderful great show here in Feb. I am working for it. All the moderns sending over, the most important show ever in America or anywhere else, Arthur Davies President, & the Armory for it, a great sensation, best thing for the americain sub-consciousness that's ever happened. Mabel Weekes [i.e., Weeks] is coming to me soon.‡ I can't get out to her. Engage the Picassos & yourselves to me at Curonia for June, make it a date as won't have others to spoil things.

Yours—

M.

Love to all.

---

*This likely refers to Hutchins Hapgood's "Material and Art" that appeared in the *New York Globe* on 10 January 1913, although the article does not mention either Stein or Dodge. Jo Davidson is quoted as saying, "The material should master the artist, not the artist the material." Hapgood expands this idea to the writer, possibly, although not explicitly, informed by Dodge's explanations of Gertrude Stein's work: "So the modern writer of words may . . . refrain from trying to express his personal ideas, but merely allow the words themselves to fall into forms and groups peculiar to their nature, and thus produce certain profound and primitive effects" (10).

† In *Movers and Shakers*, Dodge explains her role in Edwin's banishment: "I persuaded good Dr. Sachs, the psychiatrist who was attending me, that Edwin was the cause of my weakness and depression, so he . . . explained to Edwin that it would be better for him to stay away until I was stronger" (23–24).

‡ This meeting took place on 21 January 1913, according to Mabel Weeks's letter to

My dear Mabel,

I was born Feb. 3, 1874 at 7.55 a.m.* There it is xactly. What is the end of the [Isidor and Lily] Brag[g]iotti story you left it unfinished. Did you go to Boston. And by the way did you find the silver cups in the piece of furniture, the silver cups and the crucifix. Grant Watson turned up the other day. We had a very good time together. He was only in Paris two days. The second day he brought with him a perfectly delightful Hungarian patriot poet† of 18 who is being educated in England. He was charming. We are going to see Watson in London and I will tell you more about him later. He seemed to have quite lost his heart to Muriel Draper and at the last Paul [Draper] came and took her home and he did not see Paul but all this is not to be mentioned. It was let out by accident. He was quite taken aback when he heard Muriel had a child. She had not mentioned that fact. Your account of Paul's sister is interesting.‡ Will she be coming over. If you hear any more about Mabel Weeks let me know. I have not heard anything about it from anybody in New York. The portrait of you seems to have made a hit in England alright. Its a good time to see publishers but I am awfully cold-footed about it. Like [Jo] Davidson I haven't got much courage. I wrote to [H. G.] Wells among others and he has written back most delightfully saying that he does think my work crazy but as he does not think me crazy he will be glad to meet and have me xplain. I guess thats all just this minute but I will write again soon

Gertrude.

⌐Alice B. Toklas's only extant letter to Mabel Dodge included enclosures of some writings by Leo Stein that appear from the context of the letter to be related to "Portrait of Mabel Dodge at the

---

Gertrude Stein in which she reported on her mixed feelings about the event: "I am very much impressed by her, Gertrude. She seems to me a very real person with some very remarkable qualities, and I find it true of her that her appeal is emotional. . . . Her most overwhelming quality is her capacity for devotion: her faith in you is beautiful. . . . As a spectacle for me the meeting was very satisfying—as a real meeting it was a failure . . . . The visit this afternoon made me quite quite unhappy. When I know why I'll tell you" (Mabel Weeks to Stein, 21 January 1913, GLSC).

* This is in reply to Dodge's request in her 18 December 1912 letter for Stein's hour, day, and year of birth so that Dodge can obtain Stein's horoscope from Evangeline Adams.

† Unidentified.

‡ Dodge described the monologuist Ruth Draper in a letter to Alice B. Toklas dated 29 December 1912.

Villa Curonia." These writings may have included Leo's parody of the word portrait, quoted from earlier, and the following "criticism" of the portrait that he sent in a letter to Mabel Weeks dated 4 February 1913:

> Size is not circumference unless magnitude extends.
> Purpose defined in limitation projected. It is the darkness whose center is light.
> Hardly can the movement arrest. Formality is subservience. Liquidation confluent with purpose by involution elaborates the elemental. Its significance protracts but virtue is dissimulated.
> All men are so but not in all ways. It is the thought process but not detached. Relations may be elaborated and hence illumination. Though the mole is blind the earth is one.[4]

Leo then comments to Mabel Weeks: "Gertrude and even Alice have the cheek to pretend that they understand this (which I can do in part sometimes) but as Gertrude thought it very nice and I had very sarcastical intentions we evidently didn't understand it the same way."[5]

Toklas also mentions her upcoming trip to London with Gertrude during which they planned to approach publishers about Stein's writing. They were to stay for over a month, without success in securing a publisher, and meet representatives of the *English Review* and the *Oxford Fortnightly*, as well as the English publisher John Lane and the art critic Roger Fry. In her own letter, Stein mentions having recently contacted the English writer H. G. Wells, to whom she had sent a copy of *Three Lives* in 1909, the year it was first published. Wells did not reply until 7 January 1913, when he wrote that he had finally gotten around to reading Stein's book:

> At first I was repelled by your extraordinary style, I was busy with a book of my own & I put yours away. It is only in the last week I have read it—I read it with a deepening pleasure & admiration. I'm very grateful indeed to you for sending it to me & I shall watch for your name again very curiously & eagerly.[6]

❧

4TH JANUARY [1913] 27 RUE DE FLEURUS

Dear Mabel,

Mr. Grant Watson turned up to-day. He is to be here only two days but will lunch with us tomorrow. We hope to see him in London. His coming in to-day reminded me that after you sent his parody* Leo wrote these things and asked me to send them to you. Immediately I typed them and forgot all the rest. You wont blame me I know.

We are going to London in about ten days. The Siege of London. Gertrude doesnt know what you say to publishers. So we think of asking them all to tea, separately, bien entendu. Gertrude is not only afraid of publishers but she is scared of being mistaken for a suffragette and arrested. There are also a half dozen minor fears. So there is no room for any fears of my own that I might have had, on the contrary. I'm one excitement at the thought of the adventure and am sure that something will come of it.

Mildred [Aldrich] was going to go to the country to live, but now a Miss [Myra] Edgerly† wants her to live with her. Miss E. is miniaturist, successful, energetic, Californian and good looking. She has a weakness for making homes she doesnt find it convenient to live in but in which she installs some "poor dear thing" to be a mother to her when she finds herself in that town. Among other houses she has one apartment here and she wants Mildred to move into it and be her Paris mother. Mildred is considering the idea, but isn't at all pleased with the easy way every one feels her capable of mothering a woman so apparently thirty five years old.

With fondest love

Yours

Alice.

~In the spirit of Gertrude and Leo Stein's celebrated salons, Mabel Dodge began hosting gatherings at her Fifth Avenue apartment in late January 1913, providing a setting for the exchange of ideas among intellectuals and activists. Dodge remembers that it was the journalist Lincoln Steffens who suggested the idea of these Evenings, as they were called:

> "You have a certain faculty," Steff told me one autumn afternoon as we drank tea together. . . . "It's a centralizing, magnetic, social faculty. You attract, stimulate, and soothe people, and men like to sit with you and talk to themselves! You make them think more fluently, and they feel enhanced. . . . Now why don't you see what you can do with this gift of yours? Why not organize all this accidental, unplanned activity

---

* This parody was sent to Gertrude Stein with a letter in November 1912.

† Myra Edgerly, a miniaturist who painted portraits, often of European royalty. Like Mabel Dodge, "the Edgerly," as she was referred to by her friends, had first been introduced to Gertrude Stein by Mildred Aldrich.

around you, this coming and going of visitors, and see these people at certain hours. Have Evenings! . . . Let everybody come! All these different kinds of people that you know, together here, without being managed or herded in any way! Why, something wonderful might come of it! You might even revive General Conversation!"[7]

Dodge lists the range of guests she had at her 23 Fifth Avenue home:

Socialists, Trade-Unionists, Anarchists, Suffragists, Poets, Relations, Lawyers, Murderers, "Old Friends," Psychoanalysts, I.W.W.'s, Single Taxers, Birth Controlists, Newspapermen, Artists, Modern-Artists, Clubwomen, Woman's-place-is-in-the-home Women, Clergymen, and just plain men . . .[8]

And she describes her presentation of herself at the Evenings:

I had a little formula for getting myself safely through the hours without any injury to my shy and suspicious sensibilities. As people flowed in, I stood apart, aloof and withdrawn, dressed in long, white dresses with maybe an emerald chiffon wrapped around me, and gave each one my hand—and a very small smile. It was the merest mask of cordiality—impersonal and remote. . . . "I hope you will come again if you enjoyed it."[9]

Contemporary newspaper accounts of Dodge's Evenings called her "a live ringer for the sphinx" and "Mona Lisa Mabel Dodge," made such quips as "The Italian Butler Lent a Suggestion of Democracy," and listed among her guests Florence Bradley, the artists Andrew Dasburg, Myra Edgerly, Marsden Hartley, Grace Johnson, and Arthur Lee, birth control advocate Margaret Sanger, and Alfred Stieglitz.[10]

At Mabel Dodge's salons, the avant-garde ideas circulating about art and politics were often indistinguishable from one another in their revolutionary fervor. Most Evenings had a specific topic and many had invited speakers. There was an Evening dedicated to poetry, one in which the psychoanalyst A. A. Brill talked about Freud and psychoanalysis, one in which anarchists such as Emma Goldman and Alexander Berkman argued for the superiority of direct action over negotiation or attempts to change the laws. Dodge was particularly drawn to those who were important in some way: "I wanted . . . to know the Heads of things. Heads of Movements, Heads of Newspapers, Heads of all kinds of groups of people. I became a Species of Head Hunter, in fact."[11] She greatly enjoyed the controversies generated and the emotional stirrings that resulted from such varied groupings of people. Dodge admitted: "I felt I was playing with dynamite and though I liked it dangerous, yet I was scared sometimes."[12]

In her next letter, Mabel Dodge prophetically predicts the force of the impact of the upcoming controversial Armory Show. She provides Stein with the details of how she came to write the first important and wide-reaching piece of publicity about Gertrude Stein, her article "Speculations, or Post-Impressionism in Prose," which appeared in a Special Number of *Arts & Decoration* in March 1913. ✎

JAN. 24 [1913] ATLANTIC CITY

Dearest Gertrude—

Behold the above address. I am here for two or three days with John & a nurse. He has had the grippe & I am just getting over it mixed with nervous prostration. But in the midst of nerves we are in mad excitement just the same. This letter will give you news and end up with a fearful confession so be prepared for the wurst. Mabel Weekes [i.e., Weeks] came to see me & I talked of you & your work for two hours without stopping. She says I throw light on you & it. I ought to for I don't talk of much else to anyone. I liked her & we will meet again soon.* But I <u>don't</u> think it was she in the case of divorce I sent you.

I hadn't been in New York long before I found out why I had come. I had been waiting to find out! There is an exhibition coming off the 15 March to 15 Feb,† which is the most important public event that has ever come off since the signing of the Declaration of Independence, & it is of the same nature. Arthur Davies is the

---

* In spite of their initial enthusiasm for each other and Weeks's invitation for tea that she extended to Dodge after their first visit—"I find myself very eager to continue our conversation in many directions, or rather I am eager to hear you talk about Gertrude's work" (Weeks to Dodge, c. February 1913, MDLC)—the two women did not meet again at this time, as Weeks reported to Stein in a letter dated 4 May 1913: "You are becoming a lion, aren't you? All the papers and magazines are interested. Mrs. Dodge has done a lot to bring it about. I have never seen her since I wrote you. She became absorbed probably in the International Exhibition, and I never saw or heard of her again. I don't think I quite suited her anyway" (Weeks to Stein, 4 May 1913, GLSC). However, a letter from Dodge to Stein on 14 January 1917 indicates that she saw Weeks again at that time.

† The Armory Show ran in New York from 17 February to 15 March 1913. Some discrepancies exist in the date commonly given as the opening one. In *The Armory Show: International Exhibition of Modern Art 1913*, a reprint of the original catalogues from the show, the dates are listed in the table of contents as 17 February to 15 March. However, in the facsimile of the actual catalogue for the New York part of the show, the opening date is given as 15 February. According to Milton Brown in *The*

President of a group of men here who felt the americain people ought to be given a chance to see what the modern artists have been doing in Europe, America & England of late years. So they have got a collection of paintings from Ingres to the italian futurists taking in all the french, spanish, english, german—in fact <u>all</u> one has heard of. This will be a <u>scream</u>! 2000 exhibits,* in the great armory of the 69th Regiment! The academy are frantic. Most of them are left out of it. They have only invited modern artists here who show <u>any</u> sign of <u>life</u>. They call themselves the Association of Americain Painters & Sculptors. They have badges (buttons) distributed all over New York with an uprooted pine tree on it & "The new spirit" underneath. In all the catalogues is a phrase from "Iffigenia" [i.e., Iphigenia] something like "It is better to be hideously (? I don't think it is hideously) alive than magnificently dead."† And this group of men decide which are alive & which are dead—not a dead one is going to show. Somehow or other I got right into all this. I am working like a dog for it. I am <u>all</u> <u>for</u> <u>it</u>. I think it splendid. They don't say the public are to like or not to like the stuff—they simply offer it to them to show <u>what</u> has been done & lets them decide what they will. There will be a riot & a revolution & things will never be quite the same afterwords.

Now I have been talking a great deal about the Gertrude Stein portraits. I have got right into the group of men who are bringing off this show. So one day the man who has charge of all the press work, an awfully intelligent little irishman‡ came to me & asked me if I would write an article for him. He said that two or three art magazines had offered their whole February numbers, to be made up exclusively of stuff about the show, articles about artists foreign (& domestic), about the new movement, the new spirit, about modern art, etc., all round. I talked a long time to him. I told him I couldn't write him an article about any special artist or movement because while I believed in the whole thing & was giving all my time & energy to helping on the show, still it was the <u>idea</u> of it all that interested me more than anything, not any conviction about any one artist, rather the relation of it <u>all</u> to all that is going on everywhere in spots, <u>here</u> in painting, there in some little isolated sheltered girl (Ruth Draper) here in politics, there in literature. Then he flung up his hands & exclaimed "Oh! I'm all up in the air

---

Story of the Armory Show, the press preview was on 16 February and the show officially opened to the public on 17 February.

   *The number of works of art displayed was closer to 1300.

   † According to Bernard Karpel in his introduction to *The Armory Show: International Exhibition of Modern Art 1913,* this quotation is from Euripides's *Iphigenia in Aulis* (405 B.C.) and appeared in the Armory Show catalogue in Greek, translated as "To die well is better than to live poorly" (2).

   ‡ F. J. Gregg.

about this post-impressionistic literature—now this Gertrude Stein!—" I said—"Well, you believe that there is too much smell of death in most of the painting you know. You want the new spirit. You want fresh life. Why don't you see that you can apply that to words? Words originally in primitive man were pure sound expressing directly an emotion. That is some time since. The life has gone out of them, their meaning is lost, blurred—Gertrude Stein—" "Why don't you write me an article about Gertrude Stein's post-impressionism," he broke in. "I'l have a shot at it if you like" I said. "All right, have it ready by Monday noon, will you?" (This was Saturday.) "Certainly" I agreed, as tho' I'd done it all my life!

Now, my poor darling Gertrude I have written an article called "Speculations" somehow drawing a comparison between you & Picasso & it is going to come out in some art magazine in February & be on sale for a month at that show unless they change their minds, because they accepted it! And there you are, pinned down, by me who am absolutely made, quote[,] to do it—"interpreted" by Mabel Dodge not at the Villa Curonia & thousands will read it & probably I've said it all wrong & that's not at all what you mean!!! I don't mind telling you that I am petrified at having done it & in my dreadful dead language! At the same time, as you perceive it will make your name known by & large—as the writer of "post impressionistic literature" which is my only consolation & then perhaps Mitchell Kennerl[e]y who likes innovations will get out a small book of portraits or something. I wish I had more of your stuff on hand in case anything happened & I could do anything about it! Will you ever forgive me if you find I've done you all wrong? I didn't go into it very deeply nor at great length, but I quoted from my portrait & from one of Constance [Fletcher]'s & I said "the writing of Gertrude Stein" in every paragraph so as to hammer it in! Edwin says it's good and he hates all post impressionistic painting, sculpture or writing, but he says it's the only thing that's been written that makes 'em seem plausible to him but I fear that's because he's biassed in my favor as he has been living all this time two doors from me at the Brevoort House* & looks upon me as a "Princesse Remote"—something quite fascinating, elusive & interesting. He only comes when I have parties, which is rather often, but it's all by doctor's & trained nurses' orders which makes it all right. Don't tell tho' because no one is on at all. We telephone & write notes to each other.

* The Brevoort Hotel and Café was located on Fifth Avenue and Eighth Street, one block from 23 Fifth Avenue. The café was a popular gathering place for artists, writers, and Village bohemians, including the painters Charles Demuth, Arthur Dove, and John Marin, the sculptor Jo Davidson, and the writers Theodore Dreiser, Hutchins Hapgood, and Eugene O'Neill (Emily Farnham, *Charles Demuth: Behind a Laughing Mask*, 106).

So there Gertrude is my confession. I am your faithful &
incomprehending Boswell.* If I dare, I'l send you some copies. I
don't know what it's going to be in yet! The cheaper the better as
more people will buy it!! I couldn't have stood it without the show
over here. Now I feel of use—& am.

I am going to fall in love soon—as soon as I get better—with
Hutch [Hapgood]. "You do love ideas" he said the other night, "don't
you?" "Yes, alternately with emotions!" I felt impelled to reply—
which he understood & laughed long at! I had a party the other
night all made of artists & art critics with a dash of social reform &
anarchists. Picabbia [i.e., Francis Picabia]† the Spanish Picasso was
there with a nice wife. Charlotte Becker has named him Picubbia,
which all have adopted!

I have some more letters & parodies of the portrait. Many people
have it now. All my letters come to Mrs. Mabel Dodge where last
year they came to Mrs. Edwin Dodge—that's what you've done for
one thing! Let me know all about your english experiences. I will
reserve sequence of Braggiotti story until next time. You will get
your horoscope some day. I feel things are moving. Anyway I'm
shoving! But promise beforehand to forgive my article—won't you?

Ever yrs—

Mabel.

———

Jan. 27 [1913] Hotel Traymore
Atlantic City N.J.

Dearest Gertrude—

Amazing things are happening! Private things with really no
consequences as far as I know but queer—you will admit. I mailed
you my last letter upon my arrival here, describing to you that I
had written about you & Picasso & telling you Edwin rushed in
from his hotel—awfully excited—saying it was creative because I
had made post-impressionism plausible (to him!) for the first time.
He has evidently reread it since, & I transcribe his telegrams of
yesterday—literally!

(Morning one) "Am still amazed at the realization that your

* Named after James Boswell, the untiring Scottish biographer of Samuel Johnson,
meaning someone who chronicles in detail the life of a contemporary.

† Francis Picabia, French painter who was represented by four paintings in the
Armory Show. When he first met Gertrude Stein in 1913, the two did not immediately
take to one another, as Stein relates in *The Autobiography of Alice B. Toklas:* "In those
days Picabia and Gertrude Stein did not get to be very good friends. He annoyed her
with his incessantness and what she called the vulgarity of his delayed adolescence"

first name coupled with my last name is to be engraved among the inspired "Roadbreakers" who have "pursued truth to eternity"

E. S. D.

In the evening, another one saying
"Am still overcome with shame at my stupidity. "Cocksure Eddy"—Hope you will get better down there"

Dodge—

This morning comes the following letter
["]Dearest M. I am still thrilled at the certainty of your fast approching recognition. I am still humiliated by the knowledge that its arrival has been so long delayed by my blundering interference. You have been right these years, eternally right, I have not understood you. And nothing pleases me more in "Speculations" than its vibrant note of splendid optimism—for interest in vitality & distrust of the diseased are the highest & finest of human gifts. I marvel that you have been so good to me. Humility has entered the portals of Casa Edwin Dodge"

Now my darling Gertrude I can't make out anything about this! I don't know what he means! It seems a splendid capitulation but why? How has he retarded my now "fast approching recognition?["] What "blundering interference?" How have I been good to him? And why has humility entered him? I long to know but do not want to dash him with questions! It seems—even for his own happiness!—I should receive these assertions with a kind of gentle sadness, as tho' I had felt that some day I would be justified tho' it comes now a trifle late! Shall I ever know what he means? I know when he had just finished reading it he rushed in & said "What kept me awake all night was the realization that I had lived with you for eight years without knowing you had passion." How does he find this out in my poor little article & not in all I have told him of Paul? I am all mixed up—indeed I am. Does this article really help him to understand me better or has it covered me up more & more to him? I wish I knew. I am going back to N.Y. this eve. I wonder what he's going to be like. Don't tell a soul but Alice not even Leo—I wouldn't have sent copies of these to anyone but you.

Best love—

M.

P.S. Of course all this is no criterion for the article. It's only personal to him.

---

(134). It was not until the 1930s that they became friends. At this time, Picabia gave Stein a chihuahua named Byron, who died quickly, and then another chihuahua that Stein and Toklas called Pépé, after Picabia (*EA*, 48–49).

In *European Experiences,* Mabel Dodge mentions the occasion of the publication of her article on Gertrude Stein as "the real break" in her relationship with Stein and blames Alice B. Toklas for dealing the final blow to the friendship:

> Gertrude—for some obscure reason—was angry. Leo told me it was because it appeared to her that there was some doubt as to which was the more important, the bear or the one leading the bear, but I felt that it was Alice's final and successful effort in turning Gertrude from me—her influencing and her wish, and I missed my jolly fat friend very much.[13]

Inspired and energized by her increasing public recognition, Mabel Dodge quickly mobilized to create more publicity for herself and her portraitist. She proposed an issue of *Arts & Decoration* that would include Stein's word portrait of her along with a reproduction of Picasso's famous portrait of Gertrude Stein. This issue never materialized, but in a Special Number issue of *Camera Work* in June 1913, Stieglitz published Stein's portrait of Dodge together with a reproduction of Picasso's portrait and a reprint of Dodge's article on Stein.

[Whitman motto]

Monday Jan. 27 [1913] 23 Fifth Avenue

Dearest Gertrude

Yesterday I wrote you from Atlantic City & today in the early morning I got an idea. I got up & hurried up to the office of F. J. Gregg, the man who has charge of <u>all</u> the press work of the show, & who placed my article on you. I put my idea before him. He said "Splendid" & added "You know that Mabel Dodge article on Gertrude Stein is going to make a lot of talk. I've already seen two editorials on it. So <u>this</u> idea of yours fits in splendidly."

So upon that I hurried to the Editor of the Magazine that the article is to appear in. It is, I believe, a ten cent magazine, perhaps 25-cent, I forget. Its whole Feb. number* is devoted to articles on the show with reproductions of the pictures. It will be sold in thousands at the show at the Armory & also <u>after words</u> in Chicago where the show goes. I bearded [berated?] the editor in his traditional "den." I showed him a copy of "Portrait of Mabel Dodge . . ." & I said <u>You</u> say you introduce <u>my</u> article called "Speculations or Post-Impressionistic Literature" with an editor's note saying "This

---

* It was actually the March 1913 issue of *Arts & Decoration* that was devoted to the Armory Show. The magazine sold for twenty cents.

162

is an article about the only woman writing impressionistic literature by the only woman in America who fully understands it."
Now why don't you realize that those extra thousands of people
who read the magazine for March, which they will buy at the show
here & in Chicago, will have their curiosity (I would <u>like</u> to think
<u>interest</u>) aroused by my article & quotations from G. S. & if you
<u>add</u> to your editor's note "To be followed in our April number of
"The Portrait of Mabel Dodge["] by Gertrude Stein illustrated by
a reproduction of a portrait of Gertrude Stein by Picasso." You would
<u>thus</u> insure the same <u>large</u> sale of your magazine for April as you
will have in March?" My darling he saw it!!! Then I said "Of course
Miss Stein is a professional & you must pay her for the article
even if it is only a nominal sum otherwise I cannot consider it. In
the meantime I shall write her <u>at</u> <u>once</u> & have her send me a photograph of the portrait by Picasso." So there you are! In circula-
tion. Already people tell me that everywhere, on account of my
judicious scattering of the Portrait <u>everyone</u> is saying "<u>Who</u> is
Gertrude Stein? <u>Who</u> is Mabel Dodge at the Villa Curonia." Tomorrow I go down for the night to Mrs. [Clarissa] Davidge* daughter of Bishop Potter, head of a community where Edwin Arlington
Robinson† & other poets & artists live & she is most prominent in
working for the show—in order to <u>read</u> them my article about you,
& explain things, as a result of having lent them the portrait. The
ed. of "Arts & Decorations" said—as well as Gregg "I know already of three editorials on this new thing." I said "Splendid. We
don't care what anyone says. Our motto is "<u>Any</u> comment." I only
pray I'l be up to the mark enough to meet the tide & handle it all
right. I hope to answer every letter by a return one in the papers. I
am determined to make the most of this Heaven sent opportunity.

Everyone in writing circles knows of Gertrude Stein. They are
going to know more. Send me a photograph <u>at</u> <u>once</u> of that portrait
by Picasso. It's worth having done over <u>larger</u> so they can reproduce it <u>well</u>. They must have it as soon as possible. So do this up
hurry & I hope you see how things are <u>humming</u> here—

Mabel

P.S.

I should have told you before that about a fortnight ago I wrote
P.[aul] for the first time because I had learned from a mutual friend
that he is flunking all his examinations, & his family are thinking
of taking him out of Columbia because he doesn't study, & his
health is even worse than mine as he has a steady unceasing cough

---

* Clarissa Davidge, honorary treasurer for the Armory Show who lived in an old
mansion on Staten Island.

† Edwin Arlington Robinson, American poet.

& losing weight all the time. So I wrote him how ill I was too, with nervous prostration & nurses & specialists, & how upset E.[dwin] was banished to a hotel by them & I said that this sort of love that did all this couldn't be a good love that nothing justified it, that I was going to try, for the first time, to get over it, work & put it out of my mind & that I wanted him to <u>not</u> look forward to the spring or any time but to just work & try & find some girl to get interested in. Since then I've been worse & a hundred yrs old but have worked (wrote the article!) etc. & I hear he is suffering awfully. We both feel the same I suppose—

M.

～Mabel Dodge's description of her first meeting with the critic and writer Carl Van Vechten at a dinner party held in the winter of 1913 was not particularly flattering and certainly does not predict the close friendship, albeit with its ups and downs, that developed between them. In her memoirs, she elaborately provides details of Van Vechten's initial appearance to her:

> At dinner a funny-looking man sat opposite me. He was about thirty-five years old and his evening clothes looked a little queer to me, maybe because of his shirt, which was frilly, full of little tucks. He had nice brown eyes, full of twinkling, good-natured malice. . . . His mouth was his most difficult feature, because of the large teeth with slits showing between them that jutted out and made him look like a wild boar, though the rest of him looked quite domesticated. . . . He was really queer-looking, I thought, his neck never seeming able to hold up his head, or his knees his body. When he laughed, little shrieks flew out between the slits in his big teeth.
> "Really, those teeth," I thought. "They seem to have a life of their own apart from the rest of him. They are always trying to get on to the outside of his face."[14]

Bruce Kellner, Van Vechten's biographer, reports that Dodge was not alone in having a powerful and ambivalent first impression: "Carl was alternately put off and fascinated by Mrs. Dodge's remoteness and sphinxlike silence."[15] However, despite her strong response to his physical appearance, Dodge soon invited Van Vechten to visit her at 23 Fifth Avenue. She claimed that he was "the first person who animated my lifeless rooms" with his whimsy and vitality. From her meticulously decorated and carefully arranged apartment, "there was an instant response from all those inanimate things and the place became alive for us and for all others who ever afterwards entered there. He set it going on its changing round of appearances." The friendship between Dodge and Van Vechten developed quickly. He adopted a nickname for her, calling her "Mike" (for an unknown reason), and they established a routine of speaking each morning on the telephone.[16]

On 15 April 1913, Dodge wrote a poem about Van Vechten, paying tribute to the privileged place he had come to hold in her heart as she allowed him to see beneath her surface. In an apparently playful way of indicating their overlapping and mutually involved lives, Dodge swapped their last names in both the title of her poem, "Chiaroscuro—Portrait of Carl Dodge," and in her signature "M.V.V. (D.V.)," for Mabel Van Vechten, "D.V." possibly standing for Deo volente, or God willing. The last stanza of the poem reads: "Only your laughter reaches to my heart./ Laughter at love & grief! . . . / Insuperable laughter at your rôle / Of laughing while the unveiled gods depart./ But none may ever see in my glad eyes/ The tears I weep with your poor weeping soul."[17]

Van Vechten wrote an article about Gertrude Stein, entitled "Cubist of Letters Writes a New Book," that appeared in the *New York Times* on 24 February 1913, according to his notation next to the clipping in one of his scrapbooks at the New York Public Library. He also noted in the margins around his article that it was "one of the very first pieces" in print about Stein and that his writing had been "much abridged" by the newspaper.[18] The article begins by mentioning the recent appearance of Stein's "Portrait of Mabel Dodge at the Villa Curonia" and includes quotations from "a friend," an unnamed Mabel Dodge, who asserts that Stein

> "has made an attempt at creating a new art form. She is tired of the limitations of literature, and she wants to create a new field. . . . One will get a great deal of pleasure in reading Miss Stein whether one understands her or not. You will find that her work when read aloud has a musical cadence."

Van Vechten provides brief biographical details about Stein, discusses *Three Lives*, and includes a number of passages from her work, including excerpts from the word portraits of Picasso and Dodge.

At around the same time that Dodge first met Van Vechten, she also made her first trip to Alfred Stieglitz's gallery, 291. Dodge claims that it was Hutchins Hapgood who introduced her to the gallery, an essential gathering place for the avant-garde American artists and their supporters. Dodge recalls that it was at 291 that she met the American painters Marsden Hartley and Andrew Dasburg. She became an enthusiastic supporter and patron of their work, and they were to be her friends for years. Dodge describes what she found on her frequent visits to the gallery:

> There were always attractive people at Stieglitz's place. And strange, alluring paintings on the walls that one gazed into while he talked, until, gazing, one entered them and knew them. . . . In those early years he launched nearly all those painters who count today in America and without a particle of apprehension he hung up the work of artists whom the physicians diagnosed as paranoiacs and *dementia-praecox* cases.[19]

13 FEB. [1913] 23 FIFTH AVENUE

Dearest Gertrude,   ∼

You are just on the eve of <u>bursting</u>! Everybody wherever I go— & others who go where I don't say the same thing—is talking of Gertrude Stein! There is an article about you coming out in the N.Y. Times this Sunday* & the editor sent a young man around to see me & talk about you as he (the ed.) had got hold of a copy of yr portrait of me & he said he <u>must</u> get hold of it all <u>first</u> as it was new, etc., etc. I had met the young man who came to see me about it, at dinner, & found him temperamental, musical & absolutely stupid but rather nice! So I got Hutch [Hapgood] to be here—this was yesterday—when he came so that between us we could try & get something into him that wouldn't make it seem a mere <u>pie</u>. So he arrived & we talked at him & he couldn't understand a word we said but he carried away the portrait & a photograph of <u>me</u> (!) & my promise to get him some of <u>you</u>. I telephoned Mabel Weeks & your cousin Mrs. [Bird] Gans† & secured a variety (one sitting on a sundial!) & sent them to the young man. His name is [Carl] Van

---

* Van Vechten's article actually did not come out on Sunday but appeared on Monday 24 February 1913. Its full title was "Cubist of Letters Writes a New Book / Miss Gertrude Stein Calls It a 'Portrait'—Should Be Read for the 'Impression' / Need Not be Understood / Wherein It Appears to be a Great Success—Friend Says It Requires a New Point of View."

† Bird Stein Gans was Gertrude Stein's cousin through her father's side, as she was the eldest child born to Solomon Stein, one of Gertrude Stein's father's brothers. She was married to Howard Gans and founded the Child Study Association of America, of which she was president for forty-one years.

Vechten. So on Sunday you will be in the Times & Monday the show opens where they will sell that idiotic article of mine on you! And now Stieglitz is trying to get The Portrait* away from Dubois [i.e., Guy Pène du Bois]† who took it for his April number—because Stieglitz says he <u>must</u> have it. It was very funny the other day, just after I left Stieglitz's where I had been for the first time he turned to Jo Davidson & said "Now I understand the portrait perfectly, now I've seen her!" Just as <u>easy</u>!!! [Francis] <u>Picabia</u> the painter is here & very intelligent & understands it all perfectly. I asked him to write down what he said & I will send it to you. I will give him a letter to you as you & Leo will <u>both</u> (strangely enough) like him.

I am much better & have been very busy over the Exhibition—of which they have made me an Honorary Vice-Pres. It is going to be great fun & the papers will simply have a riot over it.

I have done myself proud in the way I have distributed those Portraits so that they have penetrated in this sort of way [drawing of a half-circle with spokes radiating out from a center appears here in original letter] from this house! I have been expecting letter from you lately. Let me hear what you hear. E.[dwin] is living at a hotel next door‡ but comes to dine sometimes.

Love to Alice & Leo.

M. D.

⌐Gertrude Stein writes to Mabel Dodge from London with enthusiastic praise for her publicity efforts and provides details of her current writing projects and publishing attempts. "Many Many Women," a work dealing with lesbian relationships that Stein completed around 1912, was being considered by Mitchell Kennerley. At the same time, John Lane was going back and forth about whether to publish Stein's *Three Lives*. On 28 January 1913 he wrote to Stein at the Knightsbridge Hotel, London: "Whilst I think it [*Three Lives*] is quite interesting yet as it is cast in the shape of short stories there is absolutely no sale in this country for such, but I think I might be able to create some little interest by skilful advertising, but this is a costly luxury."[20] However, three days later he wrote to Stein again: "Unfortunately I have come to the conclu-

---

*"Portrait of Mabel Dodge at the Villa Curonia."
† Guy Pène du Bois, American painter who was editor of *Arts & Decoration*.
‡ The Brevoort Hotel.

sion that I am unable to use your book here, I am therefore return-ing it."[21] A couple of months later, Lane was still interested, as he explained in a letter to Stein received on 4 April 1913: "I have this a.m. seen Mr. Roger Fry and I have decided to take your 'Three Lives' if you will agree to the following terms."[22] Lane spelled out a number of conditions, including a title change and royalty per-centages. Stein did not sign a contract with Lane for *Three Lives* until July 1914 and did not agree to the title change. The English edition of *Three Lives* finally came out in 1915.

In the final paragraph of her letter to Dodge, Stein mentions a number of works in progress: "the long gay book" refers to "A Long Gay Book," usually dated earlier than 1913 and published in *Matisse Picasso and Gertrude Stein with Two Shorter Stories* ; "Another one of the five" likely refers to "Jenny, Helen, Hannah, Paul and Peter," published in *Two: Gertrude Stein and Her Brother and Other Early Portraits,* a work Stein described in a letter to Dodge written almost a year earlier as "a description of a family of five who are all peculiar and are in a peculiar relation each one to every other one of the five of them;"[23] "the one of the Two" refers to "Two: Gertrude Stein and Her Brother," also included in *Two,* a portrait of the relationship between Gertrude and Leo at the time that their bond was weakening as Gertrude became closer with Alice; "Scenes" refers to "Scenes. Actions and Dispositions of Relations and Positions," published in *Geography and Plays;* "two very short ones about the English and about the Publishers, the British Mu-seum and the Portrait Gallery" can be read as referring to either two or three works—one about the English and one about the Pub-lishers, or two about the English plus one about the Publishers. It is likely that the work (or works) about the English includes "En-gland," published in *Geography and Plays.* "The Publishers, the British Museum and the Portrait Gallery" refers to "Publishers, the Portrait Gallery and the Manuscripts at the British Museum," also included in *Geography and Plays;* "the long one about the whole Paris crowd" seems to be, according to Jayne Walker,[24] "Matisse Picasso and Gertrude Stein," or "G.M.P.," a work about Stein and the artists in her circle, featured as the title piece of *Matisse Picasso and Gertrude Stein.*~

My dear Mabel

I am completely delighted with your performances and busting to see the article, send it as soon as it is printed. You must be having an awfully amusing time and there will be lots of stories to tell. It takes lots of shoving to make them take me but I guess you will do it. The portrait has been invaluable as you will see over here also. Mitchell Kennerl[e]y has a thing of mine Many many women which he has had about four months now. He said he wanted to see something of mine because Stieglitz had spoken of me to him and so I sent him that but he has never written anything about it. I have not hurried him because I supposed he was making up his mind. I will send you a little bunch of short things so that you will have something if you get a chance to place it but make them pay for them because I don't want to get known as giving them away. Then we can have more money to travel with and I love traveling. We are having a very amusing time here and as yet nothing is decided but John Lane and the English Review are nibbling. John Lane is an awfully funny man. He waits round and he asks a question and you think he has got you and then you find he hasn't. Roger Fry is going to try to help him land me. Perhaps it will succeed. By the way some one told me that [Arthur B.] Davies was interested in my work. That might help Mitchell Kennerl[e]y. But the most unxpected interested person is Logan Pearsall Smith.* He went quite off his head about your portrait and is reading it to everybody. Never goes anywhere without it and wants to do an article on it for the English Review. Among other things he read it to [Israel] Zangwill† and Zangwill was moved. He said "And I always thought she was such a healthy minded young woman, what a terrible blow it must be for her poor dear brother." And it seems he meant it. Then when Logan would persist in reading it and rereading it Zangwill got angry and said to Logan. "How can you waste your time reading and rereading a thing like that and all these years you have refused to read Kipling." And the wonderful part of it was that Zangwill was not fooling.

* Logan Pearsall Smith, American essayist who lived most of his life in England. Smith had approached the *Oxford Fortnightly* with one of Gertrude Stein's works. He reported to Stein in a letter dated 26 February 1913 that the paper found the manuscript too long but wondered if it could print the word portrait of Constance Fletcher (Included in *FF*, 75).

† Israel Zangwill, English playwright and novelist who was a noted Zionist.

We have been seeing all kinds of people and last night we had an evening with Paul & Muriel [Draper]. We were there for dinner. [Robert de la] Condamine* and the younger Rothenstein† were there and Condamine and I got along beautifully and were pleased with one another. Paul and Muriel have done it alright. But to begin at the beginning. We went to the Opera to see the first night of the Russian ballet and there in a box was a woman who had we thought the most effective head dress in the house and it was a very gorgeous house too. We were interested and we found she had fire opals and a gorgeous pink thing to go with them. We laughed and wondered if it was there that Paul had gotten the fire opal idea. Not at all, when we dined with them two nights after lo and behold it had been Muriel. They gave us a handsome dinner, the table a complete scheme in white only broken by the vivid color of food and wine. Their big room is very comforcable and very beautifully lighted with electricity and enormous candles. Paul so he said had just that day sworn off betting now that the house was complete and paid for. Muriel gathers the men and keeps it all going on steadily xtraordinarily well. We had a very good time. Paul sings and on the whole better but as sadly as ever. They know a considerable number of amusing people and the place is attractive.

For a while I saw quite a good deal of Grant Watson. He gets rather monotonous. Its good but it lacks variety. I don't know that he has seen Muriel. Paul owns all the things he gave us a list of and some more and he is awfully fond of the list.

Roger Fry is being awfully good about my work. It seems that he read Three Lives long ago and was much impressed with it and so he is doing his best to get me published. His being a quaker gives him more penetration in his sweetness than is usual with his type, it does not make him more interesting but it makes him purer. Your portrait is being considered by the English Review at Logan

---

* Robert de la Condamine, English actor whom Muriel Draper pronounced as "one of England's great actors" (Draper, *Music at Midnight*, 10). Dodge described him as a "strange, wonderful fellow" who "had beautiful hyacinthine eyes with a lift at their corners, and eyebrows that darted like fishes" (*EE*, 264). According to Dodge, Robert de la Condamine attempted to live a life of celibacy in order to combat his leanings toward homosexuality (*EE*, 265–66).

† It is very possible that Stein is referring to Sir John Rothenstein, an English art historian who was the son of Sir William Rothenstein, an English artist and writer whose work as a portrait painter was famous in Paris. I am grateful to Leon Katz for suggesting this identification.

Pearsall Smith's suggestion. You won't mind their publishing it if they decide to do so will you. The things I am sending you are not at all selected, they are short things I happened to have with me here.

I am doing a good deal of work. The long gay book goes on very well. Another one of the five is finished, so is the one of the Two. I am doing a short thing of Scenes. Then I am doing two very short ones about the English and about the Publishers, the British Museum and the Portrait Gallery, the long one about the whole Paris crowd goes on slowly.

I guess thats all for just now. Respects to Edwin.

Always yours
Gertrude.

〜Before Dodge received Stein's letter from London, she wrote again, impatiently requesting news of her and the photograph of Picasso's portrait of Stein. Another letter from Dodge urges Stein to visit the Villa Curonia that summer and fills her in on responses in the United States to Stein's writing.〜

FEB. 18 [1913] [23 FIFTH AVENUE]

Dearest Gertrude—

I can't understand why I don't hear from you unless you are in the South as someone said. Just when everyone is excited over you & your "works" we don't know where you are! I cabled you today to ask you to send immediately a photograph of Picasso's portrait of you which Stieglitz will probably publish with "Portrait of Mabel Dodge" & perhaps my rotten article on you, (in which magazine by the way is selling like hot cakes at the Armory.) The show is a terrific success! We are all wild over it—& <u>everyone</u> in N.Y. is saying "<u>Who</u> is Gertrude Stein?" For heaven's sake get that photograph over to me. Have <u>Mike</u> [Stein] get a <u>good</u> one done of the portrait, a bigger one than yours is that you gave me. Mitchell Kennerl[e]y is seriously thinking of "Many many women"—I am having a <u>great</u> time being your advance agent & <u>I</u> <u>do</u> <u>it</u> <u>very</u> <u>well</u>. Hutch [Hapgood] is going to do an article on you soon. Send to Paris for your letters.

Best love,
Mabel.

Dearest Gertrude,

I want you to decide if you can if you'l come to me this summer
& where & how long you can stay—so if I ask anyone I'l know
about rooms. You're the most important to me, so I give you first
choice. Mabel Weekes [i.e., Weeks] said you were going to Spain
but you [illegible] this summer—please. We'l have Mabel Weekes
come to the Curonia too—so you write & tell me.

Everyone in N.Y. is now (in literary & artistic circles) talking
about you & the Portrait. It has been cleverly managed. [F. J.] Gregg
who knows all the writing & painting people here has carefully
distributed it. Editorials & criticisms will be forthcoming. As in
every movement we may expect the vilest interpretation put upon
it by some. I have heard of two men who read it aloud to others
reading into it merely obscenity and the worst constructions.
Hon[n]i soit qui mal y pense!* Jo Davidson says he can only see
this in it now since it was pointed out to him. Someone else said it
all had an ulterior meaning & was a peculiar form of Yiddish hu-
mor. Hutch [Hapgood] is indignant as I am. He knows you so well
& comes <u>very</u> near to understanding your intention. Did you see
his article about you after Stieglitz published you?† Hutch will
doubtless write a good one this time. Do not mind the other remarks. If they knew you or me they wouldn't say them.

Yours—

Mabel.

⮜Gertrude Stein wrote to Dodge after returning from London,
bringing her up-to-date on the activities of some of their mutual
acquaintances in Paris and Florence, among them Florence Blood.
In the early months of 1913, Stein wrote a word portrait of Blood,
entitled "A Portrait of F. B." It recalled the portraits of Constance
Fletcher and Mabel Dodge in its apparently haphazard collection
of images. Upon receiving a copy of the portrait, Blood wrote to
Stein around May 1913:

---

* Shame on him who evil thinks.
† Dodge is referring to Stieglitz's August 1912 publication of Stein's word portraits
of Picasso and Matisse in *Camera Work*. Hapgood's article about Gertrude Stein was
entitled "A New Form of Literature" and appeared in the *New York Globe* on 26 September 1912.

Oh! dear Miss Stein—oh! am I really like that & what—oh! What does it mean? I feel like a person who has rushed eagerly to the looking glass to see themselves with new eyes, but alas alas, all the familiar landmarks have been quite swept away— eyes, mouth, hands, feet, & the rest all gone!—I feel convinced you know me better than I do myself & if your knowledge is contained in these leaves do do give me the key—

Blood was particularly pleased by a phrase in her portrait, "the distaste of pink pepper," and, referring to one line that begins "There is no squeak," she continues in her letter: "You say there is no squeak—but I wish you could have heard the one I gave when I came to the pink pepper."[25]

Although in her next letter Stein agreed to visit the Villa Curonia in August, she ended up not traveling to Florence that summer. Instead, she and Dodge met for several days in Paris in July.⌇

[CIRCA FEBRUARY 1913] 27 RUE DE FLEURUS

My dear Mabel,

You must have had a good time at the opening. I guess I would not have minded being there with you. We have just gotten back from London. We did have an awfully good time. I will send you the photo of my portrait by this mail. It would take considerable time to get a larger one done as the only man who photographs Picasso's things well is xtreme[ly] dilatory. He says that this one will enlarge very well. As to our summer plans, owing to stress of poverty we will be staying in Paris surely through June. Then we will go somewhere for a month of high altitudes and then we will come to you which will be August if that will suit you. The Picassos have taken a house in the South of France so they probably won't be able to get away as he has to go to Spain part of the time on account of his parents, who are alone and getting very old. Miss [Florence] Blood is in town. She was delayed some time as one of the dogs had eczema and then as he got well he bit the other dog. They are now both well and Miss Blood is here to stay for some months. She says that [Bernard] Berenson seems very feeble. He is very sweet is polite and amiable to Mary [Berenson], very kind to the Italians and intimate with [Charles] Loeser. Everybody in Florence is afraid that he is going to die soon. She says that the Berensons and the Loesers visit and dine with each other and come to see her together. I am awfully glad you like Mabel Weeks, it would be nice if she came to the Villa this summer. She is a very pleasant companion, steadily so. Did I tell you that I hea[r]d Electra in London.* I enjoyed it completely. It made a deeper impression on me than anything since Tristan in my youth. He has done what [Richard] Wagner† tried to do and couldn't he has made real conversation and he does it by intervals and relations directly without machinery. After all we are all modern. I guess thats all. I am waiting for your article

Always yours

Gertrude.

———

[CIRCA LATE FEBRUARY 1913] 27 RUE DE FLEURUS

My dear Mabel

I am sending the photographs off by this mail. I had a new and bigger one made after all and this one ought to reproduce very well. I am also enclosing a little thing I did last spring, its so short it might be useful to you. My work has been going very well ever since I have been home. I am awfully anxious to hear all the news

Yours

Gertrude.

⌒Dodge sent Stein newspaper and magazine clippings about the Armory Show and all the publicity she was generating about Stein through the publication of her article "Speculations" in *Arts & Decoration.* Dodge collected many of these clippings in scrapbooks that are now at the Beinecke Rare Book and Manuscript Library, Yale University. Stein was eager to receive Dodge's article as well as the press material and inquires about the status of her manuscript that had now been in the hands of Mitchell Kennerley for months.⌒

[CIRCA MARCH 1913] [23 FIFTH AVENUE]

Dearest Gertrude

Don't throw away any of these but send 'em all back as I want to make a book of 'em. The musical critic on the N.Y. Times‡ said to

---

* *Elektra,* written by the German composer Richard Strauss in 1909, was performed at the Royal Opera House in Covent Garden on Friday 21 February 1913.

† Richard Wagner, German composer of romantic operas. *Tristan und Isolde* was written in 1857–59.

‡Carl Van Vechten was assistant music critic for the *New York Times* at the time.

174

me today "The name of Gertrude Stein is better known in New York today than the name of God"—!

M. D.

———

Dear Gertrude,

Enclosed is a fine ad. Don't lose <u>any</u> of these clippings because we will make a book of them.

M. D.

———

My dear Mabel,

Nothing has come yet not your article nor clippings but I guess they are on the way and if you have not sent a catalogue of the show will you send one. Sometime look up the work of an Englishman Harry Phelan Gibb, He is a man I like very much personally and his work has some quality. He is the only person I have ever know[n] who has anything of the quality of Hutch [Hapgood].

I wonder if Mitchell Kennerl[e]y is going to do anything with my ms. Will you ask him sometime. There is no use my writing to him as he does not answer. Perhaps you can find out. Miss [Florence] Blood has just told me that Mary Berenson wrote to her that she has heard from New York that you are getting everybody to read the portrait and know my name. My big thing about the whole crowd over here* is getting along nicely. I think you will like it. I guess thats all

Gertrude.

〜It looked for a while as if Mitchell Kennerley was finally going to publish Gertrude Stein's "Many Many Women" as well as publicize her work in other ways. At the same time that Dodge was unflaggingly engaged in promoting Stein's writing, she was also drumming up generous amounts of attention for herself both in

---

* Most likely Stein is referring to "Matisse Picasso and Gertrude Stein," or "G.M.P.," which is usually dated as having been completed in 1912, but if this reference is correct, then it may have been finished in 1913 (Bridgman, *Gertrude Stein in Pieces,* 367; GSC, 46–47).

relation to Stein and apart from her. In her memoirs from this period, Dodge explains her passionate interest of the moment, which involved organizing a group of people for a common purpose:

> I had been brought up in an environment where altruistic attitudes were unknown, and afterwards the life in Italy had been all too concerned with aesthetics to be troubled about reforms. But I wanted a life in common with others. For instance, the idea we had for a small modern art gallery and art magazine in Paris!
> With Jo Davidson and Yvonne, Maurice Aisen, . . . the Picabias, I practically agreed to leave the desert that New York seemed to us all and to go with them and start a really altruistic group life in Paris where we would be devoting all our vitality to an understanding of modern art, for the benefit of artists, giving them a vehicle of expression somewhat along the same lines as Stieglitz's *Camera Work,* and a little place as much like "291" as possible, where their work could be seen, and where our own "vie intérieure" would have a chance to deepen.
> In Paris there was no one like Stieglitz who fostered the new art, and no way of educating the public so it would understand it. The only place in Paris where anyone could hear anything about modern art was at the Steins'.[26]

Despite all her initial excitement about this idea, Dodge finally admitted "I couldn't make up my mind to go [to Paris]."[27] The project itself then lost its motivating force and failed to materialize. However, it was in the height of her enthusiasm for the idea that she wrote to Stein. ∽

[Whitman motto]

[CIRCA MARCH 1913] [23 FIFTH AVENUE]
Dearest Gertrude

Too rushed to write. But [Mitchell] Kennerl[e]y told me today he will publish "Many many women" & he will publish an article about you in the Forum & he is holding down other stuff of yours— & furthermore this. I got some copies of "Three Lives" from Mrs. [May] Knoblauch & sent a few about. I took one to Kennerl[e]y. He said today he would like to get all the copies he can & put them on sale. He says you are well in the air now, due to first Stieglitz then to my judicious distribution of "Mabel Dodge." Everyone is after that. He <u>begged</u> me to let him have it for the Forum* & then reprint in book form after—<u>this</u> latter he <u>may</u> do but I have promised Stieglitz <u>he</u> may have the first printing of it. He (S.) is getting it out in Camera Work, (I having snatched it back from "Arts & Decorations") & he means to bring out a Stein-Dodge number†— with <u>that</u>, <u>my</u> article (in full) on you reprinted from Arts & Decs. & an article on <u>you</u> & <u>Matisse</u> by a <u>very</u> brilliant object here named Dr. [Maurice] Aisen‡—a roumanian chemist & poet mixed. <u>He</u> is against it so the number of Cam. Work will be balanced & amusing. I am sending you some clippings about show. I will send you some about <u>you</u> later. I have several.

It is madly exciting here now. We are cooking up a plan which I will tell you later for a winter in Paris—a sort of laboratory for ideas, a magazine edited by me <u>called</u> "L'idée", a showroom like Stieglitz's & magazine like his, & it will mean a real live movement forward in Paris. The [Francis and Gabrielle Buffet-] Picabias, [Jo] Davidson, Aisen & others are getting it up. The Steins, Picassos, [Manuel] Manolo§ & others will be in it. I am working like a dog over you. It has to be done subtly. I have made all N.Y. as well as suburbs talk about you. Now is the time for the publishers & <u>they</u> know it. E.[dwin] & I are about to get a divorce.¶

Best love—
M.

————

[French Telegram]

[POSTMARK: 15 MARCH 1913] [27 RUE DE FLEURUS]

DELIGHTED [MITCHELL] KENNERL[E]Y TAKING MANY MANY WOMEN DOUBT ADVISABILITY SELLING NOW COPIES THREE LIVES THINK IT WILL CONFUSE ISSUE.

GERTRUDE

* "Portrait of Mabel Dodge at the Villa Curonia" did not appear in *Forum*.
† This idea took form in the Special Number of *Camera Work* in June 1913.
‡ Maurice Aisen, Rumanian-born American chemist who was a patron of the arts and close friends with Jo Davidson, Hutchins Hapgood, and Lincoln Steffens. His article, entitled "The Latest Evolution in Art and Picabia," was published in the Special Number of *Camera Work*, June 1913, and did not mention either Stein or Matisse.
§ Manuel Manolo, Spanish sculptor who was represented by seven bronzes in the Armory Show.
¶ Mabel and Edwin Dodge were not officially divorced until 1916.

～Hutchins Hapgood wrote a column about Gertrude Stein's "Portrait of Mabel Dodge at the Villa Curonia" that appeared in the *New York Globe* on 21 March 1913. Entitled "Democratic Criticism," the article offered his view on criticism and reprinted comments by Max Weber on Stein. Hapgood also admitted his own lack of understanding of Stein's portrait of Dodge, a point that his editors would take up with him in their column the following day. Some excerpts from Hapgood's article follow:

> Understanding is impossible without sympathy, and democratic criticism consists largely in having so much respect and sympathy for the thing criticized that you look at it from its own viewpoint. . . .
>
> I myself do not understand this piece of writing ["Portrait of Mabel Dodge"]. I am sure that Miss Stein is attempting to express something, but I cannot get it. But I happen to have read earlier things by Miss Stein and to know something about her moral and mental and imaginative equipment, which is unusual and distinguished. This helps me to do what I ought to do anyway—try sympathetically to get her and her material, not from the standpoint of my own habits and prejudices as a thinker and writer, but from hers.

Hapgood praises Weber's criticism of Gertrude Stein's writing, calling it "not easy, but . . . eminently democratic. He does not try to be authoritative. He is full of doubt, and of complexity." Here is a sample of Weber's comments on Stein's portrait of Dodge:

> In counting up an endless number of objects, one falls into a rhythm, a drowsiness, and one counts even automatically after a while—so much so that one counts and thinks other things. That is what Miss Stein makes possible in her work. Such trance-throwing is needed for a change. All is good. All is bad. The bad becomes in time the good, etc., etc.
>
> It is like the experience one would have in walking through a great crowd of philosophers who would talk—and hearing stray sentences here, there, and from there, here. . . . Recording the audible stray sentences would make just as interesting a piece of literature as this pamphlet, and you could call it a portrait of a woman, the cry of a seal, the flute in an Ionic column, snowflakes in the sun, square spheres of air.
>
> One cannot criticize it with the old use of verbal criticism. . . . Criticism is comparison. Why compare? It is what it is. It is good, it is bad. It is useful. . . . Why must I understand it? I doubt whether it was meant to be understood.[28]

In Dodge's next letter to Stein, she enclosed an editorial that appeared in the *New York Globe* on 22 March 1913, in which the editors responded to Hapgood's article with criticism of his assertion that he should be able to understand Stein:

> We wish we could persuade Mr. Hutchins Hapgood, whose articles in the Globe we read with interest always, and often with understanding, to address himself to the task of making us understand a little oftener. . . . Now, it so happens that we, too, believe Miss Stein's equipment to be unusual and distinguished, in the good sense of both words. Yet such of her writings as have come in our way have proved quite beyond our comprehension. That, you may say, is neither here nor there, and we admit it. What we are worried about is Mr. Hapgood's feeling that he "ought to . . . try to get her and her material" from her point of view, or, in other words, that he ought respectfully to like what she writes. We cannot for the life of us see any ought about it. Why is the disrespectful reaction less estimable than the respectful? . . . Now, Miss Stein's writing affects us like an attempt to play ball with a trout rod, or to unlock a door with a toy balloon. Of course, this proves that we do not understand her, but why need we try?[29]

∾

[22 MARCH 1913] [23 FIFTH AVENUE]

Dearest Gertrude,

I am sending off to you a precious book of clippings about the show & some about you, & some letters & things I have had about you. <u>Don't</u> <u>lose them, any</u> of them, as they are the only ones saved. I am mailing you tonight's "Globe" with a whole ed. about us! Hutch [Hapgood] who is on the "Globe" will reply to it in a day or two & I will send it to you.* Things are moving along well. Your book will soon be out at [Mitchell] Kennerl[e]y's! I never was better or happier. Life in N.Y. is one long, protracted thrill. You must spend next winter here & be the fashion. I rcd the photos & Stieglitz has them. Too excited to write more.

Love—

M. D.

* Hapgood's reply to the editorial was not located in the *New York Globe*'s columns from the next three weeks.

⌒When Gertrude Stein finally received Mabel Dodge's article about her that was published in *Arts & Decoration*, she wrote to Dodge with generous and grateful praise.⌒

[CIRCA MARCH 1913] 27 RUE DE FLEURUS

My dear Mabel,

Your letter via Joe [i.e., Jo] Davidson has just come but not your article. Please send that, I want to see it, surely I will like it. Please send it quick. There was a delay about the photo because Mike [Stein] had it done over as he said the other was no good for reproduction, he thought this one very satisfactory. I am sending you another copy in case you want it for anything. I am delighted about Mitchell Kennerl[e]y. I have not written to him about it because I knew you could do it for me so much better. I cannot tell you how happy I am about it all. Those Oxford men are going to print the two last pieces of the Constance Fletcher in the Oxford Fortnightly in April.* I have sent her a copy of it but have not heard from her since. I have just finished a rather amusing short thing about my London publishing xperience.† I am sending it on for you to read but I don't suppose it would do for American publication so perhaps it will be best not to show it to anyone. I have gotten some clippings about the show that Stieglitz sent to a man named [Marsden] Hartley,‡ they all seem afraid to say much all xcept Hutch [Hapgood] who enjoys himself.§ Send on anything that is amusing about the show. It sounds like an awfully good one.

Yours

Gertrude.

---

* Stein's word portrait of Constance Fletcher did not appear in the *Oxford Fortnightly* as she had hoped.

† "Publishers, the Portrait Gallery and the Manuscripts at the British Museum," included in *Geography and Plays*.

‡ Marsden Hartley was given his first one-man show by Stieglitz in 1909. Two of his paintings and six drawings were included in the Armory Show. According to his letter to Stein written in the fall of 1912, Hartley had first visited 27 rue de Fleurus in the spring of 1912. In the spring of 1913, he reportedly asked Stein to write to Stieglitz about her opinion of his painting. Stein wrote: "In his painting he has done what in Kandinsky is only a direction. Hartley has really done it. He has used color to xpress a picture. . . . He deals with his color as actually as Picasso deals with his forms" (Stein to Stieglitz, c. spring 1913, ASC; Haskell, *Marsden Hartley*, 30).

§ Stein is likely referring to one or two of Hapgood's articles about the Armory Show that appeared in the *New York Globe*: "Life at the Armory Show," 17 February 1913, and "The Picture Show," 17 March 1913.

My dear Mabel,

I have just gotten hold of your article and I am delighted with it. Really it is awfully well done and I am as proud as punch. Do send me half a dozen copies of it. I want to show it to everybody. Hurrah for gloire.

Yours

Gertrude.

———

[CIRCA MARCH 1913] 27 RUE DE FLEURUS

My dear Mabel

I have just read your article over again quietly and I am startled to see how completely and fully you have told your story. It is admirable in its measure and amplitude.

Your sentences are full and simple. I am delighted and more than delighted. I expected to be pleased and I am really stirred.

Always yours,

Gertrude.

✍As she had with Grant Watson before and would soon with Carl Van Vechten, Mabel Dodge enjoyed providing letters of introduction to Gertrude Stein for her friends.✍

APRIL. 10 [1913] AT "291" [NEW YORK]

Dear Gertrude,

I am at Stieglitz's writing to you, to give you the pleasure of meeting M. et Mme. [Francis and Gabrielle Buffet-] Picabia who I am certain will be happy to know you & talk with you. It is a great moment here in New York.

Mabel Dodge

✍Complications arose concerning Mitchell Kennerley's plans for publication of Gertrude Stein's "Many Many Women" and the sale of *Three Lives.* Dodge and Stein exchanged a number of letters about Kennerley, his handling of Stein's manuscripts, and other publishing opportunities.✍

[New York Telegram]

[POSTMARK: 13 APRIL 1913] [23 FIFTH AVENUE]

SEND [MAX] WEBERS CRITICISM* IMMEDIATELY FOR REPUBLICATION
= MABEL

[CIRCA APRIL 1913] 27 RUE DE FLEURUS

My dear Mabel,

I am sending you the [Max] Weber ms. by letter and not with the other things that I am sending you this week as in that way you will get it quicker. Dod gast it will you tell me whats happening, its kind of tantalising just to know that something is doing but not to know what, its highly satisfactory to know that something is doing but I would like to know what. I have not heard anything at all from [Mitchell] Kennerl[e]y. The reason I cabled was that I had had an offer from England for Three Lives.† Of course if Kennerl[e]y is going to do other things of mine I would rather keep Three Lives to give him as he ought to have that too in that case. Anyway for the present I have refused the English offer but I would darn well like to know whats doing, whether the new book of mine that you referred to is Many Many Women whether he is doing any short things and what the terms are. I saw Florence Bradley the other day on the street, with her sister, they make a strange pair having a very singular quality. Matisse is having a show here, he is xhibiting all the things that he did in Tangiers this winter, they are lovely and quite simply gentle.‡ There is no other news xcepting that I got so xcited with all the gloire that I have had to take a week's vacation from work. Since then I have begun again and am doing some things that are interesting me very much. Surely you will be going back to Italy via Paris and then I'll find out whats been happening to you,

Goodnight, respects to everybody

Yours

Gertrude.

---

* Dodge is likely referring to Max Weber's criticism of Gertrude Stein's "Portrait of Mabel Dodge at Villa Curonia" that Hutchins Hapgood reprinted in part in his column "Democratic Criticism" in the *New York Globe* on 21 March 1913. Hapgood wrote that he had to "omit parts, because of illegibility or obscurity." It is not known where the criticism was intended to be republished.

† John Lane wrote to Stein on 4 April 1913 and offered to publish *Three Lives* if she would agree to certain terms.

‡ Matisse exhibited his Moroccan paintings at the Bernheim-Jeune gallery in Paris in April 1913. The show included a dozen paintings as well as many sculptures and drawings.

[POSTMARK: 1 MAY 1913] NEW YORK

[MITCHELL] KENNERL[E]Y REFUSED INFORMATION NOW IN HANDS
LAWYER WILL CABLE RESULTS SOON

[MABEL DODGE]

———

[2 MAY 1913] 27 RUE DE FLEURUS

My dear Mabel,

Your cabel has just come. What is it all about. Is [Mitchell]
Kennerl[e]y in financial difficulties. You have never told me anything about him since the time you said he had accepted Many
[Many] Women. What has he and under what conditions. You see
I got nervous as I had refused John Lane's offer and was hearing
nothing about Kennerl[e]y. You have so wonderfully created a public
for me that I can't help wanting them to have a book of mine to
read. Do write me all about it.

I have been seeing the [Francis and Gabrielle Buffet-] Picabias
this last week. I like him. He has no genius but he has a genuinely
constructive intelligence and solid harmony. I was awfully glad to
hear all about you from him. The things he did in New York are
much more interesting than the things he did here just before. I
saw Janet Scudder the other day. She is about to give a large garden
party for the Danes and herself. She has grown years older. I was
quite shocked when I saw her. The other evening Maud Crut[t]well*
turned up. She too has changed she has gotten in a strange way to
look like Constance [Fletcher]. I could not believe that she was the
red faced lady who smoked a cigar. Picabia says you are seeing a
good deal of Neith [Boyce] as well as Hutch [Hapgood] give her
my love. There is a man coming here to dinner to-morrow, Eugene
Ullman,† he too is New York mad and much taken with your salon. [Max] Weber's photograph man who has 20 of his pictures is
coming here to-morrow evening.‡ That seems to be all the news. I
like the clippings you send but I wish you would write. When are

* Maud Cruttwell, a writer whom Mabel Dodge described as a "red-faced English-
woman with teeth stained brown from the long, dark cigars she smoked continually"
who was "the authority on Botticelli" (EE, 282).

† Eugene Ullman, American painter.

‡ Alvin Langdon Coburn, an American photographer, wrote to Stein on 30 April
1913 asking if he could visit 27 rue de Fleurus to see the Matisse paintings. He reported in his letter that he "first became interested in the work of the modern school
through my friend Mr Max Weber of New York whose work you no doubt know, and
about twenty of whose paintings are in my collection" (included in FF, 78). Stein's

you coming and are you coming to Paris. Picabia is wonderfully enthusiastic about New York.

    Good night,

Much love,

Gertrude.

[Whitman motto]

MAY 2 [1913] [23 FIFTH AVENUE]

Dearest Gertrude

    I wrote you & cabled again that we are now having a lawsuit with [Mitchell] Kennerl[e]y. He refused to see me, talk over the phone or anything so I have sent a lawyer who has tried to get in touch with him to ask him <u>when</u> yr book was coming out, <u>what</u> terms, & to get him to give up the other mms. [i.e., mss] You see he has <u>all</u> the stuff now. An editor of the International & sub ed. of Current Opinion wanted to see yr long book as he is writing an article for the Boston Transcript* so I phoned Mrs. [May] Knoblauch to know where to find it & behold—! Kennerl[e]y has that too! He is holding them all for some purpose of his own. The lawyer expects today a reply from K. as he has now delivered an ultimatum. He must deliver up <u>all</u> the mms. & take or reject the one he wanted, & state terms. I want also a statement of <u>what</u> terms he is selling "Three Lives" under. I want <u>at once</u> your written authority to get possession of the Long book of Americains,† & give that and all the short mms. to a good agent here—a Miss [Flora] Holly‡ that Hutch [Hapgood] & everybody employs. She will place the stuff if it is possible. You see from what I send you that there is much "doing." James Frederick [i.e., Frederick James] Gregg is, as you remember the main press agent of the International Show. I sent six copies to him today in Boston. Yesterday I sent photographs of you & me to the person in Chicago. Next month Georgianna's [i.e., Georgiana King] article on you will come out in the International.§Yesterday

---

reply to Coburn is postmarked 1 May 1913: "I will be pleased to have you see the pictures Saturday evening," which would have been on 3 May 1913 (Stein to Coburn, 1 May 1913, GLSC). This information thus dates this letter from Stein to Dodge at 2 May 1913.

    * Not located.

    † *The Making of Americans.*

    ‡ Flora Holly, American literary agent who during her career represented such authors as Theodore Dreiser and Edna Ferber.

    § Georgiana Goddard King's article "Gertrude Stein" appeared in the *International: A Review of Two Worlds Combined with "Progress"* in June 1913. In this piece, King

Hutch was invited to a "Gertrude Stein evening"—at the house (next week) of a Mrs. Edith Jarmuth* who has all lions & prominent people, & where a notorious man named Frank Pease† is going to read a story he has composed in the Gertrude Stein manner. So things go on. The air is full of it. I send you this interpretation of the portrait done by a clever greek anarchist named [John] Rompapas.‡ As you see, he is is [in?] on more than some others. Hutch says I've been a clever press agent. He knows about such things so I guess it's true. It's up to you now. I advise your authorizing me to put all your stuff in Miss Holly's hands. You didn't send back letters etc. about you and I didn't go thro' the clippings to see if you sent back the ones about you. I think that now all matter relating to you should be pasted in one book to show to agents, editors & publishers & if you will send over all the stuff of this kind that you have that I have sent you & that you had anyway I will get to work on it.

I may not get over this summer. My private affairs are more complicated than ever & I don't yet know the outcome; so don't count on me for August. I want to go but I want to stay here to[o] because so much is happening. I would advise your coming over & being interviewed sometime next autumn when everyone is back. I now know men & women on every paper & this will be simple & effectual—then you will be asked to lecture on the new literature, etc., & meet everyone & be invited to luncheons at women's clubs, & probably commissioned to do portraits. Please send all stuff over at once. And return these personal mms. of mine. The Post Impressionistic poems are done by a pretty good "pote" here.§ All legs are used—I can tell you!

"The name of Gertrude Stein is better known in New York today than the name of God."¶

Goodby, best love always, yours,

M. D.

P.S. I think Hutch is coming out for Christ soon!

---

calls *Three Lives* "an astonishing little book" and describes Stein's word portraits of Picasso and Matisse as being composed of "sentences [that] sang themselves like an air on a shepherd's pipe" (157). She praises Stein for her powerful and daring writing that is characterized by "certainty and seriousness" (158).

* Unidentified.

† Frank Pease, listed in a list of contributers to the July 1914 issue of *Camera Work* as "daredevil soldier in Philippines, ex-labor agitator, writer; New York."

‡ John Rompapas, Greek radical, writer, and founder of the Rabelais Press, a New York publishing house.

§ Unidentified.

¶ Carl Van Vechten was the one who said this about Stein.

[MAY 1913] 27 RUE DE FLEURUS

My dear Mabel,

Who do you think came in last evening. Mrs. [Alice] Thursby and the little Carey [i.e., Cary] boy and a young man and another woman. Mrs. Thursby is a strange creature, she was pretty drunk but wonderful, she interested me enormously and drew me very much. As I told you I had not sent your letter to Mrs [Emily] Cary* supposing that she would be gone so I was considerably astonished when Mrs. Thursby [appeared], I imagine she wanted me to diagnose the boy. I did a short sketch of her just an impression of her as she was that evening.†

I have just gotten your long letter. Oh dear why do publishers have such an intricate way of doing business. Perhaps he [Mitchell Kennerley] has come to by this time and let you know what he means to do I guess his method is to get hold of everything so that if he decides he wants anything he will have that thing handy. One would suppose he would have sense enough to know that you had made a market. However you are making the market more solid all the time so it is alright. What short ms. has he, just the things I sent you from London. And what has he in the way of Three Lives. Has he all the unbound copies as well as what remained of the bound. Oh and another thing when you do get a contract from him they say you should put in a bankruptcy clause so that if he goes bust the property in the book does not go to the creditors. I was much pleased with [Frederick James] Gregg's letter, he seems a very sympathetic person. I suppose the show is all over everywhere by now.‡ I have been working a lot, among other things I have done a five act play but don't be nervous it is only eight pages long.§ I am very pleased with it. It is very lively. I also have been photographed by [Alvin Langdon] Coburn at his request along with the other

---

* This letter from Dodge to Emily Cary was enclosed in her letter to Stein dated 11 December 1912. Dodge urged Stein to make her acquaintance.

† This "sketch" is Stein's word portrait "Mrs. Th——y," which was written in 1913 and published in the December 1916 issue of *The Soil*. In its manuscript form at the Beinecke Rare Book and Manuscript Library, it is entitled both "Mrs. Th——y" and "Mrs. Thursby," dated 1913, and begins, "A landed break. The blown crane in a cane that is not personal, the only crest that is a criminal girdle, the absence of the blessed and the presence . . ."

‡ The Armory Show traveled from New York, where it ran from 17 February to 15 March 1913, to Chicago (24 March to 16 April 1913), and then Boston (28 April to 19 May 1913).

§ "What Happened. A Five Act Play" is included in *Geography and Plays*.

celebrities.* I have not seen the results yet. I am awfully sorry that we are not going to meet this summer. What are the private complications and what is the present state, can you tell me or would you rather wait till we meet. I would like very much to know what is happening to you. What will you do during the hot weather. Mrs. Thursby says she likes you a whole lot. Oh about that authorisation, will you tell me what kind of form it should take seeing as I have never given Kennerl[e]y any authority to keep it, what kind of an authorisation would be effective and would it have to be witnessed or anything. About Miss [Flora] Holly I don't imagine she would be any good. She had the Three Lives and she kept it for six months and could never think of anybody to whom to show it so she never showed it to anybody.† At last she asked me if I could suggest anybody. I suggest[ed] McClures as I knew a reader on it‡ and she sent it with a note from me and got a very nice note back which she never sent me but just wrote that she had gotten a nice note but that McClures could not use it and could I suggest anybody else. I wrote back that I supposed it was the agents business to do the suggesting and then she said she could not and so I told her to send the things to Mabel Weeks and paid Miss Holly 5 dollars for the privilege, so unless you think she is really interested and has some ideas I don't think it would do any good to employ her. She has been very good for Hutch [Hapgood] and Neith [Boyce] and it was through them that I gave her the things.

Anyway I continue very hard at work and very hopeful. It has all gone so much faster than I ever dreamed it could in every way. I do hope Kennerl[e]y will have turned out to be alright. I am sending you by this mail all the clippings and letters that you sent me

* Coburn photographed Gertrude Stein on 7 May 1913, according to his typewritten note on her letter to him, postmarked 6 May 1913, that offered two days that he could come to take her picture (Stein to Coburn, 6 May 1913, GLSC). In his lifetime, Coburn photographed many famous figures in the arts and politics, including Matisse, George Bernard Shaw, Igor Stravinsky, and H. G. Wells.

† Flora Holly had written to Stein on 3 January 1907 about her impressions of *Three Lives*: "I doubt very much if I could find a publisher who would consider these three stories for book publication. They seem to me to be more character sketches than anything else, while the characters themselves would not appeal to a large audience. I suppose you know that a publisher wants to feel sure that a book will sell from three to five thousand copies before he cares to undertake it for publication" (included in *FF*, 38).

‡ This reader at *McClure's Magazine* was "Miss Roseboro'," as indicated in Flora Holly's 3 January 1907 letter (included in *FF*, 39).

including the copies of the old criticism of Three Lives as I have not got the originals here just now.

Goodnight much love

Gertrude.

[Whitman motto]

[CIRCA MAY 1913] [23 FIFTH AVENUE]

Dearest Gertrude,

[Mitchell] Kennerl[e]y sent back six stories which are
    "Rue de Rennes"
    "Elsie Surville"
    "Gallerie Lafayette"
    "Pauline Claudel"
    "Flirting at B.M."
    "Portrait of One."*
He says he is willing to publish them altogether in the fall giving you a royalty of 10%.

He told the lawyer he had rcd <u>no copies</u> of "three Lives" and does not care to take them on except in connection with some <u>new novel</u> by you that will excite the public. He told lawyer "All copies of "Three Lives" are still with Mrs. [May] Knoblauch." <u>I have seen</u> Three Lives <u>on sale</u> at "The Little Bookshop" which used to be <u>his</u> & now belongs to Mr. [Laurence] Gomme,† tho' K. still has his office there. You should write <u>at once</u> to Mrs. Knoblauch & Mr. Gomme asking about this. I know it has been sold there & that <u>I</u> told Kennerl[e]y <u>she</u> had them & that they <u>communicated</u>. Kennerl[e]y also told lawyer that the book he had rcd direct from you ("Many many women"?) he would hold until authorized by you to send it elsewhere. <u>Do you want</u> him to hold it indefinitely?

---

* These six titles refer to the following works by Stein: "Rue de Rennes," included in *Two*; "Elsie Surville" is "Elise Surville," included in *Two*, and is Stein's pseudonym for Nina Auzias, Leo Stein's lover at the time whom he eventually married in 1921; "Gallerie Lafayette" is "Galeries Lafayettes," included in *Portraits and Prayers*; "Pauline Claudel" was the original title of "Julia Marlowe," included in *Two*. Bruce Kellner suggested that the original title may playfully refer to both Paul Claudel, a French experimental writer of poems and plays, and to one of Stein's cars that was named Pauline (pers. comm., 11 July 1994); "Flirting at B.M." is "Flirting at the Bon Marche," included in *Two*; "Portrait of One." is "A Portrait of One. Harry Phelan Gibb.," included in *Geography and Plays*.

† I am grateful to Robert Wilson for providing me with Mr. Gomme's first name. No further biographical information has been located.

Do you want these six published together in the fall? Have you a new novel to excite the public? Do you want to work thro' an agent? Do you want him to hold "Long long book"* which he got from Mrs. Knoblauch?

Now will you please write him & me full instructions?

I have changed my mind again & hoping to sail early in June, to be over there about 6 weeks or 2 months—will you & Alice come June when I get there? Will you decide all this at once? About K., I mean. I have various young enthusiasts writing articles about you now. Will you paste yr press clippings in a book altogether?

In haste, ever yrs,

Mabel

[CIRCA LATE MAY OR EARLY JUNE 1913] 27 RUE DE FLEURUS

My dear Mabel,

Don't worry. I have written to [Mitchell] Kennerl[e]y. Who are the youngsters writing articles. I was delighted that you had gotten Georgiana [King]'s placed.† When is it coming out. I am awfully anxious to see it. You have made an audience for me alright, its been a real triumph. I can't thank you enough. I have not seen the [Francis and Gabrielle Buffet-] Picabias since I wrote you about them in the letter that was belated. There have been such quantities of people here, most of America and a great deal of England seems to be in Paris just now. I am pretty tired but I have had a very good time. [Paul] Chalfin is here among others. He told me he was at your place, he went there with Mary Foote. Did Haisen [i.e., Maurice Aisen]‡ come over, the Picabias xpected that he would shortly. I will see them next week, as I hope by that time things will have quieted down a little.

Good night. Oh I have sent all the clippings on to you you must have received them by this time. Good night again, Always yours

Gertrude.

---

* *The Making of Americans.*

† Georgiana Goddard King's article, "Gertrude Stein," appeared in the *International* in June 1913.

‡ Maurice Aisen's "Latest Evolution in Art and Picabia" appeared in the Special Number of *Camera Work* in June 1913, along with Stein's portrait of Mabel Dodge and Dodge's "Speculations."

Gertrude Stein was delighted by an article about her work, entitled "Gertrude Stein's Fiction," that appeared in the *Mirror* on 16 May 1913. The author, Robert Allerton Parker, conveyed an understanding and appreciation of Stein's writing that must have been particularly heartening to her at a time when her publishing ventures were full of conflict and uncertainty. Parker offered an evocative description of Stein's style:

> But what are the characteristics of Gertrude Stein's "fiction?" It breaks all academic rules. It dispenses with our old friend, the "concrete detail." It does not search for the "significant." It ignores *le mot juste*. It knows not climax. It almost dispenses with beginning, middle and end. It leads you nowhere. You feel yourself carried forward towards an expected climax only to find yourself sinking away from one that has not occurred. Events do not crystallize. Characters do not develop or disintegrate in the approved fashion. Narrative structure is lacking. Subjectivity and objectivity are hopelessly confused. In a word, the reader of the purposive, highly unified, dramatic novel finds himself confronted with unrelieved monotony, a ceaseless rise and fall of aimless, futile incidents and sparse, empty events.

In his article, Parker also grasped the significance of Stein's unique approach to traditional grammar:

> And she [Stein] has, fortunately, realized that any effort to present Life in its more persistent, constant, elementary, phases must dispense with the mechanical and imprisoning medium of formal grammar, not because of its intrinsic deficiencies and limitations, but rather because Life itself in its more unconscious expressions has found it an impossible feat to be logical and grammatical. So that even if her sole accomplishment had been to make our system of punctuation and grammar more plastic in following or suggesting human nature, Gertrude Stein would be worthy of high honors.[30]

❧

[CIRCA MAY 1913] 27 RUE DE FLEURUS

My dear Mabel,

Are you coming. Are you on the way. Anyway we will be glad to see you. I got the Mirror with [Robert Allerton] Parker's article which I liked very much. The bit about my punctuation pleased me particularly. It was all very well done and well understood. Who is he.

We dined with the [Francis and Gabrielle Buffet-] Picabias the other day. They are very pleasant. I have done a sketch of him.* The young [Marcel] Duchamp the one who did the nudes falling down stairs was there.† He looks like a young Englishman and talks very urgently about the fourth dimension.

If you come over you will surely be staying all summer and we will come to you at the end as I am very tired from the varying emotions and the many people of this very xciting winter and I must go quietly some where quite new and besides I have started something that must go on being worked out.‡ So we will go down to some new places and come to you at the end of the summer.

Have you seen Mrs. [Alice] Thursby yet. She is one of my most delightful memories. She was that way. There isn't any other news. I have never heard from Constance Fletcher at all, have you.

Everybody is xcited here about a big sale of Goyas [El] Grecos and Cezannes that is coming off shortly.§ [Paul] Chalfin is here with a millionaire, they are buying antiquities. Chalfin is getting worn with the work. He told us about you all as they say in the South. Also we have the inevitable relatives in town but they will be gone soon. When are you coming

Gertrude.

⌁In her letters to Gertrude Stein from this time, Mabel Dodge only once mentions the notorious Paterson Strike Pageant that she inspired and helped organize. This spectacle generated an enormous amount of publicity for Dodge that highlighted her involvement with radicals and revolutionaries. In May 1913, Dodge went to a

---

* Stein is likely referring to "Article," a piece unpublished until 1993 when it appeared in *A Stein Reader*. In her introductory notes, Ulla Dydo states that "Article" was most probably written in the spring or early summer of 1913 and that the title appears in one of Stein's lists of early works as "Article (Picabia)," although in all other lists, it appears simply as "Article" (Stein, *A Stein Reader,* 276).

† Marcel Duchamp, French artist who was one of the original Dadaists and creator of ready-mades. His *Nude Descending a Staircase* #2 (1912) was one of the most controversial and mocked works of art exhibited at the 1913 Armory Show. Stein wrote a word portrait of Duchamp entitled "Next. (Life and Letters of Marcel Duchamp)" that was included in *Geography and Plays*.

‡ According to both Leon Katz and Ulla Dydo, it is possible that the "something that must go on being worked out" may be Stein's writing of plays, which she began around this time (pers. comm., 22 January 1995). Stein and Toklas went to Spain in the summer, thus not going to a place "quite new," as they had traveled there the previous summer. They did not visit Dodge in the summer or fall of 1913.

§ Unidentified.

meeting in Greenwich Village of those who sympathized with the striking silk workers in Paterson, New Jersey. Bill Haywood, one of the leaders of the Industrial Workers of the World, presided over the meeting, appearing to Dodge as "a great battered hulk of a man, with one eye gone and an eminent look to him."[31] Haywood spoke about the police brutality toward the strikers, a worker who was shot by a policeman and his subsequent dramatic funeral at which each striker dropped a red flower on his coffin, and the refusal of the New York newspapers to cover the strike. In *Movers and Shakers,* Dodge recalls the sequence that led to her idea of the pageant, beginning with Haywood's account of the worker's funeral with the red-flower-covered coffin:

> "The grave looked like a mound of blood. As they marched they sang the 'International.' By God, if our people over here could have seen it, we could have raised a trunkful of money to help us go on. Our food is getting mighty scarce over there."
>
> "Can't you get any reports of it into the papers by hook or crook?" someone asked.
>
> "Not a damned word," answered Haywood.
>
> "Why don't you bring the strike to New York and *show* it to the workers?" I asked in a small, shy voice.
>
> Haywood, who hadn't noticed me before, turned his eye on me with an arrested look. I went on. . . .
>
> "Why don't you hire a great hall and re-enact the strike over here? Show the whole thing: the closed mills, the gunmen, the murder of the striker, the funeral. And have the strike leaders make their speeches at the grave as you did in Paterson—you and Elizabeth Gurley Flynn and Tresca!"
>
> "Well, by God! There's an idea!" exclaimed Bill Haywood. "But how? What hall?"
>
> "Madison Square Garden! Why not?"[32]

In the next moment, according to Dodge's account, John Reed, the journalist and poet who was on the staff of the radical magazine the *Masses* and was soon to become Dodge's lover, volunteered to organize the pageant.⌒

[Whitman motto]

Dearest Gertrude—

Just a word to say you & Alice must come & spend <u>July</u> at Villa as I will be there only for July—I leave here June 19, & go at once to Florence. Please arrange this. We will have a great time. No news to speak of except in revolutionary circles here. Am working on the giant Pageant scheme, and see only red now.* [Mitchell] Kennerl[e]y holds "Many many women" from me, with no information about it. He will print other 6 in fall if you wish. I <u>love</u> Neith [Boyce] now, & she loves me; But Hutch [Hapgood] is <u>the</u> one, of course, for us both.

M. D.

⌒The Paterson Strike Pageant was held at Madison Square Garden on 7 June 1913. Approximately twelve hundred strikers traveled to Manhattan from Paterson in order to illustrate their dramatic plight. Through their acting, they demonstrated the strenuous quality of their work and reenacted the shooting of one worker and his funeral where they put red carnations on his coffin. An estimated audience of fifteen thousand had lined up for blocks to purchase tickets to the event, some paying between twenty and thirty dollars for box seats and others getting in for free if they showed their "little red cards" to indicate their working status.[33] Despite the large turnout, the Pageant failed to raise the funds its organizers had hoped for and ended up losing money.

At the same time that Mabel Dodge was fervently at work organizing the pageant and beginning her relationship with John Reed, she supplied Carl Van Vechten with a letter of introduction to Gertrude Stein, thereby initiating one of the most important connections that she made between her various friends and acquaintances. At that time, Van Vechten was writing for the *New York Times*. He became a lifelong friend to both Stein and Toklas and later served as Stein's literary executor.⌒

---

* The "red" Dodge mentions refers to the event's decorations and sets, which prominently featured the color associated with socialism, including red lights that spelled out the initials of the Industrial Workers of the World, red banners, and hundreds of red carnations to be dropped on the coffin of the dead striker.

Dear Gertrude

This letter is brought to you by Carl Van Vechten—he can tell you all about your sucès here—he wrote one of the columns I sent you, the one that said your work, sociologically, was like the orchid!*

Hope to see you soon.

Hope you'll like Carl. Hutch [Hapgood] & I do.

Ever yrs,

Mabel Dodge at the Villa Curonia.

꜒Max Weber wrote an imitation of Gertrude Stein's writing, entitled "Portrait of Mabel Dodge at 23 Fifth Avenue," that Stein refers to in the following letter. The work is an abstract word portrait of Dodge and her circle in New York and begins: "There was one living in an apartment who was delightful. There was one living in an apartment who was delightful to others. There was one living in an apartment who was delightful for others." In the spring of 1913, Dodge had sent it to Stein who was quite taken with it. Included among Dodge's papers at the Beinecke Rare Book and Manuscript Library, Weber's parody is typed with Dodge's handwritten underlining and notations in the margins indicating which person is represented by each of the various images. For instance, in the following excerpt, "the searchlight" refers to "H. H." or Hutchins Hapgood, "the jellyfish" is "Mr. [Albert?] Einstein," and "the Shetland" is "Jo" Davidson: "There was reaching. There was not that result. There was the searchlight. There was its appendage. That is intuitive. There is the Shetland which is beguiling. This is adorable. There is the jellyfish which is secretive. There is not that openness. There are shadows."[34] Max Weber himself appears as "the tadpole" and Mabel Dodge as "the prism."

Stein had heard from Van Vechten, who had arrived in Paris on

---

* Dodge is referring to a passage in Van Vechten's article, "Cubist of Letters Writes a New Book," *New York Times,* 24 February 1913, included in one of his scrapbooks at the New York Public Library, in which he wrote: "Miss Stein, like all radicals, started out rather mildly. She might have been a symbolist at one time. The symbolists, mind you, would regard an orchid as something pathological because it is a symptom of property, speaking sociologically."

Thursday 29 May 1913 and had forwarded Dodge's letter of introduction to Stein.[35] They arranged to meet soon at 27 rue de Fleurus.〜

[CIRCA LATE MAY 1913] 27 RUE DE FLEURUS

My dear Mabel,

I have just gotten through the clippings, golly there were a lot of them. I was delighted with the letters to you from the total strangers. Who did the type written parody about you and your entourage, it was thorough and intelligent and at times xtremely good. Who did it. Do answer this question. And what book is Mitchell Kennerl[e]y doing and when is it coming out. He has an interesting handwriting and seems to have an xtremely hopeful temperament. He sounds alright.

The other day I got a note from the representative of the New York Times who lives in Paris asking for an interview. He wants me to tell him about myself. I hope I will be satisfactory. He is coming here Saturday. There is no particular news here, I get awfully xcited about the gloire but this last batch has quite filled me up. I have done a lot of work since I have been back from London. A good deal on long things and I have finished several short things. I am sorry that Georgiana [King]'s thing was not what Kennerl[e]y wanted, she was one of the very first to see the direction in Melanctha.* When will the Stieglitz thing be done. Will it be a volume with the three things.† They are selling copies of the magazine out in San Francisco and my old schoolmates are much taken with your article. I have given away all the copies you sent me. Miss [Florence] Blood was some surprised. Oh by the way [Charles] Loeser or Mrs. Loeser is going to have a baby. B. B. [Bernard Berenson] is getting much better. Their secretary got smashed up in Switzerland so Mary Berenson is secretary again. I guess thats all. I will send the things all back by next mail. Bully for us, we are doing fine

Gertrude

Respects to Edwin & Hutch [Hapgood].

---

* "Melanctha" is the second of the three stories in Stein's *Three Lives*.

† Stein is referring to Stieglitz's June 1913 issue of *Camera Work* that included her "Portrait of Mabel Dodge at the Villa Curonia," Dodge's "Speculations," and a reproduction of Picasso's portrait of Stein.

~There are a number of varying accounts of the first meeting between Gertrude Stein and Carl Van Vechten. The most colorful and amusing version turns out to be incorrect, asserting that they unknowingly shared a box at the second performance of Stravinsky's *Le Sacre du Printemps,* which had its premiere at the Théâtre des Champs-Elysées on 29 May 1913 with a second performance on 2 June 1913,[36] and subsequently had a prearranged dinner engagement at 27 rue de Fleurus the following Saturday, at which they recognized each other from the ballet. Van Vechten first offered this myth about his first meeting with Stein in *Music After the Great War and Other Studies* (1915), mentioning her presence only in passing in his description of his experience at the revolutionary ballet:

> I was sitting in a box in which I had rented one seat. Three ladies sat in front of me and a young man occupied the place behind me. He stood up during the course of the ballet to enable himself to see more clearly. The intense excitement under which he was laboring, thanks to the potent force of the music, betrayed itself presently when he began to beat rhythmically on the top of my head with his fists. My emotion was so great that I did not feel the blows for some time. They were perfectly synchronized with the beat of the music. When I did, I turned around. His apology was sincere. We had both been carried beyond ourselves.[37]

In *The Autobiography of Alice B. Toklas,* Stein then perpetuates this myth about their initial encounter:

> Just before the performance began the fourth chair in our box was occupied. We looked around and there was a tall well-built young man, he might have been a dutchman, a scandinavian or an american and he wore a soft evening shirt with the tiniest pleats all over the front of it. It was impressive, we had never even heard that they were wearing evening shirts like that. That evening when we got home Gertrude Stein did a portrait of the unknown called a Portrait of One. . . .
> The next Saturday evening Carl Van Vechten was to come to dinner. He came and he was the young man of the soft much-pleated evening shirt and it was the same shirt. . . .
> Gertrude Stein and he became dear friends.[38]

In Stein's memory as recorded above, she first saw Van Vechten on 2 June 1913, which would place their meeting at dinner after that date. However, according to a number of extant letters and a carefully detailed account by Edward Burns, Stein and Van Vechten certainly had met earlier than this date. A letter from Stein written on 30 May 1913 and postmarked 31 May 1913 at 7:00 A.M. invited Van Vechten to dinner the following evening.[39] Van Vechten responded immediately on 31 May 1913: "I'll dine with you with pleasure this evening."[40] In addition, a letter Van Vechten wrote to Fania Marinoff, his lover at the time, postmarked 2 June 1913 but written the day before, confirms that he was at 27 rue de Fleurus on 31 May 1913: "Last night I had dinner at Gertrude Stein's. She is a wonderful personality. . . . She lives in a place hung with Picassos and she showed me some more sketches of his including men with erect Tom-Tom's much bigger than mine."[41] These letters illustrate that Stein and Van Vechten first met at 27 rue de Fleurus on Saturday, 31 May 1913. Therefore, when they both attended the second performance of *Le Sacre du Printemps* on Monday, 2 June 1913 and shared a box, they had already met.[42]

In the middle of June 1913, soon after the Paterson Strike Pageant was over, Mabel Dodge set sail for Europe with her companion Miss Galvin, her son John, John Reed, and the scenic designer Robert "Bobby" Edmond Jones. They planned to travel to Paris and then journey south to the Villa Curonia. Bobby Jones had designed the sets for the Pageant, inspired by the dramatic work of the English stage designer Gordon Craig. Jones was eager to meet and work with Craig, who lived in Florence. However, Craig refused any association with Jones upon discovering that he was a friend of Dodge's. According to Mabel Dodge, Craig still harbored bitterness over a failed pageant scheme they had devised together in Florence and that she had abruptly abandoned after her characteristic initial enthusiasm.[43]

Having passionately worked together on the Paterson Strike Pageant, Dodge and Reed had developed an intense yet unspoken connection. In *Movers and Shakers*, Dodge describes their mutual understanding and her role in inspiring Reed:

> That we loved each other seemed so necessary a part of
> working together, we never spoke of it once. There wasn't time,
> and that it was no time for lovemaking was accepted without
> words between us. We grew so sensitive to each other's will
> and thought that we were able to shorthand our communica-
> tions and almost do without words. . . .
> I knew I was enabling Reed to do what he was doing. I knew

he couldn't have done it without me. I felt that I was behind him, pouring all the power in the universe through myself to him.[44]

While aboard the ship bound for Europe, Dodge experienced a powerful urge to thwart Reed's amorous advances, in spite of being certain of her love for him. She was acutely aware of the reasons for these feelings, as she describes in her memoirs:

> We were free and ready to turn to each other. But, strangely, something in me resisted him strongly. I wanted a lover and I wanted to be loved, and Reed was entirely lovable. . . . Yet something in me held back from taking that step into love. . . . I didn't want to lose Reed, though I would have been glad if I had known how to preserve the intense life that we created together without (as I felt it would be) descending into the mortality of love. My blood longed for its share, too, of course, it longed for mortal life; but something in me adored the high clear excitement of continence, and the tension we had known together that came from our canalized vitality.[45]

Dodge appealed to Reed to wait—"'Oh, Reed, darling, we are just at the Threshold and nothing is ever so wonderful as the Threshold of things, don't you *know* that?'"[46]—but he became increasingly frustrated with her refusals. On the third night of being rebuffed, Reed wrote a poem to Dodge entitled "The New Age Begins" that ends with the following line: "But the speech of your body to my body will not be denied!"[47]

According to Dodge, they were not to wait much longer to consummate their love, only until their first night in Paris at the Hôtel du Pas-de-Calais.[48] On 20 June 1913, Stein had written to Van Vechten in Paris: "I have heard nothing more from Mabel and I am afraid of not seeing her as we have to be in Ceret on the 28th and so leave here the 27th."[49] However, it seems that Stein delayed her departure, as she sent a telegram to Van Vechten from Paris dated 28 June 1913 stating, "Mabel Dodge is at Hotel Pas de Calais Rue Saints Pères Paris,"[50] information that Stein likely gathered from the first of the following notes from Dodge.⟿

[POSTMARK: PARIS, 27 JUNE 1913] HOTEL DU PAS-DE-CALAIS
RUE DES SAINTS-PÈRES, 59
PARIS

Dearest Gertrude

Today spending taking John & my "companion"* around to see sights—send 'em to Florence tomorrow & come to you after dinner with John Reed who "did" my "idea" of the Pageant & "coming artist," Bobby Jones.†

Best love,

Mabel.

———

[POSTMARK: PARIS, 30 JUNE 1913] HOTEL DU PAS-DE-CALAIS
RUE DES SAINTS-PÈRES, 59
PARIS

Dearest Gertrude

We are free all day tomorrow except evening—going, I <u>think</u>, on Wednesday, to London.

M. D.

---

* Miss Galvin was Dodge's "nurse-companion," assigned to her by her psychiatrist at the time, Dr. Bernard Sachs. Dodge had come to rely upon Miss Galvin's organizational abilities, sensitivity, and good judgment (*M&S*, 23–24, 40).

† Robert Edmond Jones was a classmate of John Reed's at Harvard who had designed scenery for the Paterson Strike Pageant at Reed's urging. Dodge described Jones as a "pale, nervous fish with . . . long-fringed, eager brown eyes behind his spectacles, and a heavy thatch of hair falling over" (*M&S*, 204). She wrote of their relationship: "He said I had created him, that I was his real mother; and there seemed to be, truly, a psychic bond between us" (*M&S*, 318). Dodge wrote a nine-page undated, unpublished biographical sketch of Jones that is among her papers at the Beinecke Rare Book and Manuscript Library. In this piece, she writes: "The most interesting thing about Robert Edmond Jones is his capacity for work, the second most interesting thing is his single minded love of the theatre. . . . As he says of himself: 'too weak to live life but strong enough to make it.'" (Dodge, "Robert Edmond Jones," MDLC, 2.)

[CIRCA 30 JUNE 1913] HOTEL DU PAS-DE-CALAIS
RUE DES SAINTS-PÈRES, 59
PARIS

Dearest Gertrude

All right. I think now won't go to London. So will come Thursday & see you before then. But you don't expect me tomorrow for lunch, do you?

M. D.

———

[POSTMARK: PARIS, 1 JULY 1913] HOTEL DU PAS-DE-CALAIS
RUE DES SAINTS-PÈRES, 59
PARIS

Dearest Gertrude

All right for Wednesday & Thursday nights. See you tomorrow at 7.30?

M. D.

Telephone if I have the hour wrong.

᠃Once she was no longer holding herself back, Mabel Dodge immersed herself in her relationship with John Reed with a singular focus and an all-consuming passion that was soon to prove destructive due to her easily sparked jealousy of all of Reed's many interests outside of her. Dodge herself admits:

> As soon as I gave myself up to Reed I was all for love and everything else well lost! Nothing else in the world had, any longer, any significance for me. I had built up an interest in life, a love for beautiful things, for noble ideas, and for interesting people; I had learned to be satisfied with flattery and adulation and influence. . . . And in one night I threw it all away and nothing counted for me but Reed.[51]

On their motor trip from Paris to Florence, accompanied by Carl Van Vechten and Bobby Jones, Dodge found herself distressed and threatened by Reed's energy and curiosity: "I hated to see him interested in Things. I wasn't, and didn't like to have him even *look* at churches and leave me out of his attention. . . . Everything seemed to take him away from me, and I had no single thing left in my life to rouse me save his touch."[52] The destructive jealousy that emerged in her love affair with Reed was also to characterize Dodge's later relationship with the sculptor Maurice Sterne.

During their journey to Italy, Dodge, Reed, Van Vechten, and Jones stopped at Fontainebleau, the popular resort southeast of Paris. ◇

[Postcard: Grand Hôtel de la Fôret, Barbizon, Fôret de Fontainebleau]

[POSTMARK: GARE DE MELUN, 6 JULY 1913]

So this is Fontainebleau!

> M. D.
> J. S. Reed
> Carl Van Vechten
> Robert E. Jones

◇ Installed at the Villa Curonia for the remainder of the summer, Mabel Dodge continued her custom of surrounding herself with others, although this time she sometimes viewed their presence as distracting from her consuming passion with Reed. When Paul and Muriel Draper arrived with the renowned Polish-American pianist Arthur Rubinstein, Dodge wrote in her memoirs that they "descended upon us" and that she experienced their visit as an "interruption."[53] Rubinstein had become enamored with Muriel Draper in London during their many outings together, both with and without Paul. In his autobiography, he describes his visit to the Villa Curonia that summer and his impressions of Mabel Dodge:

> If Muriel and I had been alone in the villa, it would have been heaven. In reality, it was hell.
> Mabel Dodge was a young woman of around thirty with a pleasant face, a slightly too generous figure, and the fixed, absent smile of a Mona Lisa. She spoke in monosyllables, save when addressing her servants, and she answered any query with a short nod. Life at her Villa Curonia was a constant carousel. Our hostess showed a gift for gathering together the most incongruous combination of guests in the world. There was the art and music critic Carl Van Vechten, a genius at arguing; Robin de la Condamine, a charming, stuttering actor whom nobody had seen on a stage; . . . John Reed, a journalist and poet, and a militant Communist, was sullen and very aggressive. He was Mabel's choice companion. . . . We had Gertrude Stein, engaged in some interminable vocal battles with Van Vechten, Reed hating everything and everybody, . . . and last but not least, myself, persistently jealous and irritable. Whenever or whatever I played, whether Beethoven or

Stravinsky, some of those present would leave the room in protest, hating the one or the other.

Paul Draper, disgusted by it all, decided to return by himself to his lessons in London. Muriel was the only one who kept her unruffled poise amid the general hubbub. . . . Her loud voice and shrill laughter got on my nerves, and I hated the way she dressed à la Scheherazade, with turban and all. Besides, I could never see her alone, as our rooms were on different floors. After ten days of this ordeal, we all had had enough of it. . . .

As we took our leave, Mabel Dodge gave us another of her enigmatic smiles and a significant nod, and we were on our way.[54]

Although Rubinstein's account mentions Gertrude Stein as a guest at the villa that summer, there is no other evidence to suggest that she and Alice B. Toklas visited at that time, in spite of Dodge's many invitations and pleading. Stein and Toklas had spent the early part of the summer in Paris and the later summer and early fall of 1913 in Granada, Spain. Bruce Kellner further disputes Rubinstein's claim, asserting that Stein and Van Vechten never argued about anything.[55]

[CIRCA JULY 1913] VILLA CURONIA
VIA DELLE PIAZZOLE
ARCETRI

Dearest Gertrude,

<u>Please</u> come down here soon—the house is full of pianists, painters, pederasts, prostitutes & peasants. Great material. The [Paul and Muriel] Drapers, their "great" [Arthur] Rubenstein [i.e., Rubinstein], [Robert de la] Condamine, Mary Foote, Bobby Jones, Karl [i.e., Carl Van Vechten], & [John] Reed . . . <u>Do</u> come—we are all sailing back on Aug. 30. So please manage it—tell Alice to get the tickets & arrive. You won't be sorry. Leo brought an awfully nice friend of yours out here. The house party is just like a bunch of red geraniums & black & mauve orchids. Come.

Best love to both—

M.

Back in New York in the fall of 1913, Mabel Dodge openly lived with John Reed at 23 Fifth Avenue, a radical statement of female independence for that time. Although she still felt wholly immersed in her affair with Reed and continually abandoned by his limitless interest in the world, Dodge again found time and energy to try to get Gertrude Stein's work published. This time she focussed on Stein's plays and asked Florence Bradley, who had several, to send her one for publication. Stein was adamantly against this proposal, wanting her plays produced before they were published. Stein's tone in her next letter is demanding and annoyed at having been misunderstood by Dodge. In line with Stein's thinking, Bradley wrote to Dodge on 12 October 1913 that she thought it might be better to produce the plays first in New York and then publish them with an introduction by Dodge. Bradley also wrote to Stein on the same date, including a copy of her letter to Dodge and explaining that she was still interested in working on getting the plays produced.[56] ⁓

[CIRCA OCTOBER 1913] 23 FIFTH AVENUE

Dearest Gertrude,

I asked Florence Bradley to let me publish one of yr plays with an introduction by myself in the Sunday edition of the New York Press. Carl Van Vechten is dramatic critic on that paper now & editor of dramatic news—they have an interesting 8 page dramatic news supplement Sundays. He ordered this from me so I wrote Florence (or had a friend write as I was sick) to ask her if she would give me one of the plays but tho' I said I was sure you wouldn't mind & that I would take the responsibility in regard to you. You see what she answers.* However as she says it's perfectly true that if one is to be produced it's better to have it come out with a crash, but I didn't know she had any such intentions as she hadn't told me. She is coming in tomorrow & we will have a talk. I don't understand her last sentence at all—the P.S. I mean.† But it sounds all right, I think. The interest is still up in you. I will enclose later on when I get it from Hutch [Hapgood] a clipping comparing his

---

* This letter from Bradley to Dodge must have been included in Dodge's letter to Stein.

† The P.S. reads: "You can easily understand that Miss Stein writer of portraits makes Miss Stein writer of plays—plays which have not yet been published a practical interest that can not be ignored by the producer & quite apart from any personal enthusiasm he might have" (Florence Bradley to Dodge, 12 October 1913, MDLC).

story about [David] Edstrom* (now running serially) with your work!† Amusing? Says you are going in opposite directions & will cross! [Marsden] Hartley is expected for a show at Stieglitz's‡ & [Charles] Demuth§ is here somewhere.

Best love,

M. D.

⟍Hutchins Hapgood's story about the Swedish sculptor David Edstrom that Dodge refers to in her letter is entitled "David, the Story of a Soul." It appeared in a 1913 issue of the *Musical Advance* and is an abridged version of Hapgood's lengthy unpublished biography of Edstrom.[57] Begun as a collaboration between the writer and the sculptor that was to result in Edstrom's autobiography, the project went awry when Edstrom read Hapgood's notes from their months of work together. Upset by their content, Edstrom fled to Paris with the notes, telling Hapgood in a letter: "I do not consider you capable of handling a character like mine in a literary work, and will never therefore give you the notes I have." Edstrom had initially relied heavily upon Hapgood to write his autobiography, reportedly saying to him, "I cannot work without you. You give me the impulse, you make me see this thing, and I am dying to begin the work." However, the picture that Hapgood portrayed of Edstrom was so unflattering that the sculptor burned the manuscript in Paris.[58] Edstrom certainly had reason to feel betrayed and exposed, as the following excerpts from one of Hapgood's later drafts illustrate: "a man naturally of extreme sensibility and of extreme egotism . . . a cold, inhuman egotism, which is the real thing in the man"; "the man with the flabby face and beautiful but repulsive

---

* David Edstrom was featured in one of Stein's word portraits, "A Man," and included in another, "Men," both included in *Two*. "Men" is a description of three homosexuals, the other two subjects identified as Maurice Sterne and Hutchins Hapgood (*GSC*, 197). In *The Autobiography of Alice B. Toklas*, Stein describes Edstrom as "the fat swedish sculptor who married the head of the Christian Science Church in Paris and destroyed her" (115).

† The clipping has not been located.

‡ Hartley had an exhibition of abstractions and Berlin paintings at Stieglitz's Photo-Secession Galleries in New York, 12 January–12 February 1914. The brochure for the show included writings by Dodge, Stein, and Hartley.

§ Charles Demuth, American painter. Although some accounts assert that he later dedicated one of his poster portraits to Gertrude Stein, entitling it *Love, Love, Love: Homage to Gertrude Stein* (1929), Barbara Haskell argues that it was the art dealer Edith Halpert who erroneously assigned the title to Demuth's previously titled *Design for a Broadway Poster* based upon the superficial similarity of the repetition of words in both Demuth's and Stein's work (Haskell, *Charles Demuth*, 189).

hands"; "David talked about the women he had loved, and wept constantly"; "he wanted vehemently to convince me of his infinite capacity for sin, and how sin and the higher morality were often one"; "He often has a profound pity for himself."[59] In addition, Hapgood portrayed Edstrom as a man who frequently boasted about his sexual abilities and treated women in destructive ways.〜

[CIRCA OCTOBER 1913] 27 RUE DE FLEURUS

My dear Mabel

No decidedly not, I do <u>not</u> want the plays published. They are to be kept to be <u>played</u>. Florence Bradley understands about that perfectly. I am glad that you are all interested in [Marsden] Hartley. I hope he can get money enough so that he can be comfortable for a couple of years to work. I have a nice drawing of his hanging here now.* Do send the thing Hutch [Hapgood] is publishing of David Edstrom. David was in here the other day and very anxious to see it.†

I want the short things you have to be published in magazines as I told you, I think that is the important step now. If you cannot arrange that send them back to me and I will do it from over here, but it must be in good <u>monthlies</u>. I definitely do <u>not</u> want anything of mine published in newspapers or weeklies.

Always yours

Gertrude.

〜Realizing the error of her quest to publish Stein's plays, Dodge then asked Stein to contribute one of her stories for publication in the *Masses*, a journal devoted to arts and politics that had been founded in January 1911 and folded in December 1917. The monthly publication was based in New York and appealed to the radical avant-garde with its socialist leanings and revolutionary outlook on art, politics, and life. The journal featured political cartoons, realist illustrations by such artists as John Sloan and George Bellows, edi-

---

* According to Barbara Haskell in *Marsden Hartley,* in 1913 Stein purchased one of Hartley's drawings that had been exhibited at the Armory Show. In April 1913, Hartley had left four of his works at 27 rue de Fleurus while he traveled to Germany and this drawing is likely one of these. Its present location is unknown (141 n. 102).

† In a 1913 letter to Stein, Edstrom explains that the pain of what happened with Hapgood makes it difficult for him to continue his friendship with her: "After the Hapgood episode the association with you will always be remindfull of it. You will always continue your relations with him. . . . I have only the sweetest and finest kind of thoughts to you and your sister [Toklas?] and it done me real good that you received me so kindly" (Edstrom to Stein, c. 1913, GLSC).

torials on such topics as working conditions, women's issues, the proposed income tax, and strikes around the world, fiction, poetry, and advertisements for organizations such as the Rand School of Social Science, "Where Socialism is taught." Max Eastman was its editor and John Reed joined the staff in 1913. In his fiery journalism, Reed wrote about the injustices levied on the working class and provided vibrant accounts of the strikes organized by the Industrial Workers of the World. Dodge contributed money toward the running of the journal and for a time was active in soliciting articles for it.

Meanwhile, in Paris, Gabrielle Buffet-Picabia was on the verge of opening her gallery that was the outgrowth of earlier discussions that she had had in New York with Picabia, Dodge, Jo and Yvonne Davidson, and Maurice Aisen, among others. Their initial plans for a gallery and magazine based on 291 were abandoned in the late spring or early summer of 1913. In a letter to Stieglitz on 17 November 1913, Gabrielle Buffet-Picabia informs him of her renewed plans:

> I am organizing a gallery in Paris on the order of the idea we all talked about in New York last year, but with much more restrained proportions. . . . Do I need to tell you that the memory of "291" is a great source of strength for me in this enterprise? . . . I hope very much that you can help me in discovering & that we can maybe make some interesting exchange between "291" and "l'Ourse," (the name of the new child!)[60]

The gallery opened in Paris around January 1914 and did not survive for long, its plans for a journal headed by Jean Cocteau still unrealized.[61] ∾

[CIRCA NOVEMBER 1913] [23 FIFTH AVENUE]

Dearest Gertrude,

I never communicated so quickly with anyone across the ocean before. I believe it was a record. Florence Bradley has been staying with me & we all understand each other now. You were both right— absolutely. Now will you allow one of the short stories—the Bon Marché one*—or one like that to be printed in the "Masses Maga-

---

* This story is likely one of two: "Bon Marche Weather" or "Flirting at the Bon Marche," both included in *Two*. Although Dodge added an accent to "Marché" in her letter, Stein did not accent French words (Stein, *A Stein Reader*, 149).

zine." They do not pay for <u>any</u> of their stuff—it is all voluntary contribution. It is now thought to be the best, most fearless & modern, in America. Which isn't saying much. I send you a couple of numbers to judge of it. Of course it's all done (run) by youngsters who are too deadly <u>earnest</u> & the tone is a little <u>moral</u>. Everything in it seems to want to teach a lesson—with the editors it seems to be Art for Reform's Sake. But they will get over that. John Reed whom you met is managing editor. I send <u>one</u> number with Arthur Brisbane's picture in it!*

Alice Thursby sails soon to be in Paris all winter. She is more crazy & interesting than <u>ever</u>. Let me hear of your meetings. I also send you first number of Musical Courier with Hutch [Hapgood]'s David [Edstrom] in it & a clipping about <u>Hutch</u> & <u>you</u>!!!† The second no. I will buy & send immediately.

Stieglitz is waiting for [Marsden] Hartley, but he seems to feel (this is confidential) that Hartley is getting too autocratic about money & feeling too much that he <u>should</u> have it. But you know Stieglitz.

I believe Hartley is the man who will see, feel America & paint it. I hate National Art but I believe Hartley will be the great americain <u>painter of America</u>.

There was something identical in his stuff with America. It seemed somehow that the personality & the expression were identical with this place. I wonder if I am right. There is something ineradicably <u>Astec</u> in the americain <u>combination</u> that <u>persists</u> . . . that thing I call Astec for want of a better name is the essence of Hartley to me. Remember when I say Astec I mean what I mean to mean to myself. Anyway <u>the thing</u> that is in America & persists is what Hartley's work is <u>all</u> of. So I am awfully anxious to have him come . . . It seems so wonderful that he was perfectly untouched by

* Dodge must have sent Stein the November 1913 issue of the *Masses* that included a caricature of Arthur Brisbane lecturing to the editors of the magazine, entitled "Brisbaine's lecture on Political Science for 'Impractical Idealists'" (4). This drawing accompanied an article by Max Eastman, "Knowledge and Revolution," that attacked Brisbane's recent editorial in the Hearst newspapers. Taking a drawing by Art Young that appeared in the August 1913 issue of the *Masses* and depicted a worker handing his employer a piece of fruit, with the caption "He hands over the fruit of his toil on a silver platter and then gets about one eighth of the juice" (3), Brisbane criticized the ideas behind Socialism. In his piece, Eastman attacks Brisbane as one who "reject[s] Socialism without understanding it" and accuses him of "intellectual indolence" (5).

† It is possible that Dodge was mistaken about the journal in which Hapgood's article about Edstrom appeared, as "David, the Story of a Soul" was published in the *Musical Advance* in 1913. The article was not found in issues of the *Musical Courier* from this time. The clipping about Hapgood and Stein has not been located.

Europe or anyone over there—he seems to have kept himself absolutely unmixed, pure.*

I wish you'd come over. There is a lull in the world just now. This is an interval. Don't smile facetiously—I mean that. Everyone is waiting. I am looking up Negro literature.† Will send you some of their papers. I think "Something is coming out of them!"

Ever yrs,

M. D.

[NOVEMBER 1913] 27 RUE DE FLEURUS

My dear Mabel,

No Mabel not Masses. I know the paper very well, they send it to me regularly, thats where I had seen writing of John Reed's before I met him. I am glad you are all interested in [Marsden] Hartley, he is an interesting person alright, he ought to have time given him, he will need plenty of it, he is not a quick developer, he does need time given him, but you are probably seeing something of him now. The autumn salon is opening in a couple of days.‡ [Francis] Picabia is sending two big pictures,§ the place just swarms with chefs d'ecole, each one of them with his chosen name and introduction. Mrs. [Gabrielle Buffet-] Picabia is about to start her shop and review, they are very amusing about it, its hers he says he has nothing to do with it, not that he isn't willing to sell her a picture, in fact he has sold her a picture which he hopes she will sell again, but really its her affair[.] She intends to start it in a small way.

---

* Other critics of Hartley's work would disagree that he was "untouched" by his experiences in Europe. Barbara Haskell emphasizes the way that Hartley's art from this time period reflects his exposure to the primitive art he saw at the Trocadero Museum in Paris and to the mystical and spiritual components of German art (Haskell, *Marsden Hartley*, 26–32).

† Carl Van Vechten was Dodge's likely source for her curiosity about "Negro literature," as he had expressed a strong interest in African-American culture from an early date. He had arranged for two black performers to be featured at one of Dodge's Evenings.

‡ According to Apollinaire's review in *L'Intransigeant*, the Salon d'Automne opened in Paris on 15 November 1913 (Apollinaire, *Apollinaire on Art*, 325).

§ Picabia's two works included in the salon were *Edtaonisl* and *Udnie*, both painted in 1913. According to Apollinaire, they were "ardent, mad works that recount the astonishing struggles between pictorial substance and the imagination" (Apollinaire, *Apollinaire on Art*, 332).

Mildred [Aldrich] is probably going to settle down in the country, she will find that better for her old age, and she is very happy about it, Constance Lounsbury [i.e., Grace Constant Lounsbery]* has some Malayan Marionnettes that sound interesting. Miss [Myra] Edgerly is in New York now, we had an amusing letter from her telling all about it, that is what happened, Matisse kind of don't want to go winters any more. He wants to rent his place at Clamart and come back to Paris.† Picasso in spite of his two weeks illness has worked a lot. I have a new one of his that interests everybody very much. Its road making again. Mrs. [Mary] Berenson's daughter Karin‡ is in Paris, she is not as amusing as her mother, she is to be here a couple of months. She is trying sculpture. I guess thats all.

Always yours

Gertrude.

[CIRCA DECEMBER 1913]§ [23 FIFTH AVENUE]

Dear Gertrude

Just a word to tell you that this has been a wonderful month which brought together [Marsden] Hartley, Florence Bradley, one Helene Jungerich,¶ myself, & Andrew Dasburg**—all of the same

* Grace Constant Lounsbery, a Bryn Mawr graduate whom Stein had known in Baltimore as part of the circle of women she met with regularly. Lounsbery had a salon in Paris at which Stein had met the poet Ezra Pound (CC, 79, 304). I am grateful to Bruce Kellner and Ulla Dydo for pointing out that Constance Lounsbury is the same person as Grace Constant Lounsbery.

† In 1909, Matisse had moved from Paris to a house near Issy-les-Moulineaux, a suburb of Paris. His address was 42, later 92, route de Clamart. In the fall of 1913, Matisse moved back to 19 Quai St. Michel in Paris after finding the winters difficult in Issy. He continued to return to Issy to paint during the summer months (Alfred H. Barr, *Matisse: His Art and His Public*, 103–4).

‡ Karin Berenson, Mary Berenson's daughter from her first marriage, was raised by her maternal grandmother when Mary left her husband and two daughters in order to be with Bernard Berenson, whom she later married. Karin married Adrian Stephen, Virginia Woolf's brother, in 1914.

§ This letter must be from the end of 1913, as Hartley had returned to New York in November 1913 after having lived in Berlin since May 1913.

¶ Unidentified.

** Andrew Dasburg had exhibited three paintings and one sculpture in the Armory Show. He and Dodge developed a particularly strong attachment around this time and Dasburg painted a number of abstract portraits of her. Dodge described him as "one of the most touching people I met at '291.' Lame, but slender as an archangel and with a Blake-like rush of fair hair flying upward from off his round head" (M&S, 73).

party—somehow, & all constantly feeling <u>you</u> should be here, & almost feeling you were—all the time. Things are awfully in motion.

I am sending you today yr short stories. Did Donald Evans* write you yet? I <u>love</u> Hartley more & more. The [Myra] Edgerly is here, & toooo amusing. Is being married today to a cowboy!†

I find myself wishing to see you & be with you every day in the week.

Yrs,

M. D.

～Dodge's possessiveness of Reed and her jealousy of everything that took him away from her soon drove him away. In her memoirs, she reprints the note that she found from him one fall morning: "Good-by, my darling. I cannot live with you. You smother me. You crush me. You want to kill my spirit. I love you better than life but I do not want to die in my spirit. I am going away to save myself. Forgive me."[62] Dodge suffered for several days and was just beginning to appreciate her solitude when Reed returned. According to Dodge, he proclaimed: "'Oh, I couldn't *bear* it. . . . I can't live without you. I missed your love, your selfish, selfish love.'"[63]

Dodge and Reed resumed their relationship. In several weeks, Reed was asked by *Metropolitan Magazine* to travel to Mexico and write articles about the revolutionary Pancho Villa, who was fighting with the Constitutionalists to overthrow President

---

* Donald Evans, American poet and owner of a small press called Claire Marie through which he published Gertrude Stein's *Tender Buttons* in 1914. Dodge described Evans as a "strange genius. . . . with that Welsh type of slabsided face that is as flat as a board" (*M&S*, 74). Evans had become a regular attendee of Dodge's Evenings and was very taken by Stein's "Portrait of Mabel Dodge at the Villa Curonia." In April 1913, Evans had set out to write, as he explained in a letter to Dodge, "a thousand and one sonnet portraits of you—Of course, I only hope to do ninety nine, but that will be enough" (Evans to Dodge, 14 April 1913, MDLC).

† A search of the *New York Times* marriage announcements from December 1912, January 1913, and November 1913 through March 1914 did not yield any mention of Myra Edgerly's marriage. The "cowboy" she married most likely had the last name "Burt," as a clipping from one of Mabel Dodge's scrapbooks from this time, "Many Inventions!," reports on an exhibition of "Portraits on Ivory" by "Mira Edgerly-Burt" (6). This marriage did not last long in any case, as in January 1919 she married the semanticist Count Alfred Korzybski (*FF*, 139).

Victoriano Huerta and his military dictatorship. Dodge was immediately thrown back into her former clinging dependency and pleaded with Reed not to leave. Reed insisted on going and, as soon as he left, Dodge decided to follow him to Chicago and then travel with him to Mexico. She relates her feelings at seeing him in Chicago: "When we met I was disappointed that he looked merely rather glad instead of overjoyed. The man in him was already on the job. The woman's place was in the home!"[64] Although she felt threatened by his active seeking out of male companionship on the train to Texas, Dodge resolved not to complain or get in the way. However,

> as soon as we arrived in El Paso and had rooms in the large ugly hotel, I began to wonder why I had come. Reed rushed out, was all over the town, making arrangements, trying to see his way ahead. He wanted to get down into Mexico immediately. . . . I couldn't see what I was going to do in El Paso while he was over there, for I saw soon enough, I couldn't go with him. He was going to be with Villa's army, riding on troop trains and God knows what.[6]

⌀

[Postcard: Indian Scout with Villa's Army]

[POSTMARK: 22 DECEMBER 1913] EL PASO, TEXAS

Couldn't keep away when such amusing things are happening here. Am on the Texas border.

M. D.

⌀ Within a few days of her arrival in El Paso, "feeling very much out of sorts,"[66] Dodge traveled back to New York where, with her permission, the Evenings had taken place without her under the direction of Hutchins Hapgood and Lincoln Steffens. Upon her return to 23 Fifth Avenue, she discovered Andrew Dasburg's *The Absence of Mabel Dodge* that he had painted while she was in Texas. Dodge was thrilled by the abstract portrait and asked Hartley to write a letter to Reed describing the painting and the circumstances of its creation:

> It came out of a vivid experience which he Dasberg passed through here in the house at a recent Thursday evening when Mabel was off in Texas. . . . I could see D. was quite troubled and asked me secretly where M. D. was. I replied "in Texas."

D. was evidently wholly amazed inside—evidently disappointed with her absence—so much so that he threatened to go home. I insisted that he remain and stick the evening out which he consented to do—and did—but evidently it gave him one of those definite inner shocks. . . . To describe [the painting] is difficult. It is full of the lightning of disappointment. It is a pictured sensation of spiritual outrage—disappointment carried way beyond mediocre despair. It is a fiery lamentation of something lost in a moment—a moment of joy with the joy sucked out of it—leaving the flames of the sensation to consume themselves.[67]

Hartley's description of *The Absence of Mabel Dodge* as a direct record of Dasburg's disappointment at Dodge's absence contrasts with another account of the creation of the painting in which the artist, at Bobby Jones's suggestion, supposedly retitled one of his recent abstractions.[68] Whatever its origin, Dodge was enthralled by this painted homage to herself, its location now unknown, and began an intense relationship with Dasburg while Reed was in Mexico.

Stein wrote to Dodge about her current plans to move with Alice B. Toklas to the Palais Royal, plans that never materialized. The increased tension between Leo and Gertrude at the beginning of 1913 had led to their decision not to live together. The exact date of their separation is not clear. Mellow suggests it was in the fall of 1913, after Gertrude and Alice had returned from Spain and Leo decided to move to Italy year-round.[69] In a letter to Mabel Weeks dated 7 February 1913, Leo had acknowledged Alice's role in the separation while at the same time expressing relief at being freed from his enmeshed relationship with Gertrude:

One of the greatest changes that has become decisive in recent times is the fairly definite "disaggregation" of Gertrude and myself. The presence of Alice was a godsend, as it enabled the thing to happen without any explosion. As we have come to maturity, we have come to find that there is practically nothing under the heavens that we don't either disagree about, or at least regard with different sympathies.[70]

Stein and Toklas's consideration of a move away from 27 rue de Fleurus was not in response to the tensions with Leo. Their apartment needed many renovations and their landlady opposed making them.[71]

[Whitman motto]

[CIRCA DECEMBER 1913] 23 FIFTH AVENUE

Dearest Gertrude,

Am better since two days. [Hutchins] Hapgood dined here last night, a great boy.
Enclosed find news of Mabel Weekes [i.e., Weeks]?*

Yours—

Mabel

Happy New Year to all!

[CIRCA DECEMBER 1913 OR JANUARY 1914]
27 RUE DE FLEURUS

My dear Mabel,

Happy new year to you and Hutch [Hapgood] and Neith [Boyce] and all. Its almost quite New York here its so cold, the Seine has not frozen yet but it might. Mabel please send those short things of mine to me right away.† I have to have them. What are your plans for the spring. We are going to move. We have after much hunting found an apartment in the Palais Royal with a balcony that promises to be very nice. We don't move until July. I guess we will see you before then.

Always yours

Gertrude

Will you register those things when you send them.

Gertrude

* Unlocated enclosure.
† Stein may be referring to the six stories that Mitchell Kennerley had returned to Dodge around May 1913 and that Dodge lists by name in a letter to Stein from that time.

213

~

1914

Dodge and Stein's writings were united in a catalogue for Marsden Hartley's exhibition of abstractions and Berlin paintings that appeared at Stieglitz's Photo-Secession Galleries from 12 January to 12 February 1914. The brochure for the show included a foreword by Dodge, an essay by Hartley on his own work, and excerpts from Stein's play, *IIIIIIIIII*, in which Hartley was the character M——N H——. All three texts also appeared in the January 1914 issue of *Camera Work*. In her foreword, Dodge lists all the possible comments critics could make about Hartley's paintings and concludes by stressing that the pictures "must be seen and felt directly in order to be received. No other introduction is necessary; or can be anything more than futile. As futile as the description of music."[1] Hartley's statement begins:

> The purpose of this foreword is to state merely the uselessness in art of forewords—of theses. It is to state that in the present exhibition there is nothing in the way of a theory of art of aesthetics or of science to offer. The intention of the pictures separately and collectively is to state a personal conviction—to express a purely personal approach. . . . It has not intellectual motives—only visionary ones.[2]

In Gertrude Stein's play, the character M——N H—— has such speeches as: "A cook. A cook can see. Pointedly in uniform, exertion in a medium. A cook can see." and "A sound is in the best society." The excerpt in the catalogue ends as follows: "A cape coat, in bold shutters, in bold shutters shutting and not changing shutters not changing climaxes and peelings and hold over the switch, the binding of a pet and a revolver, the chosen loan, the owned cake in pieces the way to swim."[3]

Hartley's exhibition was well received by the critics and resulted in enough sales of his paintings to enable him to meet expenses for another year in Europe. He left New York in March, traveling to London and Paris before settling back in Berlin at the end of April.〜

[Whitman motto]

[CIRCA EARLY JANUARY 1914] [23 FIFTH AVENUE]

Dear Gertrude,

I am sending you some sonnets engendered by yourself. Let me hear what you think of them. "Year's End" is about a year old baby.*

I <u>love</u> [Marsden] Hartley more & more. He is just like a cooky. Will send you soon copy of your & his union in print about to come out for his show at Stieglitz's.

Best love & New Year's greeting,
Mabel.

Would you & Alice go to India with Florence Bradley & me in April? <u>In the air.</u>†

〜Gertrude Stein wrote Mabel Dodge about a celebrated sale in Paris of paintings by modern masters, including works by the Fauves and the Cubists. According to Guillaume Apollinaire in his column "Anecdotiques" in *Le Mercure de France,* this public sale was held on 2 March 1914 and was the first offer of Fauve and Cubist works of art at auction. The sale also marked the first time that a percentage of the sale price was given to the artists.⁴〜

---

* These sonnets were likely by Donald Evans, whose "Year's End," written in Dodge's hand, was attached to this letter. The sonnet's full title is "Portrait of Michael Peter Norton—the Year's End." In a letter to Dodge dated 13 August 1913, Evans sent four sonnets including this one, commenting that "The Michael Peter Norton sonnet, I think, is worthy in half manner of Gertrude Stein. Do <u>you</u>?" (Evans to Dodge, 13 August 1913, MDLC). This sonnet is composed of sentences that echo Stein's style, such as "There is what is, and what there is is fair," and "And here is there what there is here begun."

† Dodge seems to be referring to airplane travel, which was just beginning to be offered as a means of transportation.

In his letter, he claimed, "I can give you a book of more distinguished appearance than any other publisher in America and I can also get more publicity for it. . . . My public also is the most civilized in this country."[6] Although Evans had heard through Van Vechten about Stein's objections to publishing the plays before producing them, he attempted to convince her that publication "would not in any way hurt the producing value; in fact, it would stimulate interest in their production in the theatre."[7] Evans also offered Stein royalties on all copies sold, the first time that she was not asked to pay for her work to be published.[8] Still refusing to publish the plays, Stein sent Evans three short works, "Objects," "Food," and "Rooms," collected under the title *Tender Buttons*. Evans wrote to Dodge in February 1914 that he had received these manuscripts and was eager to publish them.[9] However, Dodge had gathered a number of objections to Evans's press and warned Stein against publishing with him. Instead, she proposed Robert J. Coady as a publisher, at whose Washington Square Gallery copies of *Three Lives* were already on sale. Coady later wrote to Stein that *Three Lives* "has been an enormous ad for the gallery and we are being much talked of. . . . Your support has meant a great deal to us and we feel much encouraged. We shall try to prove worthy of it."[10]

At this time, in addition to her involvement with Stein's publishing ventures, Dodge became closely connected with the growing American labor movement and its flamboyant and revolutionary leaders. She had accompanied Hutchins Hapgood to the trial of Frank Tannenbaum, who had been arrested for leading hundreds of unemployed, homeless men into a number of churches on a winter night looking for food and shelter. Her attendance at this trial was mentioned in the papers, as an example of a society woman interested in the plight of the working class. One account read: "Mrs. Mabel Dodge gets a front seat! Among the crowd . . . was a sprinkling of professionals . . . Socialists and uplifters such as Mrs. Mabel Dodge and Hutchins Hapgood—who expressed the opinion that Free Speech was about to be upheld or strangled . . . !"[11] Uncertain of her own position and degree of commitment, Dodge spoke to the papers about her connection with the Industrial Workers of the World, a revolutionary labor union whose members, sometimes called Wobblies, strongly defended Tannenbaum's actions. She was quoted as saying: "'I am interested in the I.W.W. . . . as I am in other organizations. I am searching for the best way for labor to organize. The I.W.W. has consequently come in for a good deal of study on my part.'"[12] The IWW, initially founded in Chicago in 1905, organized 150 strikes in its time and contributed significantly to gains achieved in the American labor movement.

As part of her "study," Dodge invited some IWW leaders to one of her Evenings at 23 Fifth Avenue and explained her actions: "'I invited these men merely to listen to their stories. I am a student and wished to get information at first hand. I did not invite them socially nor to feed them.'"[13] The newspapers were intrigued by Dodge's involvement with the IWW:

FAIR SOCIETY WOMAN DEFENDS I.W.W.; IS NEITHER ANARCHIST NOR SOCIALIST, BUT THINKS UNEMPLOYED NOT TO BLAME. "I THINK THAT THE UNEMPLOYED ARE JUSTIFIED IN DOING ANYTHING TO CALL PUBLIC ATTENTION TO THEIR CONDITION," SAYS MRS. MABEL DODGE

"Anything that doesn't injure people," she qualified. "Of course, I don't believe in dynamite and that kind of thing," adds the Society Leader, but she would like to help in bringing about a proper organization of all labor.

Mrs. Dodge, who attends the Tannenbaum trial every day, says she is a student watching trend[s] of events. . . .

Why is a society woman from Fifth Avenue interested in such a trial? Is she an Anarchist? Is she a Socialist? Does she belong to the Industrial Workers of the World?. . .

These are some of the questions they are whispering in General Sessions: And this is what she told me:

"I am not an Anarchist. I do not belong to the Socialist Party. I am not a member of the Industrial Workers of the World. I am not a person who joins anything. I am a student and I am interested, keenly interested, in this trial and in all the circumstances of the recent I.W.W. conflict with the established order."[14]

Frank Tannenbaum was sentenced to a year in prison at the end of March 1914. Dodge's loyal attendance at the trial had thrown her for a short time into the center of debates over the plight of the unemployed. She held another Evening devoted to discussions of the "Unemployment Movement" that was attended by such radicals as the anarchist and birth control advocate Emma Goldman, the labor leader and IWW organizer Big Bill Haywood, and the anarchist Alexander Berkman. The newspaper headlines read: "I.W.W. THRONG ARE GUESTS OF SOCIETY FOLK ON FIFTH AVENUE. WOMEN IN EVENING GOWNS ENTERTAIN BILL HAYWOOD, AGITATORS AND THE UNEM-

PLOYED IN HOME OF MRS. MABEL DODGE"[15] and "I.W.W. MEN STARVE AS LEADERS EAT. LATTER MAKE MERRY IN DODGE'S FIFTH AVE. HOME."[16]〰

[New York Telegram]

[POSTMARK: 15 MARCH 1914] [23 FIFTH AVENUE]

WOULD COUNSEL HESITATION BEFORE PUBLISHING WITH [DONALD] EVANS IS GETTING NAME OF SECOND RATE AND DECADENT [ROBERT] CO[A]DY SEEMS BETTER PROPOSITION FOR PRESTIGE EVANS WILL PROCEED IMMEDIATELY UNLESS YOU CABLE.

MABEL

———

SUNDAY [29 MARCH 1914] [23 FIFTH AVENUE]

Dearest Gertrude

This is going to be a letter.

Now in the first place. About your stuff. I cabled you not to publish with D.[onald] Evans after having a long talk with E.[dwin] A.[rlington] Robinson who is our "dark poet," here, & who knows more about things than most people. He knows Evans & believes in his ability but he thinks the Claire Marie Press which Evans runs is absolutely third rate, & in bad odor here, being called for the most part "decadent" & Broadwayish & that sort of thing. He wrote Evans to get out of it, to chuck it & stop getting linked up in the public "mind" with it. I think it would be a pity to publish with him if it will emphasize the idea in the opinion of the public, that there is something degenerate & effete & decadent about the whole of the cubist movement which they all connect you with, because, hang it all, as long as they don't understand a thing they think all sorts of things. My feeling in this is quite strong. Now that quiet little [Robert] Co[a]dy man, who hates Stieglitz & "291" & has allied himself with Max Weber against him & everyone connected with him, would be a better one to publish with & have them sold at his little gallery, where he's already selling "Three Lives." I am trying to write this in bed, while Arthur Lee & "Freddie" his wife are wrangling about how she did her part last night in a socialist play. Arthur says he "wants to work" but no one sees much sign of it. They have been staying with me for six weeks—& Oh! how many arguments!*

* It may have been around this time that, according to Dodge, Freddie Lee developed a strong connection to Mabel and shared her bed, with no sexual contact. Arthur Lee reportedly sculpted his wife on her knees with head bowed, entitling his work *Adoration of Mabel Dodge* (*M&S*, 254).

The [Stanton MacDonald-]Wright-[Morgan] Russell show*
came on, & Arthur rushed down here & said it was the finest thing
since Michelangelo & that it had "freed him" & now he can work!
And the "impulse" was strong enough to last 15 years. But we
went up & pricked that bubble for him! They are going away today, & Neith [Boyce] is coming in to stay. Hutch [Hapgood] has
had sort of neurasthenia all winter & has been seeing "spirits."
(More of this when I see you.)

Lee Simonson† has become a regular habitué. He is a real "community man", & conscientiously paints for six hours a day in order to win the respect of his fellows for being a hard worker! So
much for joy! Whereas Arthur who isn't a community man at all
doesn't care what happens so long as there's something amusing to
talk about, & he need only work when all the talk is over!

I am wondering what you'l be doing this summer. I don't know
about my own plans. But I think some day soon I'l go to Paris for 3
months to get a residence to have a divorce. It is impossible over
here except for unfaithfulness & I couldn't—& wouldn't—divorce
E. for that.‡ Is it true, as Stephen Haweis, who sees Edwin, says,
that you wrote E. that your remarks in Stieglitz's Foreword—was
on [Marsden] Hartley—was a tremendous dressing down of
Hartley?§ And that you were very severe on him about himself &
his nature & his work? And that no one had understood you were
raking him over the coals in that play, & that everyone had misin-
terpreted it to be flattering? I cannot believe this because I know
how much you like H. & his work. He sails on Wed . . . for England. He is quite tierd, & needs a rest. One night here he had a
real mystical exaltation—(more of this when I see you!)

I am again being mixed up in the newspapers mind, with the
I.W.W. because of having [Big Bill] Haywood & [Arturo]
Giovannitti¶ here one eve. to discuss the meaning of the organiza-
tion, & because I am following any events which seem to bear on the

---

*The work of the Synchromist painters Stanton MacDonald-Wright and Morgan
Russell was exhibited at the Carroll Galleries in New York from 2 March to 16 March
1914.

† Lee Simonson, American scenic designer, painter, and writer.

‡ Mabel Dodge's divorce from Edwin was not final until some time around June
1916. He consented to an arrangement in which Mabel Dodge could use as the reason
for the divorce that he had deserted her, an assertion that certainly seemed far from
the truth (Rudnick, *Mabel Dodge Luhan*, 134).

§ Excerpts from Stein's play *IIIIIIIII*, in which Hartley appeared as a character,
were included in the brochure accompanying his 1914 exhibition at 291.

¶ Arturo Giovannitti, Italian-American labor leader, prominent member of the Industrial Workers of the World, and poet.

possibility of a Revolution—hence this clipping*—the names of the "leaders" are most inaccurate. Haywood & Giovannitti were the ones who were here, &, as you may imagine, I did <u>not</u> say "I did not ask them <u>socially</u>!"

Every little while a Gertrude Stein parody comes out. Stieglitz showed me one the other evening from the Sun which I have ordered & will send you.† I would like to hear your plans because I may decide to leave here at any moment. I am getting awfully tierd.

Arthur & Freddie are going to live in Paris. Lee Simonson is going abroad in May, & to Italy. Andrew Dasburg whom you used to know too,‡ is going over, and I <u>may</u> come over with Florence Bradley, or Neith or someone. So please let me hear your plans. We are thinking of renting Curonia till July 1st and I may not go to Italy till then. April May & June would be enough for divorce residence. Let me hear what you think about what I say about publishing. And tell me if this Marie Claire add. is a bluff. Best love to you & Alice and remember I think a lot tho' I don't write.

Yrs,

M. D.

——————

[Postcard: Paris—Jardin du Palais Royal—Vue Générale]

[POSTMARK: PARIS, 7 APRIL 1914] [27 RUE DE FLEURUS]
My dear Mabel,

We are not making any plans until we move which won't be for several months yet,

Yours

Gertrude.

* Dodge must have sent Stein a clipping of "Fair Society Woman Defends I.W.W.," *New York Evening World,* 27 March 1914.

† Although a search through the *New York Sun* from this time did not yield a parody of Stein, one of Mabel Dodge's scrapbooks contains an undated parody from the *Sun Dial,* entitled "Gertrude Stein on the War." It begins: "I asked of Gertrude Stein: 'Explain / Why they are fighting on the Aisne.' / She mused a space and then exclaimed, / 'What seal brown bobble can be / blamed?'" (Luhan scrapbook, "Miscellaneous #1," MDLC).

‡ Dasburg first met Gertrude and Leo Stein during his trip to Europe in 1909–10. He and Grace Mott Johnson, a sculptor who was soon to be his wife, traveled to Paris to

⌁Most likely to Mabel Dodge's dismay, a letter to her from Donald Evans at the beginning of April 1914 informs her that he had received word from Gertrude Stein agreeing to the publication terms for *Tender Buttons*. He writes, "It is [the] loveliest piece of work I have yet seen of Miss Stein's. I've decided on canary with a round green label for the board binding. Modish shades and effective!"[17] Dodge tries once more to convince Stein to change her mind, but to no avail.⌁

[CIRCA APRIL 1914] [23 FIFTH AVENUE]

Dearest Gertrude,

You will see from this notice of the third book from the Claire Marie Press how the idea of decadence is now really inseperable from its publications in the minds of the public. I really believe you will give your work a set back and make further publishing & understanding of it more difficult unless you withdraw what he has from D.[onald] Evans. Neith [Boyce] says the same & says to tell you so. With Kenyon Cox's article this month in Scribner's, ("Artist & Public") where he hammers in again his old charge of the degeneration & decadence & Cubism, & your undenied relation to it in writing*—to publish with him will only go to create, or foster an impression that will be awfully hard to get rid of. I don't want to hurt or bother Evans because I like him well enough but there are plenty of people to give him things to make sensations with, without his having yours. If [Robert] Co[a]dy would publish & sell at his gallery it would be far better but I can't do anything there as I have no influence on account of my friendship for, & allegiance to, "291" which he hates.

Best love—

M. D.

---

visit their friends Morgan Russell and Arthur Lee. Russell introduced Dasburg to Matisse and Lee arranged a meeting for him with the Steins. Dasburg was especially taken with the Cézanne paintings he saw and Leo Stein allowed him to borrow a still-life to copy (Coke, *Andrew Dasburg*, 16).

* Kenyon Cox, "Artist and Public," *Scribner's Magazine* (April 1914): 512–20. Cox does not mention Stein by name but talks about "artistic anarchists" who rebel against tradition and rails against Cubists and Futurists who destroy the customary view of reality. He ends his article by calling the new art "decadent and corrupt" (520).

Dearest Gertrude

This still goes on! Have you ever read [Frederic] Myers "Human Personality"? If not, get it & read what he says about genius & language in IIIrd chapter.* Also get April & May Metropolitan & read John Reed's mexican articles† which are making a big hit over here.

I suppose "Tender Buttons" will be out soon! What will the papers say? I wish I could see you & tell you some things. Please let me hear how you find [Marsden] Hartley & what his condition is when you see him. He was nearly disintegrated when he left. Stieglitz was very worried. I was delighted with that dirty paper you sent me!‡ What supports it?

I wish we could meet this summer but my plans are vague as usual. I may not be able to afford to open villa.

Best love,

M. D.

Did you get another clipping from the Sun I asked a man on the paper to send you?

⌒In the late spring of 1914, Mabel Dodge began to sense a real rift in her friendship with Gertrude Stein, perhaps partially due to the tension around their different opinions of Stein's publishing with Donald Evans's Claire Marie Press. The controlling and somewhat possessive tone of Dodge's letters may have put off Stein. However, by this time Alice B. Toklas had already begun to put some distance between Stein and Dodge. In *Movers and Shakers*, Dodge tried to account for the change in their relationship, repeating Leo Stein's explanation that she had also included in *European Experiences:*

> Gertrude cooled towards me after a little though we still wrote back and forth for I had business to do for her, though I

---

* Frederic W. H. Myers's *Human Personality and Its Survival of Bodily Death* was published in two volumes in 1903. Dodge directed Stein to Myers's third chapter, on "Genius," which would likely have held much interest for Stein with its discussion of ideas about the limits of language for fully expressing an individual's thoughts and feelings, the characteristics of automatic writings, and the superiority of the arts as a medium of self-expression that can go beyond the limits of language.

† Reed's article "With La Tropa" appeared in the April 1914 issue of *Metropolitan*, and "The Battle of La Cadena" appeared in the May 1914 issue.

‡ Unidentified and not located among Dodge's papers.

was the last who should have tried that—being so muddle-headed, forgetful, and self-centered. Once I asked Leo why she had changed towards me, and he laughed and said because there was a doubt in her mind about who was the bear and who was leading the bear![18]

In the following letter, Dodge appeals to Stein to respond to her, despite their differences, and seeks some reassurance of their friendship.〜

MAY 18. [1914] HOTEL CHELSEA
ATLANTIC CITY

Dearest Gertrude—

The latest plans are as follows & I hope to goodness that yours & Alice's can somehow fall in with them.

Neith [Boyce] is going to take the baby (3 yrs) & Boyce, & I am going to take John, & we're going to "Paradiso Albergo" in Vallombrosa* for six weeks or two months. Hutch [Hapgood] is taking the other two† to Provincetown for the summer. I'm not opening the villa because I can't afford to & it is rented from Oct. 1st on for the winter.

We may sail to Italy & go straight to Vallombrosa or we may sail to Cherbourg & go to Paris & down . . . If we go to Italy I'l have to go to Paris alone for a few days to "establish a residence" (—this is before getting a french divorce—don't tell, please, on account of one's not being able to get one if one wants one or shows it in any way or plans ahead, or seems to be doing it openly, or with the knowledge of the other partner or if there is any willingness on the other side.) Now Neith & I both want to have you along or near by this summer. What are the chances? Will you come to that very nice plain Albergo & join us?—We are going there to pass our time on the mountain tops (as Boyce & John wish to make a colony of americain cowboys in the Appenines—) in the sun & it will be great. I will have my motor up there & we will make trips. Will you please see what you think of this. I don't believe you realize that I'm fonder of you than of anyone else abroad & think of you more—(as I write it that doesn't sound very important any-way!) but it is! You know that as far as some things go I'm a leaf in

---

* Vallombrosa is a Tuscan resort town in the Etruscan Apennines fifteen miles east of Florence at an altitude of four thousand feet.

† Neith Boyce and Hutchins Hapgood had four children. The "baby" was Beatrix and their oldest boy was Boyce, who was John's best friend.

the wind—I make plans & some thing knocks them to pieces. So far as I am able I mean to carry out this one, & I hope nothing will interfere. What do you think of my "establishing a residence" in the Palais Royal too? Could I get two or three rooms there for about 200 fcs a month? While I'm away I could lend them to someone or something & violently send myself letters & papers there. Have you enough rooms to rent me—say two which I could begin paying for the minute I arrive? You see how it is I hope! Awfully silly. Also where <u>am</u> I going to find a lawyer? Do you know any lawyers? I think it a wonderful plan if I could rent two rooms from you. I wouldn't in that case lend 'em to anyone unless you said so. And you wouldn't mind me around for a little while while I was "getting it," would you?

Everybody is going or has gone abroad. The [Arthur and Freddie] Lees, (Superman Lee) have left. Arthur carries a copy of "Zarathustra"* in his coat pocket but has a very worried look in his eyes. His sculpture won't stand up tho' it's so strong in the muscle. Freddie, his wife, is willing he should be a superman & doesn't at all stand in the way, tho' he blames her when he misdoubts himself.

Lee Simonson has gone too. He is going to Corsica to paint. Everything he wants to paint orange & red seems to come out yellowish green. It makes him very miserable. But he goes on, & paints for so & so many hours a day so that he shall build up a position for himself, & is getting a good deal respected for being quite solid—in the community. Of course Arthur enjoys the isolation of being of the artist temperament & doesn't have to work any special hours to have the good opinion of the public but Lee Simonson is by nature a community man & is judged as such by such.

Walter Lippmann, a very intelligent young man wrote one book & has now written another, & is going abroad, too.† You will probably meet him. He is twenty five & bears himself as one who expects to be president in about 3 yrs from now. His second book is called "Drift & Mastery" & is about everything & everyone contrasted with himself! The world he represents as Drift, himself as Mastery. The americain world, that is.

* This most likely refers to the German philosopher Friedrich Wilhelm Nietzsche's *Thus Spake Zarathustra* (1883–92).

† Walter Lippmann, American author, editor, and journalist, who was Assistant Secretary of War in 1917. His first book was *A Preface to Politics* (1913), and his second book, *Drift and Mastery*, was published in 1914.

[John] Reed whom you met is going too sometime—but don't know when. Mary Foote says he is my Waterloo. This means I have gone on & on liking him! He has just "made a name for himself" as they say over here.

Your name still bubbles up on people's lips & in reviews & papers. God knows what it will do when Donald Evans brings it out again in "Canary boards with green title label." Hutch read it was going to be called "Tender Buttons" & he was very stern about it, as coming from <u>that</u> Press it would have a terrible "implication." I suppose you are guided by your star in these matters but I wish I hadn't spend all that on that cable to you. And you <u>never</u> told me why or what or <u>any</u> thing! Evans is certainly as promising a word slinger as anyone over here—but even then! He's amusing too.

Did I write you that one night when I had atropine in my eyes Hutch & Neith brought two Caines* to spend the evening with me. I talked to them for hours but never saw them. Sent 'em to Stieglitz's on the following, & then they left & to this day I don't know what they're like. Hutch had got them from you, & at a certain restaurant called "Polly's"† they had all met, along with Stephen Haweis who has what his wife calls "an honest job" over here—(it's painting lifesized screens for a certain fashionable Mrs. [Benjamin] Guinness (ale)‡ who gives em to her friends for wedding presents signed by her.)

Mrs. Caine told me, without embarrassment (as I couldn't see her) that she supplied the spark her husband uses to write with, also to any others who temporarily need it. "Her job was merely to inspire," as Reed sings in the "Day in Bohemia." But that kind of vampiring seemed to suit her very well for she seemed blooming. Husband seemed a little dissolved but still having form.

They were enjoying our current revolution—the new religions, the Free Speech Fight, & the censoring of Moving Pictures—& Stieglitz's subsequently so you can see they had jumped right into everything.

---

* Dodge is likely referring to the same Gordon Caine and her husband, Sir Thomas Henry Caine, a writer, that Stein mentions in *The Autobiography of Alice B. Toklas* (135). According to Stein, she had met the Caines in London through John Lane who was Mr. Caine's publisher.

† Polly's was a restaurant run by Polly Holladay from 1913 to 1915 that was housed in the basement of the building at 137 MacDougal Street where the Liberal Club was based from 1913 to 1918 (Watson, *Strange Bedfellows*, 124). Holladay was a self-proclaimed anarchist whose lover Hippolyte Havel was also the chef and waiter at Polly's.

‡ Mrs. Benjamin S. Guinness, prominent New York and London hostess who was also a painter.

Mrs. [Ducie] Haweis has "developed" & has written some aphorisms about Futurism which are quite good & coming out in Camera Work.*

I sent all your printed works to a professor of english at a boys school in Morristown† because he told me it had been an "experience" to read one of them sometime ago & he wrote me that one of the stories in "Three Lives" is one of the finest things ever expressed in the english language.

I have had my tonsils out & have had a bad attack of melancholia in my larynx, & am down here for a few days to get over it. If you answer—& please do—send it to 23 Fifth—& please show some sign of affection after my making up to you this way in this letter a mile long, & please say you'l come to Vallombrosa.

Love, yrs,

Mabel.

∾Stein and Toklas no longer felt the need to move from 27 rue de Fleurus, as their landlady finally agreed to allow them to make renovations that would modernize their living space, including the replacement of the cast-iron stove with a fireplace and the addition of electricity.[19] Their decision not to move to a new apartment appears to have inconvenienced Dodge in her search for a temporary residence to facilitate her divorce from Edwin.∾

[CIRCA MAY 1914] 27 RUE DE FLEURUS

My dear Mabel,

[Marsden] Hartley has been and gone, he seemed quite alright, it was delightful to see him.‡ We have changed our mind about moving, we found we liked it best here after all and so we are making ourselves a bit more comfortable and then we will go away for the summer as usual. Is [Stephen] Haweis coming over or does he

---

* Mina Loy's (or Ducie Haweis, as she was also called) "Aphorisms on Futurism" appeared in the January 1914 issue of *Camera Work* (published in June 1914), 13–15. They included such statements as: "IN pressing the material to derive its essence, matter becomes deformed," "LOVE the hideous in order to find the sublime core of it," and "FORGET that you live in houses, that you may live in yourself— / FOR the smallest people live in the greatest houses."

† Mabel's son John was attending the Morristown School in Morristown, New Jersey at this time.

‡ On his way back to Berlin, where he had arrived by 30 April 1914, Hartley stopped in London and then Paris where he visited with Stein.

go straight back to Italy. He must have had some charming adventures. Do you ever hear from Grant Watson. We see Miss [Maud] Crut[t]well every now and then. She always asks after you.

Always

Gertrude.

MONDAY LATER [18 MAY 1914] HOTEL CHELSEA

ATLANTIC CITY

Dearest Gertrude—

Just after sending off two or three pounds of letter today I got yr scrappy one tonight saying you're not moving after all. Well, do you want to see if you could rent me a couple (or one) room which most of the time I'l never be in? Or if you don't, what <u>do</u> you advise?

[Stephen] Haweis you asked about. He will stay all summer in N.Y. painting on <u>her</u> screens for $150 a month & living in her house while she is abroad.* She is english too hence this affinity. Stephen is very tierd of the Revolution & thinks the common people common. But he has to hear a good deal about it all unfortunately. No more news now. Let me hear from you soon. You see I'l have to pay a residence for about 6 months I guess or 4 anyway.

Best love—

M. D.

∽Gertrude Stein's *Tender Buttons* was published by Donald Evans's Claire Marie Press in June 1914, a yellow volume with a round green label. Writing from Provincetown, Massachusetts, where she was spending part of the summer in a cottage with John Reed, Dodge appeared to swallow her pride around her loud objections to publishing *Tender Buttons* with Evans. In her familiar role of admirer and supporter, Dodge praised Stein's new book and offered encouragement about its prospects for sale.

In the spring of 1914, John Lane had visited Stein in Paris and suggested that she consider traveling to London in July in order to

------

* Haweis was commissioned by Mrs. Guinness to paint screens, according to Dodge's letter to Stein written earlier the same day.

finalize agreements for publishing *Three Lives*.[20] On 31 March 1914, Lane had written to Stein about his continued interest in the volume: "I am still willing to undertake it, although it is a very highly speculative proposition, as I told you."[21] Stein and Toklas left for London on 6 July 1914,[22] hoping to sign a contract for *Three Lives* and not believing that the rumors of war would come true. ᔰ

[CIRCA JUNE 1914] PROVINCETOWN P.O. MASS.

Dearest Gertrude,

I don't know whether anyone has sent you these or not. They are the the first notices. The book is certainly charming. It looks lovely. People tell me it will—must—have a big sale. If it doesn't, it's only because so many are away from bookshops for the summer.

The other "nicknames" is by quite a well known writer over here who told me she did it, unconsciously under the influence of "Three Lives."* Neith [Boyce] & I will be in Florence end of July. <u>Where</u> will you be. Answer.

Love,
Mabel

[JUNE 1914] PROVINCETOWN, MASS.

Dearest Gertrude

Enclosed is a story that Edna Kenton swears is the <u>unconscious</u> result of your three lives—done after reading it & much influenced by it. I leave you to discover the relationship. See in last "Camera Work" how much the critics lug you in.† It increases. I

---

* According to Dodge's next letter, "nicknames" appears to have been written by Edna Kenton, although a work by that title has not been located among Kenton's published writing.

† The January 1914 issue of *Camera Work*, published in June 1914, reprinted the brochure for Hartley's exhibition at 291 that included excerpts from Stein's play, *IIIIIIIIII*, and forewords by Dodge and Hartley. Following these, *Camera Work* reprinted a number of critical reviews of the exhibition, in which Stein's play was favorably mentioned. The art critic Henry McBride wrote that "there is a wonderful foreword by the great Gertrude Stein, which she has made quite simple for us so we will all understand. . . . A more delicious accompaniment to the pictures cannot be imagined. Is it not wonderful the way in which Gertrude responds to every one of Hartley's moods?" (19–20).

am keeping all clippings about your Buttons as [Donald] Evans may not send em all to you. Neith [Boyce] & I sail 15 July on Stampalia for Genoa. Where are you? Where will you be? Write to me to Curonia. We are undecided in plans & might come where you are.

Yrs,

Mabel

[Charles] Demuth sits here by me & sends love to you.*

———

[CIRCA JUNE 1914] 27 RUE DE FLEURUS

My dear Mabel,

I am glad you like the book, its charmingly gotten up. I am entirely pleased with it. We are still in Paris, we are going to London for a few weeks and then are coming back here and late in August will go to Spain. The [Arthur and Freddie] Lees turned up the other day[.] They were looking for a place to live and thought they had found one. Mrs. [Alice] Thursby came to tea. I found her as interesting and attractive as before. Bryson Burroughs† is going to have a show. I haven't seen him yet, [Henry] McBride‡ is over here just now. Georgiana King has just been. Leo seems very pleased with Florence.§ My best to Neith [Boyce] and Hutch [Hapgood] and [Stephen] Haweis,

Yours

Gertrude.

⌇Dodge writes again from Provincetown where many of her friends from New York have gathered. She tells Stein about an article by Robert Rogers, entitled *"Tender Buttons,* Curious Ex-

<hr>

* Demuth had lived in Paris from December 1912 to the spring of 1914. When he returned to the United States, he spent the summer of 1914 in Provincetown.

† Bryson Burroughs, American painter who was curator of paintings at the Metropolitan Museum of Art, New York from 1909 to 1934. His paintings were exhibited in Paris in 1914 at Galerie Levesque.

‡ Henry McBride was an important early supporter of modernism and artists in the Stieglitz group. He was first introduced to Gertrude Stein at 27 rue de Fleurus in the spring of 1913 by Mildred Aldrich.

§ Leo Stein had moved to Settignano, near Florence, in April 1914.

periment of Gertrude Stein in Literary Anarchy," that appeared in the *Boston Evening Transcript* on 11 July 1914. In his article, Rogers lists the titles of some works published by Claire Marie Press and proclaims them "mad," then calls Stein's *Tender Buttons* "madder." He believes that the avant-garde writing published by Evans serves "to express anarchy in art" and introduces Stein's new book as "where literary expression as we know it jumps off into the deep waters of unintelligible derangements of words!"[23].~

[Postcard: Two women sitting on the beach]

[POSTMARK: 1 JULY 1914] PROVINCETOWN, MASS.

Hutch [Hapgood], Neith [Boyce], & I & the kids, Maurice Sterne,* Mary Foote, Bobby Jones all living together. Leo comes in a week. Address here.

M. D.

————

JULY 8 [1914] PROVINCETOWN

Dear Gertrude,

A friend has been staying with us here, Robert Rogers, & he has just written an article for "Boston Transcript" about yr book, etc. called "Anarchy in Art." I have given him your address & he will forward you a copy. I have a good many clippings in a book & will bring it over, & will probably see you in Paris early in August. Neith [Boyce] & I & two sons sail next Wed. July 15, on "Stampalia" for Genoa. I want to see you sure while over. We'l only be there about a month. Did you ever get my long letter from Atlantic City? You never said. Your letters sound very cold & faraway. I haven't heard about sales of yr book—are they going well? They should be at Brentano's in Paris. Will you see about it?

Best love,

Mabel.

* Maurice Sterne, Latvian-born American painter and sculptor who was soon to become Dodge's lover and later her third husband. He had met Gertrude and Leo Stein in Paris when he was studying painting and was one of the three homosexual men portrayed in Stein's word portrait, "Men," included in *Two.*

~At this time, the friendship between Stein and Dodge was, on Stein's part, cooling further, as she intimated, writing less frequently and more reservedly, her letters having a matter-of-fact and impersonal tone. Dodge certainly was aware of this shift, and it continued to trouble her for years.

Stein and Toklas had traveled to London at the beginning of July to meet with the publisher John Lane. While in England, they spent time in Cambridge, where they met the English philosopher Alfred North Whitehead and the poet A. E. Housman at a dinner party. Whitehead and his wife, Evelyn, invited Stein and Toklas to their London house for dinner and to spend the last weekend in July with them at their country home, Lockeridge, near the Salisbury Plain. Before leaving London to visit the Whiteheads, Stein finally signed a contract with John Lane to publish *Three Lives*.[24]~

[JULY 1914] THE KNIGHTSBRIDGE HOTEL
KNIGHTSBRIDGE
LONDON, S.W.

My dear Mabel.

We are in England and have been in the country and are going again. We will be back in Paris about the tenth. Let me know your change of plans. What are your plans.

Love to Neith [Boyce]

Yours

Gertrude.

~While Stein and Toklas were at Lockeridge, World War I broke out. Travel to Paris was not advised, since on 3 August 1914 Germany declared war on France and began approaching its borders. Evelyn Whitehead insisted that Stein and Toklas stay with them in the country rather than return to London: "She was very sweet and we were very unhappy and we liked them and they liked us and we agreed to stay."[25] What had been planned as a weekend visit stretched out for many weeks. Stein and Toklas made a quick trip to London to pick up their belongings and get money from Toklas's bank in California. Stein's funds were in a French bank, and thus unavailable, and so she wired her relatives in Baltimore to send money. They returned to Lockeridge, where they waited out the anxious first weeks of the Great War. In *The Autobiography of Alice B. Toklas*, Stein describes some of her activities and feelings from this time:

> The germans were getting nearer and nearer Paris. One day Doctor Whitehead said to Gertrude Stein . . . have you any copies of your writings or are they all in Paris. They are all in Paris, she said. I did not like to ask, said Doctor Whitehead, but I have been worrying.
>
> The germans were getting nearer and nearer Paris and the last day Gertrude Stein could not leave her room, she sat and mourned. She loved Paris, she thought neither of manuscripts nor of pictures, she thought only of Paris and she was desolate. I came up to her room, I called out, it is alright Paris is saved, the germans are in retreat. She turned away and said, don't tell me these things. But it's true, I said, it is true. And then we wept together.[26]

Meanwhile, Mabel Dodge was in Paris during the German advance upon the city. In the battle of the Marne, which took place at the Marne River from 6 September to 9 September 1914, the Germans were stopped by the Allies and subsequently retreated. Dodge's initial response to the declaration of war was markedly different from Stein's. While Carl Van Vechten and Neith Boyce hurried to book passage back to the United States, Dodge remained indifferent: "As for me, it didn't mean a thing. It didn't interest or excite me, or even reach me. I dwelt alone in a deep contempt for wars, for anxieties, for humanities. My isolation at that time was doubtless at its zenith."[27] However, when she received a cable from John Reed asking her to wait for him in Naples and then travel with him to Paris to witness the war, Dodge soon became temporarily energized by the spectacle of war. She waited for Reed while Carl and Neith accompanied her son John back to the United States, her stubborn resolve to stay creating a rift in her friendship with Van Vechten.[28] Once she was in Paris with Reed, Dodge fell back into her despair, likely fueled by seeing his excitement for all the activity around him that inevitably competed with her for his attention. Dodge wrote an article about her exposure in Paris to the soldiers of the Great War that was published in the November 1914 issue of the *Masses*. As she explained in her memoirs, her article, entitled "The Secret of War: The Look on the Face of Men Who

Have Been Killing—And What Women Think About It," described "the happiness of those men in Paris. The cafés surged with officers in brand-new uniforms and shining eyes. The male population in Paris was as lustful as the Roman mob."[29] Dodge interviewed soldiers, exposed the sexual power that is stimulated by battle, and pointed out the role of machine guns in dehumanizing warfare. She ended her article with the following statement: "The only hope of permanent peace lies in a woman's war against war."[30]

In her first letter to Stein after the beginning of the war, Dodge encourages her to return to Paris now that the danger seems to have passed. ∽

WED. 16 [CIRCA SEPTEMBER 1914] PARIS
16 RUE D'ASSAS

Dearest Gertrude,

When are you both coming back? Paris is wonderful and in fact was so all thro' the danger of the siege. You wouldn't have recognized it as the same place . . . No one can ever talk any more about "those excitable french people"—for they are, at bottom, marvels of sang froid & levelheadedness. I have been here for ten days and I never have admired the french as I do now.

Of course the danger is over now & people are beginning, some to stream back, others to trickle back. Soon they'l all be here once more . . . except the americans somewhat cursorily advised to go home by the ambassador who grew very tierd of their repeated questions.

Get a passport from our ambassador in London & come back soon. I have taken two or three rooms here & expect to stay awhile. Neith [Boyce,] boys & Carl [Van Vechten] sailed for home Aug 22 on an emigrant boat, she left her love to you.

This pen is a disaster—I can't write any more but I want just to tell you I want to see you & please answer when you think you'l come.

Best love,
Mabel.

THURSDAY. [SEPTEMBER 1914] 16 RUE D'ASSAS
[PARIS]

Dear Gertrude,

What about [Marsden] Hartley?* I wish you'd write & tell me
what you imagine his situation is. You know how he is in circumstances now. What do you suppose is happening to him? I think it's
useless to write. What do you think about wiring him to come to
Paris for the present? I have an extra room he could use.

Let me know what you think.

Yrs,

Mabel.

∼Dodge and Reed went to London, where Dodge became even
more miserable at his continual absence and decided to return alone
to New York. While in London, she saw Gertrude Stein, who had
not yet been able to leave. On 17 October 1914, Stein and Toklas
finally boarded a boat to return to Paris, in the company of Belgian
soldiers, their "first experience of the tired but watchful eyes of
soldiers."[31] Arriving in Paris late at night, they found it "beautiful
and unviolated"[32] and were relieved to be home.∼

TUESDAY NIGHT [CIRCA OCTOBER 1914] YORK HOTEL
ALBEMARLE STREET, W.
[LONDON]

Dearest Gertrude,

I couldn't sell my berth, waited all day to see if I could—& so I
am sailing tomorrow. I wish I'd seen you again.

Love & all good wishes for a
peaceful winter.

Mabel.

* Hartley was living in Berlin at this time, where he remained until December
1915 when he returned to New York.

[Postcard: Cossack officer]

[POSTMARK: PARIS, 30 DECEMBER 1914] [27 RUE DE FLEURUS]

My dear Mabel

How goes it. I had a letter from [Marsden] Hartley. He seems well and happy. Poor old [Arnold] Ronnebeck however has narrowly escaped death and is deaf in one ear and his nerves are shattered.* We are peaceful in Paris and enthusiastic. Happy New Year to you

Yours

Gertrude.

---

* Rönnebeck suffered a war injury that resulted in deafness in his left ear (Townsend Ludington, *Marsden Hartley,* 122).

~

1915–1934

Back in New York, Mabel Dodge "said good-by forever to Reed in my heart" and "turned once more to Nature and Art and tried to live in them."[1] In this quest, she was immediately drawn to Isadora Duncan's dance, identifying with its energy: "It seemed to me I recognized what she did in the dance, and that it was like my own daily, nightly return to the Source. Power rose in her from her Center and flowed vividly along her limbs before our eyes in living beauty and delight."[2] Isadora Duncan had arrived in New York in January 1915 and appealed to her audience at Carnegie Hall to provide her with a school so that she could teach dance to poor American children. Mabel Dodge, along with Walter Lippmann and the social worker and anthropologist John Collier, enthusiastically began to try to help Duncan with her plans, but soon abandoned their efforts as she emerged as "upsetting and disturbing."[3] Dodge and Collier then turned to help Elizabeth Duncan, Isadora's older sister, establish a school where she could teach, as she herself described, "'a way of living'"[4] that was inspired by art and nature. They purchased two houses in Croton, New York, overlooking the Hudson River, where the school soon opened and Dodge enrolled her son John. Elizabeth Duncan became for Dodge "one of the few great women friends I have had at intervals during my life."[5]

While Mabel Dodge had resolved to forget about Reed, he returned to New York at the end of January 1915 wanting to resume their relationship. He had left Freddie Lee after a brief involvement. According to Dodge, Reed was convinced that he "could not live without me."[6] He professed his love and promised marriage, having already purchased her a wedding ring. However, Dodge was unmoved: "But this time I was determined to go on possessing myself and not to lose my balance. . . . I would not be fool enough to lose all I had gained, for I had arrived at this security after a great deal of searching and unhappiness."[7] Despite her professed resolve, Dodge remained fitfully involved with Reed until he left again for Europe in March. When he returned in the fall, Dodge was living with the American painter and sculptor Maurice Sterne and no longer interested in Reed. In December 1915, Reed met the playwright and journalist Louise Bryant, whom he married in 1916. They both traveled to Russia and wrote about the Russian Revolution, remaining together until Reed died of typhus in Moscow in 1920.

The winter of 1915 was a time when Dodge gathered into herself, withdrawing her attention from many of the causes that she had previously supported. As she reported, "I just lost interest in that fabricated puppet, Mabel Dodge, as a Creature of Importance in her Time, and I longed only for peace and more peace."[8] However, she did not lose her interest in Gertrude Stein, as she continued her efforts at reviving their friendship.✧

[CIRCA JANUARY 1915] [23 FIFTH AVENUE]

Dearest Gertrude—

This is a great winter for me. New York is more interesting than ever, and I wish to goodness you would come over here.

I want to be where you are and when I saw you in London you were the strongest drag on keeping me over there. But I knew I had to get back & it was good that I did. I am up to my neck in [Elizabeth and Isadora] Duncans this winter. John Collier & I got a school started for one of them, & for Isadora we are engaged in the maddest project of getting her the Armory where she can teach a thousand unemployed people's poor children to <u>dance</u> & feed & clothe them & charge the rich people sums to come in & see her teach 'em. And we're going to get up some great out of door festivals for her in the Stadium at Cambridge & in New Haven's <u>Bowl</u>! We're perfectly insane in our plans but sometimes insanity works!

We hear from Marsden [Hartley] sometimes & the accounts of Berlin are stunning!* Press clippings about you still come in—it is a habit now to quote you "as Gertrude Stein would say"—

I am keeping them in a book which is <u>yours</u> & which you can have whenever you want it. And you <u>have</u> a school. People are copying you. I heard from Leo the other day. Quite jocose!

---

* Hartley had written to Dodge in October 1914: "Here in Berlin one simply knows there is a war that is all. The people are calm thoughtful and as always wonderfully undemonstrative—they know well the secret of keeping one's head. . . . Up to this hour my friends in the war are all alive—Rönnebeck his brother cousin & two others" (Hartley to Dodge, October 1914, MDLC).

Gertrude I wish to <u>goodness</u> you were here. It's no use writing that, I suppose. But you <u>would</u> be amused by New York. [John] Reed fell in love with Freddie Lee the week after I left him in Paris, & they've been going thro' horrors. But you will have heard all that. That immediately turned me into a mother to Reed, and I've been happy ever since.

Write a good letter & tell me what is going on, & how everything is.

Always yours,

M. D.

[CIRCA MARCH 1915] [23 FIFTH AVENUE]

Dearest Gertrude,

Here is a letter from the editor of "Vanity Fair."* I wrote him that I was sending you his letter & perhaps you could do something about it. Can you? Do you belong to a Press-Clipping Bureau? Hardly a day goes by that some notice of you comes in. I am keeping them all in case you don't get 'em.

[John] Reed came back & we took it up where we'd left off. He leaves again today for Russia, Constantinople, etc.

<u>Write sometimes.</u>

Yours

Mabel.

⌒Mabel Dodge provided the playwright Avery Hopwood with a letter of introduction to Gertrude Stein. Van Vechten was close friends with Hopwood and had also encouraged him to meet Stein. Although Hopwood first met Stein in Paris around 1915, they did not have consistent contact until the early 1920s.[9] Stein apparently came to enjoy Hopwood's company, as she later wrote to Van Vechten on 15 March 1923: "We have been seeing a good deal of Avery, I like him very much, there was a time in between when he seemed to have lost some of his charm but this time it has come back mellowed and increased."[10] In *The Autobiography of Alice B. Toklas*, Stein wrote that out of all the people whom Van Vechten sent to Stein with letters of introduction, "the first and perhaps the one she has liked the best was Avery Hopwood. The friendship lasted until Avery's death. . . . They were very fond of each other."[11]

*Unlocated enclosure.

Hopwood's best known play, *The Bat* (1920), was a mystery written with Mary Roberts Rinehart. His play *Our Little Wife* (1916), a farce about wife-swapping among New York's upper classes, was the inspiration for Stein's *A List. Inspired by Avery Hopwood* (1923), a play visually organized with a list of names in the left column, all beginning with the letters "Ma," which was included in *Operas and Plays* (1913–31; 1932).[12]

[Whitman motto]

[1915 ?] [23 Fifth Avenue]

Dear Gertrude,

This is to introduce Mr. Avery Hopwood. I don't need to tell you about him & his persuits because, as usual, you will know more about him in two minutes than I could in two years!

Yours—

Mabel.

In May 1915, Gertrude Stein and Alice B. Toklas traveled to Mallorca, where they planned to spend several weeks but remained for a year. They welcomed the peacefulness of the island in contrast to the chaos and hardships in Paris. This was a productive time for Stein, whose poems and plays from this period are quite personal and more approachable and readable than her earlier works. Many of the poems describe her domestic life with Alice B. Toklas. She also acknowledged the effects of war in her poems, such as, "What this war teaches us. This war teaches us to be certain of our hates" and "We have made a vow never to speak to a german."[13]

[Postcard: Saleri II]

[POSTMARK: Valencia, 12 May 1915]

My dear Mabel,

We are here at Mallorca. What are your summer plans. We are to be here awhile anyway. There is no news xcept the war which we read industriously in all languages. Continue to address Paris, that will always reach.

Always yours

Gertrude.

~When they heard that the battle of Verdun had been won by the Allies, Gertrude Stein and Alice B. Toklas decided to return to Paris in June 1916. They soon volunteered for the American Fund for French Wounded and were given the job of delivering supplies to hospitals. Stein ordered a Ford van through her cousin Bird Gans in New York and learned to drive. Stein and Toklas called their van "Auntie," "after Gertrude Stein's aunt Pauline who always behaved admirably in emergencies and behaved fairly well most times if she was properly flattered."[14]

At the same time that Stein and Toklas were working to support the war effort, Dodge was getting involved with Maurice Sterne and beginning psychoanalysis. At a dance recital given by students from the Elizabeth Duncan School in 1915, Dodge first met Sterne, who was to become her third husband in August 1917. She had spotted him immediately in the crowd:

> What I liked about him was his handsome look of suffering. A dark torture ennobled him and added a great deal of dignity to that countenance. . . . He was positively enveloped in a cloud of secrecy and caution. . . . That interested me. I wondered what it was all about.[15]

Dodge and Sterne soon began a relationship, its initial moments celebrated in Sterne's executing a series of tempera drawings of Dodge that were displayed at the Montross Gallery in New York in October 1915. In a letter to Stein dated 24 October 1915, Van Vechten described these drawings as "almost nudes" of Dodge. "In one," he wrote, "she is reading a book with her feet on the chandelier."[16] However, the union between Sterne and Dodge was ridden with desperate passion and conflict that often left Dodge feeling depressed and dependent. In an effort to find some relief from her turmoil, in January 1916 she entered into psychoanalysis with Smith Ely Jelliffe, and in the fall of the same year switched to analysis with the prominent psychiatrist A. A. Brill. Often a pioneer in new movements, Dodge was one of the early analysands in the United States and an avid promoter of the benefits of analysis. Although Freud's lectures at Clark University in 1909 had marked the formal introduction of his revolutionary theories to an American audience, the first significant popularizations of psychoanalysis were concentrated in the year 1915, which saw a flurry of articles about Freud and his ideas.

In the spring of 1915, Dodge had begun spending long stretches of time at Finney Farm in Croton-on-Hudson, which she leased for two years. The property consisted of a main farmhouse with a number of outbuildings that Dodge put to use as refuges for her artist and writer friends, who visited and sometimes needed a place to work. Among her guests from this time were Marsden Hartley, Bobby Jones, Leo Stein, and the poet Bayard Boyeson. In response to a non-extant card from Stein, Dodge wrote to her at the beginning of 1917, providing her with news of their mutual friends and of her latest interest in interior design. On 13 January 1917, Dodge ran an advertisement in the *New Republic* offering her consulting services: "Mrs. Mabel Dodge is prepared to assist in the furnishing and decorating of rooms, to supply ideas of her own, or to express those of her clients."[17].~

JAN. 14. [19]17. 23 FIFTH AVENUE

Dearest Gertrude

I was awfully glad to get your card. I had been thinking of you quite a lot lately. Mabel Weekes [i.e., Weeks] spent the day with me out on my farm yesterday & of course we talked about you.

Why don't you come over here? Leo is around all the time. He is coming in here to tea today. I wish you'd answer his letters. I think it would make him feel good. He's always reading your letters to other people. I don't think he's very happy. He tried to go to Paris but he couldn't because he was the son of an alien enemy—whatever that means!

Ducie Haweis flashed up over here—but got in almost at once with all the wrong kind of people—I mean the kind one tries & passes up finally! Muriel Draper is here working under [Paul] Chalfin & doing efficient work. I don't see her much.

[Myra] Edgerly is here—saw her last week & she's coming to dinner Wednesday. She's <u>always</u> amusing. She had a husband for a while & then she didn't. Thats all I know about that!

Stephen Haweis has gone to live in the Bahamas. Mildred Aldrich's books are having a success here.* [Marsden] Hartley is in Bermuda.†

---

* In addition to her most famous book, *A Hilltop on the Marne* (1915), which described her observations of the 1915 battle of the Marne, Aldrich had published two other books around this time, *Told in a French Garden* (1916) and *On the Edge of the War Zone* (1917).

† Hartley spent the winter of 1916–17 in Bermuda, returning to New York in May 1917.

People go on quoting you in papers, & [Robert] Coady is advertising an expensive book of yours in which you've written your name!*

Hutch [Hapgood] complains more & more. Neith [Boyce] is hardworking & the children are growing up every which way!

I have my farm at Croton overlooking Hudson river, where I have cows, pigs, chickens, etc., and where I prefer to be but I have my apartment here where I stay two or three nights a week on account of people & thinks. One can't stay here solidly more than a year or two. It's too hectic & noisy & alloverish! I have just decided to be in business because I like to fix up rooms. I enclose my card!

I'd love to see you again. There's never been a day that I haven't loved you a lot—

Mabel

Do you know about psycho-analysis?

∽Having impulsively decided to marry Maurice Sterne the morning of 23 August 1917 at Finney Farm, Dodge soon tired of the relationship and of Sterne's reportedly wandering eyes. She sent him to New Mexico, explaining: "'It's no use, Maurice. We can't make a go of it here. One of us must leave. And I want to stay here. I'm going to send you out to the Southwest. I've heard there are wonderful things to paint. Indians.'"[18] After Sterne left, Dodge went to a medium who saw the following images while holding Dodge's hand: "'Then you are surrounded by many people—they are pressing up around you ... dark people ... dark faces—they are Indians, I guess. You are to help them—you are for them.'"[19] Sterne had written letters to Dodge encouraging her to join him in Santa Fe, but she had no interest in such a journey. However, one night she had a dream in which Sterne's face was succeeded by an Indian face:

> ... before my eyes I saw a large image of Maurice's head. Just
> his face, there before me, with its handsome features and its
> alien Oriental expression. It frightened me and I shuddered.
> Then, as I gazed his began to fade and another face replaced it,
> with green leaves twinkling and glistening all around it—a

---

* Coady published Stein's "Letters and Parcels and Wool" (1916) with Stein's signature on each copy. The piece is included in *As Fine As Melanctha*.

dark face with wide-apart eyes that stared at me with a strong look, intense and calm. This was an Indian face and it affected me like a medicine after the one that had been before it. I sighed and let it take me and cleanse me. . . .[20]

Convinced that something was calling her, in December 1917 Dodge left New York for New Mexico. Disliking Santa Fe at first, she set off for Taos with Sterne and quickly decided that it would be her new home. She signed a lease on 1 January 1918 for some rented rooms in town, where she and Sterne lived until the summer. Dodge was immediately taken by the Pueblo Indians at the Taos pueblo and became a regular visitor, drawn as she was to their otherness and their rituals and ceremonies. She invited the Indians to her home where they came to play their music and dance.

Dodge became deeply involved in Indian culture in Taos, attending Pueblo ceremonies and longing to be like the Indians she observed. She cut her hair and wore shawls, joining the Pueblo women for several hours each day in order to become more like them:

> I knew I could arrive at this unconscious, full equilibrium, but that I could only do so by adapting myself. I longed to simply *be* so, as they were, but I knew I must make it for myself as I went along. Not for me, alas, the simple, unthinking harmonies of life; but for me—yes! I thought fiercely— this sumptuous peace and content. . . .[21]

Dodge was overwhelmed and inspired by her first hearing of Indian music in December 1917:

> For the first time in my life, then, I heard the voice of the One coming from the Many—I who until then had been taught to look for the wonders of infinite divisibility and variety, for the many in the one. . . .
>
> The singular raging lust for individuality and separateness had been impelling me all my years as it did everyone else on earth—when all of a sudden I was brought up against the Tribe, where a different instinct ruled, . . . where virtue lay in wholeness instead of in dismemberment.
>
> So when I heard that great Indian chorus singing for the first time, I felt a strong new life was present there enfolding me.[22]

Soon after this experience, Dodge met Antonio Luhan, a tall and striking Pueblo Indian from the Tiwa community. Dodge immediately recognized him: "[He] looked at me for the first time, with a quick glance that penetrated to the depths with an instantaneous recognition, and I saw his was the face that had blotted out Maurice's in my dream—the same face, the same eyes, involuntarily intense, with the living fire in their depths."[23] A slow courtship followed, as Luhan, who was called Tony, introduced Dodge to the wonders of his country and the ways of the Indians.

Dodge wrote to Stein from New Mexico in a further effort to rekindle their friendship.〜'

FEB. 6 [CIRCA 1918] TAOS. NEW MEXICO.

Dear Gertrude

Just rc'd enclosed & answered it as follows:

Dear Mr. Cowen*—

Your letter followed me to New Mexico. I am very glad if I can give you a little furthur news of Miss Gertrude Stein.

She has been writing continuously & her work shows great development, in depth, in significance & in technique.

She is driving an ambulance at present in the South of France. She continues her own work & recently a thing of hers relating to the war, came out in "Life."†

She has, certainly, a number of followers, in England as well as America, & her influence has been remarked in many of the younger prose writers & poets. She has influenced Donald Evans, a remarkable poet himself, Mina Loy, Louise Norton Arensburg‡ & in fact almost all of the younger writing set in England & here.

I believe that the strongest influence on Miss Stein's own expression was the art of the modern painters, Picasso, Matisse, Hartley & others, with whose pictures she was surrounded. As you remember I noted this in the article you mention having seen some time ago.§ I believe that if you will

---

* Unidentified.
† Stein, "Relief Work in France," *Life* (27 December 1917): 1076.
‡ Unidentified. It is possible that Dodge is referring to Louise Stevens Arensberg, the wife of Walter C. Arensberg, a poet and art collector.
§ Dodge is referring to her article about Stein that appeared in *Arts & Decoration* in March 1913.

write to Miss Stein herself she will be glad to help you in anyway you wish. Address her 27 Rue de Fleurus, Paris.

Sincerely—
etc——

Now Gertrude—I am writing this in bed without any lap board so don't go drawing any conclusions about the writing—which, it must be admitted, is fierce.
Long to see you again.

Best love,
Mabel

———

[Postcard: Santiago, Santa Fe Fiesta]

[POSTMARK: NEEDLES, CALIFORNIA, 12 MARCH] [1918 ?]

Do write a letter sometimes. How are you? Aren't you coming sometime?

Love from
Mabel S.[terne]*

In June 1918, at Tony Luhan's urging, Mabel Dodge purchased twelve acres of land in Taos at the foot of the Sangre de Cristo mountains that included a three-room adobe house, orchards, a large field, and a stream. In her memoirs, Dodge describes her feeling about buying the property:

> . . . when I bought the Taos place my feeling for Tony made me take root in it and I began to live in a way that was new to me. . . .
>
> Of course acquiring a piece of this land here was a symbolic move, a picture of what was happening inside me. I had to have a place of my own to live on where I could take root and make a life in a home. This earth and Tony were identical in my imagination and his, and I wanted to become a part of them, and the day the place became mine, it was as though I had been accepted by the universe. In that day I became centered and ceased the lonesome pilgrimage forever.[24]

Luhan was in charge of the Indians and Mexicans who built the

---

* Stein had written to Van Vechten on 24 March 1918: "Mabel Dodge is or is not Mrs. Sterne not that it very much matters" (CVVC).

additions to the house. Not fully completed until the early 1930s, Dodge's adobe estate, which came to be called Los Gallos because of the Mexican ceramic chickens mounted on the roof, expanded to seventeen rooms. With the same division of responsibilities that she had practiced with Edwin Dodge in renovating the Villa Curonia, Mabel Dodge concentrated on the interior while Tony Luhan directed the building of the exterior.

In her book *Winter in Taos* (1935), Dodge describes the evolution of Los Gallos:

> The house grew slowly and it stretches on and on. At one end it piles up, for over the Big Room there is the bedroom where Tony sleeps, next to my room, and a big sleeping porch off of it; and from this room one climbs a steep little stairway up into a kind of lookout room, made of helioglass set in wooden columns on all four sides, where one has the views of all the valley. . . . There is nothing on this bare, blue-painted floor but some *serapes,* and up here under the sky, winter and summer, one can lie in the sunshine and bathe in it until "untied are the knots in the heart," for there is nothing like the sun for smoothing out all difficulties.[25]

The expansive "Big Room" was built with a ceiling of saplings and mud and was filled with French, Italian, and Oriental furniture in pale colors. Its walls were hung with Indian blankets.[26] The dining room's viga ceiling was painted in earth-colored stripes to mimic an Indian blanket, the floor covered in red-brown and black tiles, and the windows hung with red-brown gauze curtains. During one of his visits, D. H. Lawrence painted over the windows in one of the bathrooms with brightly colored designs.

In *Winter in Taos,* Mabel Dodge chronicles some of the contents of Los Gallos:

> And how I have loved it, this house built on different levels, a room or two at a time. The gatherings of all my past life are deposited here. Besides the regular furniture and pictures and books that came from Italy and France and New York, letters, in packets, that date all the way back to Buffalo, are stuffed into cabinets and drawers, and all kinds of curious odds and ends that have followed me down the years are tucked away in corners and shelves. . . .
>
> In the linen room, upon the top shelves, there are piles of remnants filled with the sweet smell of cedar with which the

place is lined. Handwoven bits from Asolo, old curtains from the Villa Curonia, pieces of French embroidered dresses. . . . Presents of Indian beadwork, oddments of basketry and deerskin, Renaissance velvet, ecclesiastical gold fringe, are side by side with my Grandmother Ganson's patchwork quilt . . .[27]

In her last estate, Dodge mixed elements from her richly cultured past and her more earth-based present, succeeding in creating a harmonious environment for her many remaining years with Tony Luhan.

Mabel Dodge and Gertrude Stein had evidently lost all but sporadic contact by this time. In the fall of 1917, Gertrude Stein and Alice B. Toklas had been reassigned to Nîmes for their work with the American Fund for French Wounded. They were there the day the Armistice was declared on 11 November 1918. With the war over, Stein and Toklas were again reassigned to Alsace, where they were to provide supplies to the Alsatian refugees left virtually homeless by the war. Finally, in the spring of 1919, they had finished their work and drove Auntie back to Paris. They were forced to order a new car, a Ford two-seater, to replace Auntie, which had labored hard for the war effort. Their new car arrived in Paris in December 1920 and was named "Godiva," as explained by Alice B. Toklas's account of her first impressions of the car: "I remarked that she was nude. There was nothing on her dashboard, neither clock nor ashbox, nor cigarette lighter. Godiva, was Gertrude Stein's answer. The new car was baptised . . ."[28]

In Mabel Dodge's life, Maurice Sterne soon bowed to the competition of Tony Luhan and left Taos in August 1918. This left Dodge free to open herself to Luhan and to relinquish her old way of living, as she relates in her memoirs:

"Tony! You know if we come together now there's no turning back. Do you feel that?"

"Yes." He nodded. "I know this not play. This forever."

"I mean, I know it is like going across a deep gulf on a bridge that goes with me, is gone when I reach you. I will not be able to return because you will make all of my own kind of life unreal for me. It has always been more or less unreal—you will make it impossible."

"I give you a new life, a new world—a true one, I think."[29]

Dodge plunged into her new life with Tony Luhan, in the process transforming herself as she lessened her hold on the white world and embraced the spirituality and community of the Indian one.

Dodge sent Stein a greeting from Taos and Stein replied cryptically.〜

DECEMBER 1921. TAOS!

Best wishes for the New Year from Taos!

———

[Postcard: Ingres, Portrait de la Belle Zélie]

[POSTMARK: PARIS [?] 10 JAN 1922]

It smells but not as good as here
                                Gertrude.

〜In February 1922, Carl Van Vechten's first novel, *Peter Whiffle: His Life and Works,* was published. The book is a thinly disguised account of the Mabel Dodge circle, with Dodge herself appearing as the character Edith Dale. In the novel, Van Vechten credits Dodge with having organized the Armory Show—an exaggeration of her actual role, which included donating money and actively participating in the preparations. In *Peter Whiffle,* Van Vechten describes the atmosphere of Edith Dale's "evenings," a direct reference to Mabel Dodge's salons:

> The crowds flocked to her place and she made them comfortable. Pinchbottles and Curtis Cigarettes, poured by the hundreds from their neat pine boxes into white bowls, trays of Virginia ham and white Gorgonzola sandwiches. . . . Arthur Lee and Lee Simonson, Marsden Hartley, Andrew Dasburg, Max Weber, Charles Demuth, Bobby Jones—just out of college and not yet a designer of scenery. . . . Arguments and discussions floated in the air, were caught and twisted and hauled and tied, until the white salon itself was no longer static. There were undercurrents of emotion and sex.
>
> Edith was the focus of the group, grasping this faint idea or that frail theory, tossing it back a complete or wrecked formula, or she sat quietly with her hands folded. . . . She was the amalgam which held the incongruous group together; she was the alembic that turned the dross to gold.[30]

In 1922, Mabel Dodge sent Gertrude Stein a copy of Van Vechten's *Peter Whiffle*. On the same day that Stein wrote the following letter to Dodge, she also wrote to Van Vechten about his novel, getting in a jab at Mabel Dodge:

> "Am I in it" there is one and certainly one could never be more pleasantly more faithfully nor more gently in it than when one is put in it by you. I am awfully pleased with your book. You are indeed the most modern the least sentimental and the most gently persistent of romantics. . . . Mabel Dodge was funny. She was afraid I would miss the book so she sent me a copy. Anyway we all like it.[31]

≈

[Postcard: Aix-en-Provence—Hotel Guigou]

[POSTMARK: PARIS, 2 JUNE 1922]27 RUE DE FLEURUS
My dear Mabel,

Thanks for the book. He did you quite nicely didn't he. Come in but not out and lend a hand. Don't you want to send me a photo of yourself being an Indian

Gertrude.

∼Although there is a gap in the extant letters between Dodge and Stein from June 1922 to October 1925, references in both Stein's and Van Vechten's letters to each other indicate both that Dodge had written to Stein during this period and that Stein was curious about Dodge's activities in Taos.

In September 1921, Mabel Dodge invited D. H. Lawrence to Taos after reading *Sons and Lovers* (1913), *Psychoanalysis and the Unconscious* (1921), and *Sea and Sardinia* (1921). It was Lawrence's travel writing in particular that inspired Dodge to try to lure him to New Mexico, as she believed that he could help her articulate her experience with Indian culture, thereby broadening the scope of her audience: "I wanted Lawrence to understand things for me. To take *my* experience, *my* material, *my* Taos, and to formulate it all into a magnificent creation. That was what I wanted him for."[32] She engaged in an active correspondence with him until he arrived in Taos with his wife, Frieda, in the early fall of 1922. In a letter to Van Vechten dated 15 March 1923, Stein inquired cattily about Dodge's involvement with D. H. Lawrence: "Do you ever see Mabel any more or is she completely mired in D. [H.] Lawrence, who it seems does not want to put her in a book, Totems not being really interesting."[33] On 8 April 1923, Stein again wrote to Van Vechten: "Anyhow Lawrence seems to have left, do you think he will find Mexico calmer or just safer. It will be awful if Mabel has gotten back a taste for white man."[34] Lawrence's stay in New Mexico did not yield the results Dodge had hoped for, as their relationship was characterized by many arguments and mutual disillusionment. However, Dodge did succeed in making her way into Lawrence's novel *The Plumed Serpent* (1926), in which the character Kate is based partially on her.[35]

In December 1922, Dodge was divorced from Maurice Sterne, legally clearing the way for her marriage to Antonio Luhan on 23 April 1923.[36] Stein had heard about Dodge's marriage, as she wrote to Van Vechten in May 1923: "And Van what were Mabel's business reasons, Mina Loy suggested that Mabel was marrying for John's sake or is it to show the end of an epoch. I had a tender postal from Mabel just before the event but the event was not mentioned, I am rather xpecting to see her soon aren't you."[37] Stein seemed to enjoy any scandal concerning Dodge. She wrote to Van Vechten again on 31 May 1923: "She [Jane Heap] said that Dasburg said that Antonio deserted Mabel two days after the wedding, that might account for one's not hearing from her but it does not sound very likely does it. Business reasons are business reasons."[38] And again on 5 August 1923: "Not a word from Mabel at all. Lo, the poor Indian."[39] Van Vechten wrote to Stein on 22 October 1923 after having heard from Dodge that she saw herself in a character in his book, *The Blind Bow-Boy* (1923):

> Mabel's letter about The Bow-Boy almost knocks me flat. She identifies herself with Campaspe, which, of course, she isn't: says it's the most perfect character in fiction: "showing the perfect equilibrium which results from a soul in utter conflict." Not a word about the chief! and to this day I don't know how to spell her FIFTH name.[40]

In fact, in an earlier letter to Stein, Van Vechten had quipped about Dodge and *The Blind Bow-Boy:* "Mabel will not like this book. She is not in it."[41]

In 1924, Mabel Dodge began writing her memoirs, at the strong suggestion of A. A. Brill who believed it would be a curative process for her. Once she committed herself to writing, Dodge devoted herself to her task with fervor, as her friend the painter Dorothy Brett observed:

When she started to write her memoirs, she wrote incessantly, without stopping, day after day, lying on her sofa with a copy book and pencil. She poured herself untiringly into those books. The energy concentration was boundless, until all of a sudden the book was finished and Mabel resumed normal life—which was energetic enough, Heaven knows.[42]

In her memoirs, which were published in four volumes in 1933, 1935, 1936, and 1937, Dodge described her life from childhood to the beginning of her transformative relationship with Antonio Luhan in Taos. She was often remarkably open about her own idiosyncracies and also exposed those of others. It was a daring move to have her memoirs published at that time, as they described unflattering aspects of Dodge as well as her family and friends. As she explained, however, about her first volume of memoirs that dealt with growing up in Victorian Buffalo, "if Background can make a few grownups, with guilty, intimate childhood memories, realize theirs was a common and almost universal experience, then I have done the right thing in publishing it."[43]

Dodge wrote to Stein after learning of the publication of *The Making of Americans* in 1925 by Robert McAlmon in France.~

Oct. 7 [1925] Taos, New Mexico

Dearest Gertrude,

I remember so well leaving Paris with your big mms [i.e., mss] in my hands;—in the station I dropped it—it was open—I was reading it as I got on the train—the train jerked—some pages dropped under the wheels—Oh dear—What a horror! And now it's printed. I am so anxious to have it, but have lost the address—and anyway I want you to write in it—<u>so</u> can you get me a copy & send it C.O.D. as I also don't know the price of it.

I have been working on an autobiography since last December. The first vol. is finished, called "Background," just the first 22 years until I went to Italy. It is not to be published but put away until a few people are dead! But I am going to let some people read it. Do you want to? Willa Cather* & Carl V.[an] V.[echten] & some others who have seen it say it's the best record of that period in America ('80 & '90) ever done. Anyone who reads it must give me a criti-

---

* Willa Cather, American novelist who had first visited Taos in 1912 and stayed with Dodge at Los Gallos in 1925 (Rudnick, *Mabel Dodge Luhan*, 188). New Mexico figures prominently in two of her novels, *The Professor's House* (1925) and *Death Comes for the Archbishop* (1927).

cism to bury with it in the safety deposit box to be unearthed in better days. Do you want to or <u>da</u>?

[Arnold] Ronnebeck has been here this summer, & has just come in & sends his best regards. I <u>wish</u> I could see you again & want to hear your <u>laugh</u>. Will you get those publishers to send the book soon? I'll review it for Vanity Fair or something. Write me a nice long letter & tell me about yourself.

With the same affection as ever (in spite of the <u>terrible</u> things you said to Neith [Boyce] & Hutch [Hapgood] about me—that I was a "sweet woman from the middle west." You won't think me so sweet if you ever read the Memoirs, though!)

Affectionately,

Mabel. (Luhan)

⌁Stein's final extant communication to Dodge is a postcard with a rather impersonal message. Dodge's quick reply seems to reflect the terse quality of Stein's note.⌁

[Postcard: Hunting scene with dead deer]

[POSTMARK: PARIS, 28 DECEMBER 1925] [27 RUE DE FLEURUS]
Happy new year Mabel the season's greetings to you

Gertrude

[Postcard: Los Gallos]

JAN. 11 [POSTMARK: 12 JAN 1926] [TAOS]

Nice to get a word from you.

<u>*Mabel*</u>.

⌁From January 1926 until November 1929, there is a large gap in the existing letters from Dodge to Stein, although the correspondence between Van Vechten and Stein from this time again reveals Stein's ongoing love of gossip about Dodge. Stein wrote to Van Vechten on 11 August 1927, commenting on his strong affinity for black culture:

> I know why you like niggers so much . . . it is not because they are primitive but because they have a narrow but a very long civilisation behind them. . . . Of course Mabel and her Indian business is wrong because they were an undeveloped people

and the Indians learn but the niggers don't which is their problem.[44]

She wrote again on 20 September 1927 after having received the new edition of *Peter Whiffle:* "Thanks so much for the new Peter Whiffle. . . . Janet [Scudder?] says thanks for Mabel only it is sweeter than she was but then she was sweet . . ."[45] On 26 April 1928, Stein wrote to Van Vechten about her visit with Edwin Dodge: "Poor dear Mabel and Edwin has been with us, it is hard to know whether Edwin is or was Mabel and Mabel seems rather to lose it."[46]

In February 1929, the composer Virgil Thomson gave a private performance of Stein's *Four Saints in Three Acts* (1927), a plotless opera by Stein for which he had written the music and now was working to promote. As Van Vechten relates in a letter to Stein from that month, Dodge was enthusiastic about the joint venture:

> Virgil Thomson came & played "Four Saints in Three Acts" to a select crowd which included Mabel Luhan, Muriel Draper, les Stettheimers, . . . etc. & everybody liked it so much that yesterday I cabled you. I liked it so much that I wanted to hear it all over again right away. Mabel liked it so much that she said it should be done & it would finish opera just as Picasso had finished old painting.[47]

Dodge continued to supply letters of introduction to Stein, this time for the painter Loren Mozley, who was a member of the Taos Art Association. Mozley's letter to Stein that accompanied this note is dated 29 December 1929 and explains that he knows Dodge from New Mexico and would like to meet Stein "when you may be inclined to meet someone of such vague reccommendations."[48]⌁

NOV 12 [1929] LOS GALLOS
TAOS, NEW MEXICO

Dear Gertrude—

This will introduce Loren Mosley [i.e., Mozley] whom I believe you will like. I would "appreciate" a note from you sometime!

Affectionately
Mabel.

⌁In the intervening years before the final group of letters from Dodge to Stein in 1934, Dodge had remained in Taos and cultivated friendships with such figures as the artist Georgia O'Keeffe, the poet Robinson Jeffers, and the writers Thornton Wilder and Willa Cather. The first volume of her memoirs, *Background,* was published in 1933, the same year that Gertrude Stein's *The Autobiography of Alice B. Toklas* was published. During these years Stein and Toklas had embarked on a private publishing venture to put into print Stein's unpublished works. Stein christened the edition of works "Plain Edition" and was forced to sell Picasso's *Woman with a Fan* in order to raise the funds for their project. The first volume was published on 5 January 1931 and titled *Lucy Church Amiably,* a romantic novel. The second issue of the Plain Edition, the poem *Before the Flowers of Friendship Faded Friendship Faded,* was brought out in May 1931, and the third volume, *How to Write,* was published in November 1931.

After the critical and financial success of *The Autobiography of Alice B. Toklas* following its serialization in the *Atlantic Monthly* and its publication by Harcourt, Brace in 1933, Van Vechten encouraged Stein to travel to the United States for a lecture tour. The writer Sherwood Anderson also suggested a trip: "Why don't you and Alice come to America as a great adventure next summer, Ford around, come see us and others?"[49] In the summer of 1934, Stein decided to make the trip. She and Toklas boarded the *Champlain* at Le Havre on 17 October 1934 and landed in New York exactly one week later. Stein's celebrated lecture tour included stops in New York, Chicago, Detroit, and Pasadena, as well as many places in New England and the South. Upon learning of Stein's upcoming arrival, Mabel Dodge first wrote to her in Paris and later to addresses in the United States, attempting one more reconciliation by inviting Stein and Toklas to Taos.⌇

Oct. 9 [1934] Taos, New Mexico

Dear Gertrude—

I am glad to read every day in press clippings that come here that you are arriving pretty soon, & I told Alfred Harcourt* when he was here the other day, that he was to tell you about this place & tell you to come here & see us. You've got to! You must bury the hatchet (if it is a hatchet) & come for a good visit, you & Alice. I think we will be here until after Xmas unless it gets too cold—

---

* Alfred Harcourt, American publisher who founded Harcourt, Brace Company.

sometimes it does. Then we will likely go to Carmel to be near the [Robinson and Una] Jeffers.* Now be a good girl & write me a card like you used to & say you will. Maybe you are not mad—anyway you've never answered me for ages!

Affectionately—

Mabel—

Oct. 14 [1934] Taos, New Mexico

Dear Gertrude—

I wrote to you to the Rue Fleurus a week ago & lest it missed you, here is another.

I do want you & Alice to come out & pay us a visit, while you're here. I guarantee you will enjoy it as much as anything else. I would like to take you to a wonderful Indian Ceremony at Zuni Pueblo—the Shaliko Dance, only we never know the exact date ahead, usually the end of November or early in December. But anyway you must see Taos, & Tony, you & he will certainly like each other. Come on—do let's get together once more. Carl [Van Vechten] says you have thousands of lecture engagements & invitations but even so—!

Ever—

Mabel L.

* Robinson Jeffers lived an extremely secluded and private life with his wife Una in Carmel, in a house they had built on the cliffs overlooking the ocean. After meeting Dodge in 1930, they visited her often in Taos and a close relationship developed between Una Jeffers and Mabel Dodge. However, in 1938, Dodge was involved in orchestrating an affair between Robinson Jeffers and a female friend of hers, reportedly in order to reawaken him sexually and thus free up his blocked writing. Upon learning of the affair, Una Jeffers attempted suicide in Dodge's bathroom at Los Gallos (Rudnick, *Mabel Dodge Luhan,* 298–99). Alice B. Toklas refers to this incident in a letter to the writer Donald Sutherland dated 30 November 1947 in which she also put in a few digs at Dodge: "Thanks for the Mabel Dodge-Mrs. Jeffers story. Is that recent? It's Mabel's inevitable end because the only way she can convince the people around her that she's won the man—sometimes it convinces him too—is to have some one—she or he or his wife or an ex-lover—try to commit suicide. When we knew her best—in '12 to '14—there were then attempts and no victims. John Reed she said was one of them. Later she claimed Mrs. [Frieda] Lawrence as another. Mabel was not what Gertrude said repetition was—repeating with a slight difference. It was in Mabel just the same repetition with nothing added or taken away and she was deadly dull. But she did have a pretty old-fashioned coquetry" (Toklas, *Staying on Alone,* 92).

Oct. 14 [1934] Taos, New Mexico

Dear Gertrude—

I am sending letters all over to you! I want you & Alice to come out & visit us. I promise you you'l like it. There is a ceremony called Shaliko Dance at Zuni Pueblo near the end of November I would like to take you to—can you? Do you want to?

Also I want you to see Taos & know Tony—<u>Do</u>.

Ever yrs—

Mabel.

Dec. 11 [1934] Taos

Dear Gertrude,

Now that you didn't come for the Shaliko which was <u>yesterday</u> I suppose you won't come at all! Curses. I want to see you again very much.

Thornton Wilder* wrote me you are going to San Francisco— well we are going to Carmel about Jan. 6 & that is <u>near</u>. Can't we meet <u>some</u>where. Can you come to Carmel? Tony could go & fetch you & Alice in the automobile. Then you could meet the [Robinson and Una] Jeffers. You'd love them. Are you going to lecture in San Fran? Would you like to in Carmel? I wish you'd write a card or something. If I weren't so poor at the moment I'd go east & all— but I can't!

We must meet <u>some</u>where!

Mabel.

~Dodge had also written to Van Vechten on 4 October 1934, urging him to facilitate a reunion between Stein and herself:

What I want to know now is: are you going to bring Gertrude out here in a plane to visit me? Wouldn't that be fun! I think you could all spend Xmas here--or what about Thanksgiving? G.S. has been mad at me for ages. Someone made

-----

* Thornton Wilder became close friends with Mabel Dodge in the 1930s, leaning on her for emotional support as he was charmed by her personal qualities of liveliness and perceptivity. He did not meet Gertrude Stein until 1934 in Chicago during her lecture tour. The two developed a tight bond immediately, so much so that Stein first chose Wilder as her literary executor, a decision she later changed by appointing Van Vechten (*GSC*, 285–87).

trouble or something. Maybe it was because I sent her a spectacle case six years ago by Virgil Thompson [i.e. Thomson]! I never heard from her since. But she'd better forget all that along with other things.[50]

These appeals to Stein and Van Vechten were unsuccessful and so Dodge tried again by telephone, as Toklas recalls in her memoirs, *What is Remembered*:

We got to the Del Monte Hotel [in California] quite late that night and at once there was a telephone call from Mabel Dodge. I answered. She said, Hello, when am I going to see Gertrude? and I answered, I don't think you are going to. What? said she. No, said I, she's going to rest. Robinson Jeffers wants to meet her, she said. Well, I said, he will have to do without.[51]

One final attempt at a meeting between Stein and Dodge occurred in March 1935, on the occasion of a cocktail party for Stein given in San Francisco by Gertrude Atherton, a writer who had met Stein through Avery Hopwood. On 4 March 1935, Atherton wrote to Dodge: "I do hope you can come to the cocktail party on Thursday the 11th [of April]. . . . But I hope you can make the party, for Miss Stein wrote me that she would like to see you again . . . . The party is early, from 4 to 6, as Miss Stein lectures that evening."[52] On 16 March 1935, however, after having extended the invitation to Dodge, Atherton wrote to Stein, inquiring about her interest in seeing Dodge again:

The other day a friend of Mabel Luhan (who is staying at Carmel, an artists' colony near Monterey) called me up and said that Mrs. Robinson Jeffers was very anxious to bring about a "reconciliation" between you and the High Priestess of Taos. I suggested that Mrs. Jeffers write to you and find out whether you cared to meet Mrs. Luhan or not. If you did I'd ask her to the cocktail party. Now, please tell me frankly how you feel about it. If you don't want her she doesn't get asked; that is certain. I like Mrs. Luhan, but this is your party and I want no jarring note.[53]

Stein then wrote to Van Vechten on 20 March 1935 about the possibility of meeting up with Dodge:

Mrs. Atherton is getting so xcited about the cocktail party, she air-mails about it and the last is that Mrs. Jeffers wants to reconcile me and Mabel, and do we want to be reconciled me not Mabel and is there anything to reconcile, I have said that I am reconciled to meeting Mabel which is not what you call reconciliation but an arriving. . . .[54]

Dodge wrote to Van Vechten on 6 April 1935, providing her own version of the telephone call that Toklas recalled and recording her bafflement at Stein's treatment of her:

Well! Gertrude appeared here—staying at a hotel near by. I called her up & asked her over to meet the Jeffers—& Tony & she boisterously replied: "Oh no. I have no curiosity to see Tony & I am sure he has none to see me. Has he?" I answered "No! Of course not!" I had just thought they would like each other as human beings. Then she said she was seeing no one here but would see me in San Francisco! Gertrude Atherton is giving a tea for her & wrote me G.S. had written her she would like me there.

Then Noel Sullivan here, called her up & asked her to dinner to meet some people—She accepted & he said he would have the Flavins, the Jeffers, etc. & Mabel Luhan. She made a gurgle & said: "Do you know her well?" He said he'd been seeing me a lot lately & would she like to see me. She replied: "Well, maybe not! She is un peu difficile!"

Well! Well! Well!

At the dinner, (the Jeffers didn't go) Alice said to Mrs. Steffens: "I hear Mrs. Jeffers was to mediate & be a peace maker between Mabel & us!" [illegible]

Does all this mean anything to you? Not a thing to me! Atherton just called up to make sure Una & I would be at the tea as G.S. was counting on it! We are to be in town but of course not going to that! I am mad. First about Tony, then at all the fuss about a peace making. Over what, pray? The San Francisco paper had a weird bit this morning entitled "A snub! A snub! A snub!" Going on to report an interview with G.S. who said she wasn't going to see any "notables" in Carmel, that she only liked ordinary people, & was not going to see Robinson Jeffers, Mabel Dodge or Lincoln Steffens! Well heck![55]

In a letter to Leo Stein dated 31 April 1935, Dodge reported:

Gertrude acted like a monomaniac & meglomaniac in California and disgusted everyone & made them laugh! When she was approching she wrote Gertrude Atherton she wished to see me at the tea Atherton was giving for her. When she came to Carmel she told me on the phone she did not wish to see me <u>there</u> but in San Francisco! Naturally I did not go! What a strange end to her early years![56]

It seems, then, that Mabel Dodge and Gertrude Stein did not meet in California and only had one brief exchange on the telephone. There is no mention of their meeting in Stein's account of her travels during her lecture tour, in *Everybody's Autobiography,* or in Dodge's memoirs or correspondence with others. After Gertrude Stein's visit to the United States, which ended on 4 May 1935 when she and Toklas boarded the *Champlain* in New York to return to Paris, it seems likely that she and Dodge did not have further contact before her death on 27 July 1946. However, Stein remained interested in Dodge's affairs, as she and Van Vechten exchanged comments about her, particularly at the time of the publication in 1935 of Dodge's *European Experiences,* which included a chapter entitled "The Steins." Van Vechten wrote to Stein on 23 September 1935: "Has [Alfred] Harcourt sent you Mabel Luhan's *European Experiences?* & have you see[n] how Mabel writes (at length) about you & Alice? I think you better had. It will amuse you or something!"[57] He wrote again on 14 October 1935: "Please write me when you read Mabel's book!"[58]

When Stein finally read *European Experiences,* she wrote to Van Vechten on 25 November [?] 1935:

> We did get Mabel's book . . . and Alice deep in it reads me choice pieces, and they are pretty choice, but where are you in it, I hoped you would be in it it seems Muriel [Draper] is so mad she went back from Chicago although she was headed for Taos, a good time is always to be had by all[59]

Mabel Dodge was to outlive Gertrude Stein by almost twenty years, as she died on 18 August 1962, still married to Tony Luhan, her fourth husband.∾

~

UNDATED LETTERS

[CIRCA 1911–14]*
Dearest Gertrude,

Now they're off again!

M.D.

———

[CIRCA 1914–17]†
Why don't you write to me—you mean old thing?

M.D.

[VERSO]

Caine's [?]‡ have been added.

M.

---

* This was written when Mabel Dodge was still Dodge and most likely still in good stead with Stein, as evidenced by the greeting. This would date the letter somewhere between 1911 and 1914.

† This was written when Mabel Dodge was feeling ignored by Stein and when she was still Dodge, most likely between 1914 and 1917.

‡ This may refer to Sir Thomas Henry and Gordon Caine, whom Dodge mentions in a letter to Stein dated 18 May 1914 and whom Stein includes in *The Autobiography of Alice B. Toklas* (135).

~

APPENDIX A

Portrait of Mabel Dodge at the Villa Curonia (1912)

Gertrude Stein

The days are wonderful and the nights are wonderful and the life is pleasant.

Bargaining is something and there is not that success. The intention is what if application has that accident results are reappearing. They did not darken. That was not an adulteration.

So much breathing has not the same place when there is that much beginning. So much breathing has not the same place when the ending is lessening. So much breathing has the same place and there must not be so much suggestion. There can be there the habit that there is if there is no need of resting. The absence is not alternative.

Any time is the half of all the noise and there is not that disappointment. There is no distraction. An argument is clear.

Packing is not the same when the place which has all that is not emptied. There came there the hall and this was not the establishment. It had not all the meaning.

Blankets are warmer in the summer and the winter is not lonely. This does not assure the forgetting of the intention when there has been and there is every way to send some. There does not happen to be a dislike for water. This is not heartening.

As the expedition is without the participation of the question there will be nicely all that energy. They can arrange that the little color is not bestowed. They can leave it in regaining that intention. It is mostly repaid. There can be an irrigation. They can have the whole paper and they send it in some package. It is not inundated.

A bottle that has all the time to stand open is not so clearly shown when there is green color there. This is not the only way to change it. A little raw potato and then all that softer does happen to show that there has been enough. It changes the expression.

It is not darker and the present time is the best time to agree. This which has been feeling is what has the appetite and the patience and the time to stay. This is not collaborating.

All the attention is when there is not enough to do. This does not determine a question. The only reason that there is not that pressure is that there is a suggestion. There are many going. A delight is not bent. There had been that little wagon. There is that precision when there has not been an imagination. There has not been that kind abandonment. Nobody is alone. If the spread that is not a piece removed from the bed is likely to be whiter then certainly the sprinkling is not drying. There can be the message where the print is pasted and this does not mean that there is that esteem. There can be the likelihood of all the days not coming later and this will not deepen the collected dim version.

It is a gnarled division that which is not any obstruction and the forgotten swelling is certainly attracting, it is attracting the whiter division, it is not sinking to be growing, it is not darkening to be disappearing, it is not aged to be annoying. There can not be sighing. This is this bliss.

Not to be wrapped and then to forget undertaking, the credit and then the resting of that interval, the pressing of the sounding when there is no trinket is not altering, there can be pleasing classing clothing.

A sap that is that adaptation is the drinking that is not increasing. There can be that lack of quivering. That does not originate every invitation. There is not wedding introduction. There is not all that filling. There is the climate that is not existing there is that plainer. There is the likeliness lying in liking likely likeliness. There is that dispensation. There is the paling that is not reddening, there is the reddening that is not reddening, there is that protection, there is that destruction, there is not the present lessening there is the argument of increasing. There is that that is not that which is that resting. There is not that occupation. There is that particular half of directing that there is that particular whole direction that is not all the measure of any combination. Gliding is not heavily moving. Looking is not vanishing. Laughing is not evaporating. There can be the climax. There can be the same dress. There can be an old dress. There can be the way there is that way there is that which is not that charging what is a regular way of paying. There has been William. All the time is likely. There is the condition. There has been admitting. There is not the print. There is that smiling. There is the season. There is that where there is not that which is where there is what there is which is beguiling. There is a paste.

Abandon a garden and the house is bigger. This is not smiling. This is comfortable. There is the comforting of predilection. An open object is establishing the loss that there was when the vase was not inside the place. It was not wandering.

A plank that was dry was not disturbing the smell of burning and altogether there was the best kind of sitting there could never be all the edging that the largest chair was having. It was not pushed. It moved then. There was not that lifting. There was that which was not any contradiction and there was not the bland fight that did not have that regulation. The contents were not darkening. There was not that hesitation. It was occupied. That was not occupying any exception. Any one had come. There was that distribution.

There was not that velvet spread when there was a pleasant head. The color was paler. The moving regulating is not a distinction. The place is there.

Likely there is not that departure when the whole place that has that texture is so much in the way. It is not there to stay. It does not change that way. A pressure is not later. There is the same. There is not the shame. There is that pleasure.

In burying that game there is not a change of name. There is not perplexing and co-ordination. The toy that is not round has to be found and looking is not straining such relation. There can be that company. It is not wider when the length is not longer and that does make that way of staying away. Every one is exchanging returning. There is not a prediction. The whole day is that way. Any one is resting to say that the time which is not reverberating is acting in partaking.

A walk that is not stepped where the floor is covered is not in the place where the room is entered. The whole one is the same.

There is not any stone. There is the wide door that is narrow on the floor. There is all that place.

There is that desire and there is no pleasure and the place is filling the only space that is placed where all the piling is not adjoining. There is not that distraction.

Praying has intention and relieving that situation is not solemn. There comes that way.

The time that is the smell of the plain season is not showing the water is running. There is not all that breath. There is the use of the stone and there is the place of the stuff and there is the practice of expending questioning. There is not that differentiation. There is that which is in time. There is the room that is the largest place when there is all that is where there is space. There is not that perturbation. The legs that show are not the certain ones that have been used. All legs are used. There is no action meant.

The particular space is not beguiling. There is that participation. It is not passing any way. It has that to show. It is why there is no exhalation.

There is all there is when there has all there has where there is what there is. That is what is done when there is done what is done and the union is won and the division is the explicit visit. There is not all of any visit.

Note: Soon after Gertrude Stein wrote "Portrait of Mabel Dodge at the Villa Curonia," Dodge arranged to have three hundred copies of it printed and covered in Florentine wallpaper. "Portrait of Mabel Dodge at the Villa Curonia" was reprinted in Stein's *Portraits and Prayers,* 98–102, and in Dodge's *European Experiences,* 328–31. Carl Van Vechten also included the portrait in his edited *Selected Writings of Gertrude Stein,* 527–30.

APPENDIX B

Speculations, or Post-Impressionism in Prose (1913)

Mabel Dodge

Many roads are being broken today, and along these roads consciousness is pursuing truth to eternity. This is an age of communication, and the human being who is not a "communicant" is in the sad plight which the dogmatist defines as being a condition of spiritual non-receptivity.

Some of these newly opened roads lie parallel and almost touch.

In a large studio in Paris, hung with paintings by Renoir, Matisse and Picasso. Gertrude Stein is doing with words what Picasso is doing with paint. She is impelling language to induce new states of consciousness, and in doing so language becomes with her a creative art rather than a mirror of history.

In her impressionistic writing she uses familiar words to create perceptions, conditions, and states of being, never before quite consciously experienced. She does this by using words that appeal to her as having the meaning that they *seem* to have. She has taken the English language and, according to many people, has misused it, or has used it roughly, uncouthly and brutally, or madly, stupidly and hideously, but by her method she is finding the hidden and inner nature of nature.

To present her impressions she chooses words for their inherent quality, rather than for their accepted meaning.

Her habit of working is methodical and deliberate. She always works at night in the silence, and brings all her will power to bear upon the banishing of preconceived images. Concentrating upon the impression she has received and which she wishes to transmit, she suspends her selective faculty, waiting for the word or group of words that will perfectly interpret her meaning, to rise from her sub-consciousness to the surface of her mind.

Then and then only does she bring her reason to bear upon them, examining, weighing and gauging their ability to express her meaning. It is a working proof of the Bergson theory of intuition. She does not go after words—she waits and lets them come to her, and they do.

It is only when art thus pursues the artist that his production will bear the mark of inevitability. It is only when the "*élan vital*" drives the artist to the creative overflow that life surges in his production. Vitality directed into a conscious expression is the modern definition of genius.

It is impossible to define or to describe fully any new manifestation in esthetics or in literature that is as recent, as near to us, as the work of Picasso or of Gertrude Stein; the most that we can do is to suggest a little, draw a comparison, point the way and then withdraw.

To know about them is a matter of personal experience; no one can help another through it. First before thought must come feeling, and this is the first step toward experience, because feeling is the beginning of knowledge.

It does not greatly matter how the first impress affects one. One may be shocked, stunned and dismayed, or one may be aroused, stimulated, intrigued and delighted. That there has been an *approach* is what counts.

It is only in a state of indifference that there is no approach at all, and indifference reeks of death. It is the tomb of life itself.

A further consciousness than is already ours will need many new forms of expression. In literature everything that has been felt and known so far has been said as it has been said.

What more there may be for us to realize must be expressed in a new way. Language has been crystalized into four or five established literary forms, that up to the present day have been held sacred and intranscendant, but all the truth cannot be contained in any one or in any limited number of molds. A. E., the Irish poet, says of it:

The hero first thought it—
To him 'twas a deed;
To those who retaught it
A chain on their speed.

The fire that we kindled,
A beacon by night,
When darkness has dwindled
Grows pale in the light.

For life has no glory
Stays long in one dwelling,
And time has no story
That's true twice in telling.

And only the teaching
That never was spoken
Is worthy thy reaching
The fountain unbroken.

This is so of all the arts, for of course what is true of one must, to be justifiable, be true of them all, even to the art of life; perhaps, first of all, to that one.

Nearly every thinking person nowadays is in revolt against something, because the craving of the individual is for further consciousness, and because consciousness is expanding and is bursting through the molds that have held it up to now; and so let every man whose private truth is too great for his existing conditions pause before he turn away from Picasso's painting or from Gertrude Stein's writing, for their case is his case.

Of course, comment is the best of signs. Any comment. One that Gertrude Stein hears oftenest is from conscientious souls who have honestly tried—and who have failed—to get anything out of her work at all. "But why don't you make it simpler?" they cry. "Because this is the only way in which I can express what I want to express," is the invariable reply, which of course is the unanswerable argument of every sincere artist to every critic. Again and again comes the refrain that is so familiar before the canvases of Picasso—"But it is so ugly, so brutal!" But how does one know that it is ugly, after all? How does one know? Each time that beauty has been reborn in the world it has needed complete readjustment of sense perceptions, grown all too accustomed to the blurred outlines, faded colors, the death in life of beauty in decline. It has become jaded from over-familiarity. from long association and from inertia. If one cares for Rembrandt's paintings today, then how could one have cared for them at the time when they were painted, when they were glowing with life. If we like St. Marks in Venice today, then surely it would have offended us a thousand years ago. Perhaps it is not Rembrandt's paintings that one cares for, after all, but merely for the shell, the ghost—the last pale flicker of the artist's intention. Beauty? One thing is certain, that if we must worship beauty as we have known it, we must consent to worship it as a thing dead. "*Une grande, belle chose—morte.*" And ugliness—what is it? Surely, only death is ugly.

In Gertrude Stein's writing every word lives and, apart from the concept, it is so exquisitely rhythmical and cadenced, that when read aloud and received as pure sound, it is like a kind of sensuous music. Just as one may stop, for once in a way, before a canvas of Picasso, and, letting one's reason sleep for an instant, may exclaim: "It *is* a fine pattern!"—so listening to Gertrude Stein's words and forgetting to try to understand what they mean, one submits to their gradual charm. Huntley Carter, of the *New Age*, says that her use of language has a curious hypnotic effect when read aloud. In one part of her writing she made use of repetition and the rearranging of certain words over and over, so that they became adjusted into a kind of incantation, and in listening one feels that from the combination of repeated sounds, varied ever so little, that there emerges gradually a perception of some meaning quite other than that of the contents of the phrases. Many people have experienced this magical evocation, but have been unable to explain in what way it came to pass, but though they did not know what meaning the words were bearing, nor how they were affected by them, yet they had *begun* to know what it all meant, because they were not indifferent.

In a portrait that she has finished recently, she has produced a coherent totality through a series of impressions which, when taken sentence by sentence, strike most people as particularly incoherent. To illustrate this, the words in the following paragraph are strenuous words—words that weigh and qualify conditions; words that are without softness yet that are not hard words—perilous abstractions they seem, containing agony and movement and conveying a vicarious livingness. "It is a gnarled division, that which is not any obstruction, and the forgotten swelling is certainly attracting. It is attracting the whiter division, it is not sinking to be growing, it is not darkening to be disappearing, it is not aged to be annoying. There cannot be sighing. This is this bliss."

Many roads are being broken—what a wonderful word—"broken"! And out of the shattering and petrifaction of today—up from the cleavage and the disintegration—we will see order emerging tomorrow. Is it so difficult to remember that life at birth is always painful and rarely lovely? How strange it is to think that the rough-hewn trail of today will become tomorrow the path of least resistance, over which the average will drift with all the ease and serenity of custom. All the labor of evolution is condensed into this one fact, of the vitality of the individual making way for the many. We can but praise the high courage of the road breakers, admitting as we infallibly must, in Gertrude Stein's own words, and with true Bergsonism faith—"Something is certainly coming out of them!"

Note: Mabel Dodge's "Speculations, or Post-Impressionism in Prose" appeared in the Special Number issue of *Arts & Decoration* in March 1913, 172, 174. The two punctuation errors that appear in the original article have been retained in this reprinting. Dodge included an edited version of her article in *Movers and Shakers,* 27–29.

~

ABBREVIATIONS

Full citations are provided in the bibliography.

For works by Mabel Dodge:

B	*Background*
EE	*European Experiences*
ETD	*Edge of Taos Desert*
M&S	*Movers and Shakers*
WIT	*Winter in Taos*

For works by Gertrude Stein:

AABT	*The Autobiography of Alice B. Toklas*
AFAM	*As Fine As Melanctha*
EA	*Everybody's Autobiography*
G&P	*Geography and Plays*
LIA	*Lectures in America*
P&P	*Portraits and Prayers*
QED	*Fernhurst, Q.E.D, and Other Early Writings*
Two	*Two: Gertrude Stein and Her Brother and Other Early Portraits*
Yale GS	*The Yale Gertrude Stein*

For books about Mabel Dodge, Gertrude Stein, and their circles:

CC   James Mellow, *Charmed Circle: Gertrude Stein & Company*

CVV   *Letters of Carl Van Vechten*, ed. Bruce Kellner

FF   *The Flowers of Friendship: Letters Written to Gertrude Stein*, ed. Donald Gallup

GS/CVV   *The Letters of Gertrude Stein and Carl Van Vechten, 1913–1946*, ed. Edward Burns

GSC   *A Gertrude Stein Companion: content with the example*, ed. Bruce Kellner

JIS   Leo Stein, *Journey into the Self*

1915   *1915, The Cultural Moment*, eds. Adele Heller and Lois Rudnick

PW   Carl Van Vechten, *Peter Whiffle*

WIR   Alice B. Toklas, *What is Remembered*

For manuscript collections:

ASC   Alfred Stieglitz Collection, Beinecke Rare Book and Manuscript Library, Yale University

CVVC   Carl Van Vechten Collection, Beinecke Rare Book and Manuscript Library, Yale University

GLSC   Gertrude and Leo Stein Collection, Beinecke Rare Book and Manuscript Library, Yale University

MDLC   Mabel Dodge Luhan Collection, Beinecke Rare Book and Manuscript Library, Yale University

NOTES

Introduction

1. Gertrude Stein, *The Making of Americans*, 282–83.
2. Mabel Dodge Luhan, *European Experiences*, 327 (hereafter cited as *EE*).
3. Dodge to Stein, c. April 1911, Gertrude and Leo Stein Collection, Beinecke Rare Book and Manuscript Library, Yale University (hereafter cited as GLSC).
4. Stein, *As Fine As Melanctha*, 308 (hereafter cited as *AFAM*). In *The Biography of Alice B. Toklas*, Linda Simon claims that "Mable" refers to Mabel Dodge, although it is also possible that it represents Mabel Weeks, a friend of Stein's from Radcliffe (265).
5. Dodge to Stein, October 1912, GLSC.
6. See Appendix A for the complete text of Stein's "Portrait of Mabel Dodge at the Villa Curonia."
7. Dodge to Stein, c. November 1912, GLSC.
8. See Appendix B for the complete text of Dodge's article, "Speculations, or Post-Impressionism in Prose."
9. Stein to Dodge, c. April 1913, Mabel Dodge Luhan Collection, Beinecke Rare Book and Manuscript Library, Yale University (hereafter cited as MDLC).
10. Stein to Dodge, May 1913, MDLC.
11. Stein to Dodge, c. late May or early June 1913, MDLC.
12. Dodge to Stein, 8 July 1914, GLSC.
13. Stein to Dodge, 2 June 1922, MDLC.
14. Dodge to Stein, 7 October 1925, GLSC.
15. Dodge to Stein, 9 October 1934, GLSC.
16. Dodge to Stein, 11 December 1934, GLSC.
17. *EE*, 53, 54.
18. Stein, *Everybody's Autobiography*, 142 (hereafter cited as *EA*).
19. Luhan, *Intimate Memories: Background*, 264 (hereafter cited as *B*).
20. *B*, 264.
21. *B*, 278.
22. Stein, *The Autobiography of Alice B. Toklas*, 85 (hereafter cited as *AABT*).
23. Christopher Lasch, *The New Radicalism in America, 1889–1963: The Intellectual as a Social Type*, 118.

24. *EE*, 140.
25. *EE*, 36.
26. Luhan, "Doctors: Fifty Years of Experience," MDLC, 15.
27. *AFAM*, 245.
28. Stein, *The Yale Gertrude Stein*, 5, 41 (hereafter cited as *Yale GS*).
29. *Yale GS*, 291.
30. Stein, *Fernhurst, Q.E.D., and Other Early Writings*, 66, 102 (hereafter cited as *QED*).
31. *QED*, 63, 103, 62.
32. *QED*, 60.
33. *EE*, 324.
34. *AABT*, 124.
35. Carl Van Vechten, *Peter Whiffle: His Life and Works*, 123 (hereafter cited as *PW*).
36. Max Eastman, *The Enjoyment of Living*, 523.
37. Lincoln Steffens, *The Autobiography of Lincoln Steffens* 2:655.
38. Eastman, *Venture*, 27–28.
39. *PW*, 122–23.
40. Muriel Draper, *Music at Midnight*, 12.
41. *EE*, 267.
42. Leo Stein, *Appreciation: Painting, Poetry and Prose*, 186.
43. Stein, *Lectures in America*, 61 (hereafter cited as *LIA*).
44. *EE*, 325.
45. Max Weber to Dodge, 22 January 1913, MDLC.
46. *PW*, 124.
47. Luhan, *Movers and Shakers*, 38 (hereafter cited as *M&S*).
48. Steven Watson, *Strange Bedfellows: The First American Avant-Garde*, 38.
49. Watson, *Strange Bedfellows*, 39, 41.
50. Watson, *Strange Bedfellows*, 45–46.
51. *AABT*, 30.
52. *AABT*, 43.
53. *AABT*, 108.
54. *M&S*, 72.
55. Stein to Alfred Stieglitz, 6 March 1912, Alfred Stieglitz Collection, Beinecke Rare Book and Manuscript Library, Yale University (hereafter cited as ASC).
56. Sue Davidson Lowe, *Stieglitz: A Memoir/Biography*, 158.
57. Benita Eisler, *O'Keeffe & Stieglitz: An American Romance*, 101.
58. Watson, *Strange Bedfellows*, 68.
59. Quoted in Watson, *Strange Bedfellows*, 364 n. 29.
60. Watson, *Strange Bedfellows*, 81.
61. Watson, *Strange Bedfellows*, 72, and 364 n. 27.
62. All passages are from *Camera Work* (July 1914): Dodge, "The Mirror," 9; Hutchins Hapgood, "What 291 Is to Me," 11; Marsden Hartley, "What is 291?", 35; Lee Simonson, 48.
63. All passages are from issues of *Camera Work* that reprinted reviews of exhibitions at 291: "Henry Tyrrell in the 'N.Y. World,'" *Camera Work* (April 1912): 40; "Mr. Israel White in the *Newark Evening News*," *Camera Work* (October 1911): 34; "Mr. Arthur Hoeber in the *N.Y. Globe*," *Camera Work* (October 1911): 31; "J. Edgar Chamberlin in the 'Evening Mail,'" *Camera Work* (April 1912): 44; "Adolph Wolff in the *International*," *Camera Work* (January 1914): 23.
64. *M&S*, 142.
65. Steffens, *Autobiography of Lincoln Steffens*, 2: 655–56.
66. John C. Burnham, "The New Psychology," in *1915, The Cultural Moment: The New Politics, the New Woman, the New Psychology, the New Art, and the New Theatre in America*, eds. Adele Heller and Lois Rudnick, 120, 123 (hereafter cited as *1915*).

67. Sigmund Freud, *The Interpretation of Dreams*, 282.
68. *M&S*, 516.
69. Sanford Gifford, "The American Reception of Psychoanalysis, 1908–1922," in *1915*, 129.
70. Burnham, "The New Psychology," 120, 126.
71. Freud, *Inhibitions, Symptoms and Anxiety*, 87–96.
72. Dodge, "Consuming Energy is Keeping Well," in "Scrapbook," vol. 17, MDLC.
73. Burnham, "The New Psychology," 123.
74. Quoted in Burnham, "The New Psychology," 120, from Frederick J. Hoffman, *Freudianism and the Literary Mind*, 58.
75. Hapgood, *A Victorian in the Modern World*, 382–83.
76. Hapgood, *A Victorian in the Modern World*, 383.
77. Fred Matthews, "The New Psychology and American Drama," in *1915*, 150–51.
78. George Cram Cook and Susan Glaspell, *Suppressed Desires*, in *1915*, 283.

1911

1. *EE*, 321.
2. *AABT*, 128–29; Alice B. Toklas, *What is Remembered*, 65 (hereafter cited as *WIR*); James Mellow, *Charmed Circle: Gertrude Stein & Company*, 203 (hereafter cited as *CC*).
3. *AABT*, 129.
4. *EE*, 324.
5. There is some disagreement about the date that Alice B. Toklas moved into 27 rue de Fleurus. In *Charmed Circle*, Mellow states that the move occurred in September 1910 (187). In *Everybody Who Was Anybody*, Janet Hobhouse maintains that the move took place in 1909 (68). In Douglas Cooper's essay, "Gertrude Stein and Juan Gris," included in the Museum of Modern Art's exhibition catalogue entitled *Four Americans in Paris*, he explains in a footnote that letters from Leo Stein to Gertrude from August 1910 indicate that Toklas moved in during August 1910 (73).
6. *EE*, 324.
7. *EE*, 321.
8. *EE*, 321.
9. *EE*, 322.
10. *EE*, 405.
11. *EE*, 327.
12. *AABT*, 113.
13. *EE*, 327.
14. Bruce Kellner, ed., *A Gertrude Stein Companion: content with the example*, 45 (hereafter cited as *GSC*); *CC*, 66; Leon Katz essay in *QED*, xxii.
15. Lois Palken Rudnick, *Mabel Dodge Luhan: New Woman, New Worlds*, 33.
16. *EE*, 139.
17. *EE*, 134–35.
18. *EE*, 303.
19. *EE*, 140.
20. *EE*, 139.
21. *EE*, 174.
22. *EE*, 138–43.
23. *PW*, 119.
24. *EE*, 144, 146.
25. *EE*, 146.
26. *EE*, 147.
27. *EE*, 150.
28. *EE*, 150.
29. *EE*, 152.
30. *EE*, 164.
31. *EE*, 162.
32. *EE*, 162.
33. Whitman, *Leaves of Grass*, 34.
34. *EE*, 153.
35. *EE*, 159.
36. Quoted in *EE*, 155. These lines are from Robert Browning's poem, "The Guardian-Angel: A Picture at Fano," first published

in 1855 in *Men and Women*
2:167. As quoted in *The Com-*
plete Poetic and Dramatic Works
of Robert Browning, the lines
are punctuated somewhat differently: "O world, as God has
made it! All is beauty; / And
knowing this, is love, and love is
duty. / What further may be
sought for or declared?" (194).
37. *EE,* 159.
38. *EE,* 166.
39. *EE,* 173.
40. *EE,* 327.
41. *EE,* 326.
42. *WIR,* 66.
43. *CC,* 164–65.
44. *LIA,* 183; Quoted in *CC,* 171.
45. *GSC,* 46.
46. Quoted in Robert Bartlett Haas,
ed., *Gertrude Stein: A Primer*
for the Gradual Understanding
of Gertrude Stein, 15.
47. Quoted in *The Oxford Compan-*
ion to English Literature, 319.
48. Toklas to *English Review,* August 1911, GLSC. Toklas usually
served as Stein's secretary and
wrote cover letters when sub-
mitting works to publishers.
49. *English Review* to Stein, 25
August 1911, GLSC."You and
Me" is likely the work referred
to in Toklas's letter to the *En-*
glish Review as "someone's
reaction to the new art movement." Neither title has been
located in the Beinecke Rare
Book and Manuscript Library's
catalogue of published and
unpublished works by Gertrude
Stein.
50. *EE,* 332.
51. *EE,* 324.
52. *EE,* 389.
53. Included in *FF,* 62.
54. *CC,* 145.

1912

1. *AABT,* 132.
2. Quoted in Peter and Linda Murray, *A Dictionary of Art and*
Artists, 160.
3. *AABT,* 115–16.
4. *EE,* 281.
5. *EE,* 289.
6. *EE,* 299.
7. *EE,* 299–300. Marguerite says:
"Yes, it is I" and "No, no, Mabel
is sleeping, sleeping so well! I
am going away—I am going
away—I am going away." I am
grateful to Michael Conforti for
help in translating this passage.
8. *EE,* 288.
9. Jo Davidson made a sculpture of
Gertrude Stein in 1923 at the
same time that she wrote a word
portrait of him, "Jo Davidson,"
included in *Portraits and Pray-*
ers. Stein also wrote a portrait
of Yvonne Davidson as part of
her portrait of three women,
"And So. To Change So. Muriel
Draper Yvonne Davidson Beatrice Locher," also included in
Portraits and Prayers.
10. Jo Davidson, *Between Sittings,*
82.
11. Hapgood, *A Victorian in the*
Modern World, 349.
12. *AABT,* 129; *CC,* 203.
13. Watson, *Strange Bedfellows,* 50.
14. Included in *FF,* 57.
15. Stieglitz, "Editorial," *Camera*
Work (August 1912): 4.
16. Stein, "Henri Matisse," *Camera*
Work (August 1912): 23.
17. Stein, "Pablo Picasso," *Camera*
Work (August 1912): 29.
18. Included in *FF,* 66.
19. Beaux-arts or fine arts.
20. Session or meeting.
21. Included in *FF,* 68–69.
22. Included in *FF,* 68.
23. *AABT,* 131.
24. *WIR,* 76–77. In fact, it seems to

have been an evening during which no meaningful connections were made, as Dodge does not include Gide in her memoirs from this period and Gide's journals and autobiography do not contain one mention of either Dodge or Stein, even though he refers fleetingly to "A week in Florence" in his 9 October 1912 journal entry (André Gide, *The Journals of André Gide* 1:331).

25. Stein's original title is written on the flyleaf of the black notebook in which she wrote Dodge's portrait (HG41, GLSC). For more detailed analysis of Stein's "Portrait of Mabel Dodge at the Villa Curonia," see: Richard Bridgman, *Gertrude Stein in Pieces*, 120–22; Michael J. Hoffman, *The Development of Abstractionism in the Writings of Gertrude Stein*, 168– 69; and Rudnick, *Mabel Dodge Luhan*, 47–51.

26. Draper, *Music at Midnight*, 10.

27. *EE*, 328.

28. *EE*, 331–32.

29. *EE*, 332.

30. Stein, "Portrait of Mabel Dodge at the Villa Curonia," *P&P*, 98, 100–101, 102. For the complete text of Stein's portrait, see Appendix A.

31. *CC*, 206.

32. Stein, *A Stein Reader*, 260. Ulla Dydo's introduction to "Portrait of Constance Fletcher" provides the details of this chronology of the writing of the portrait.

33. *GSC*, 189. For more detailed analysis of Stein's portrait of Constance Fletcher, see Bridgman, *Gertrude Stein in Pieces*, 122–23, Ulla Dydo's introduction to the portrait in Stein, *A Stein Reader*, 260-61, and Wendy Steiner, *Exact Resemblance*

to *Exact Resemblance: The Literary Portraiture of Gertrude Stein*, 89-95.

34. Stein, "Portrait of Constance Fletcher," *Geography and Plays*, 157, 165 (hereafter cited as *G&P*).

35. *EE*, 332–33. Dodge's article, "Speculations, or Post-Impressionism in Prose," was published in the March 1913 issue of *Arts & Decoration* that was distributed at the Armory Show.

36. *EE*, 3.

37. Paul Ayrault to Dodge, 23 October 1912, MDLC.

38. Ayrault to Dodge, 24 October 1912, MDLC.

39. Florence Bradley to Dodge, 1 November 1912, MDLC.

40. *EE*, 295.

41. Strachey and Samuels, *Mary Berenson*, 184.

42. *M&S*, 137.

43. *M&S*, 137.

44. Leo Stein, *Journey Into the Self: Being the Letters, Papers, and Journals of Leo Stein*, 53 (hereafter cited as *JIS*).

45. *JIS*, 50. Leo Stein's parody is undated.

46. *EE*, 306.

47. *EE*, 307.

48. *EE*, 308.

49. *EE*, 309.

50. *EE*, 311.

51. *EE*, 311.

52. *EE*, 315.

53. *M&S*, 5.

54. *M&S*, 6.

55. Hapgood, *A Victorian in the Modern World*, 120.

56. Hapgood, *A Victorian in the Modern World*, 131.

57. *M&S*, 46, 45.

58. All of the above quotations from Hapgood's article, "A New Form of Literature," are from *Camera Work* (October 1912): 42, 45.

1913

1. Milton W. Brown, *The Story of the Armory Show*, 72.
2. *M&S*, 36.
3. *M&S*, 37.
4. *JIS*, 49.
5. *JIS*, 49.
6. Included in *FF*, 69–70.
7. *M&S*, 80–81.
8. *M&S*, 83.
9. *M&S*, 84.
10. Janet Vale, "The Salon Dodge," *Morning Telegraph*, 8 February 1914; Karl K. Kitchen, "Revelling with Parlor Socialists and Others At a Wednesday Evening Soiree on Fifth Avenue," *New York World*, 29 March 1914.
11. *M&S*, 83–84.
12. *M&S*, 88.
13. *EE*, 333.
14. *M&S*, 14–15.
15. Kellner, *Carl Van Vechten and the Irreverent Decades*, 64.
16. *M&S*, 16, 22.
17. Dodge, "Chiaroscuro—Portrait of Carl Dodge," Carl Van Vechten Papers, Rare Books and Manuscripts Division, New York Public Library (Box 116, f. 8). Both the date of Dodge's poem—15 April 1913—and its title suggest that it was inspired by Donald Evans's poem about her that was written on 14 April 1913 and entitled "Portrait of Mabel Dodge—Chiaroscuro."
18. It is intriguing to imagine what material the *New York Times* editors reportedly cut from Van Vechten's original manuscript, as his voice does not appear often between the many quotations from "a friend" and the excerpts from Stein's writings. The following quotations are all from his article as it appears in the scrapbook. Bruce Kellner explains that Van Vechten's article does not appear in the microfilm editions of the *New York Times* because the article was printed only in the early Monday edition's financial section (Kellner, *Letters of Carl Van Vechten*, 3 n. 3 [hereafter referred to as *CVV*]). A clipping of the article is in the Carl Van Vechten Archives at the New York Public Library in Scrapbook #8. Van Vechten's handwritten notes in the margins are dated by him 30 May 1941.
19. *M&S*, 73.
20. John Lane to Stein, 28 January 1913, GLSC.
21. Lane to Stein, 31 January 1913, GLSC.
22. Lane to Stein, c. April 1913, GLSC.
23. Stein to Dodge, c. March 1912, MDLC.
24. Jayne L. Walker, *The Making of a Modernist: Gertrude Stein from Three Lives to Tender Buttons*, 161 n. 24.
25. Both passages are from Florence Blood to Stein, c. May 1913, GLSC. "A Portrait of F.B." is included in *G&P*.
26. *M&S*, 165.
27. *M&S*, 168.
28. Hapgood, "Democratic Criticism," *New York World*, 21 March 1913.
29. "Ought We to Try?," *New York Globe*, 22 March 1913.
30. Both quotations are from Robert Allerton Parker, "Gertrude Stein's Fiction," *Mirror* (16 May 1913): 6.
31. *M&S*, 187.
32. *M&S*, 188.
33. Martin Green, *New York 1913: The Armory Show and the Paterson Strike Pageant*, 200.
34. Max Weber, "Portrait of Mabel Dodge at 23 Fifth Avenue," MDLC.
35. *GS/CVV*, 848.

36. François Lesure, ed., *Igor Stravinsky: Le Sacre du Printemps*, 163.

37. Van Vechten, *Music After the Great War and Other Studies*, 88.

38. *AABT*, 136–37. This first of Stein's four portraits of Van Vechten was entitled "One: Carl Van Vechten" and published in *Geography and Plays*. In 1923, she wrote "And too. Van Vechten. A sequel to One." that was found among her papers after she died and was published in *GS/CVV* as "Appendix B: An Unpublished Portrait of Carl Van Vechten by Gertrude Stein," 864–66. Stein also wrote "Van or Twenty Years After" and listed Van Vechten among the V's in "To Do: A Book of Alphabets and Birthdays," a group of stories purportedly for children that feature characters whose names begin with each letter of the alphabet.

39. Stein to Van Vechten, 30 May 1913, Carl Van Vechten Collection, Beinecke Rare Book and Manuscript Library, Yale University (hereafter cited as CVVC).

40. Van Vechten to Stein, 31 May 1913, GLSC.

41. *CVV*, 6.

42. For a more detailed account and documentation of this first meeting between Stein and Van Vechten, see Edward Burns's "Appendix A: The First Meeting of Gertrude Stein and Carl Van Vechten" in *GS/CVV* 2:847–53.

43. *M&S*, 218.

44. *M&S*, 205.

45. *M&S*, 212, 213.

46. *M&S*, 213.

47. Reed's poem is quoted in full in *M&S*, 213.

48. *M&S*, 215.

49. Stein to Van Vechten, 20 June 1913, CVVC.

50. Stein to Van Vechten, 28 June 1913, CVVC.

51. *M&S*, 215, 216.

52. *M&S*, 217.

53. *M&S*, 219.

54. Arthur Rubinstein, *My Young Years*, 414–15.

55. Bruce Kellner, pers. comm., 3 November 1993.

56. Bradley to Dodge, 12 October 1913, MDLC; Bradley to Stein, 12 October 1913, GLSC.

57. Two typewritten drafts of Hapgood's "David, the Story of a Soul," dated c. 1913 and labeled "A" and "B," are in the Hutchins Hapgood Collection at the Beinecke Library. Each is approximately 200 pages. The following quotations are from Draft A, which has some repeated page numbers.

58. *CC*, 587–88.

59. All of the quotations in this paragraph are from Hapgood's Draft A of "David, the Story of a Soul," 195, 167, 2 (Preface), 3 (Preface), 3 (Preface), 8 (Preface), 7.

60. Gabrielle Buffet-Picabia to Stieglitz, 17 November 1913, ASC. Translated by the author.

61. William A. Camfield, *Francis Picabia: His Art, Life and Times*, 62–63; 63 n. 16.

62. *M&S*, 242.

63. *M&S*, 245.

64. *M&S*, 247.

65. *M&S*, 247.

66. *M&S*, 247.

67. Hartley to John Reed, c. early 1914, MDLC.

68. Van Deren Coke, *Andrew Dasburg*, 29.

69. *CC*, 250.

70. *JIS*, 52.

71. *CC*, 250.

1914

1. Dodge, "On Marsden Hartley," *Camera Work* (January 1914): 16.
2. Hartley, "Forward to his Exhibition," *Camera Work* (January 1914): 17.
3. Stein, "From a Play by Gertrude Stein on Marsden Hartley," *Camera Work* (January 1914): 17–18.
4. Apollinaire, *Anecdotiques*, 151–53.
5. Quoted in Simon, *The Biography of Alice B. Toklas*, 91.
6. Included in *FF*, 95.
7. Included in *FF*, 96.
8. *CC*, 216.
9. Donald Evans to Dodge, February 1914, MDLC.
10. Robert J. Coady to Stein, 27 April 1914, GLSC.
11. Quoted in *M&S*, 97.
12. Quoted in *M&S*, 101.
·13. "Fair Society Woman Defends I.W.W.," *New York Evening World*, 27 March 1914, quoted in *M&S*, 111.
14. "Fair Society Woman Defends I.W.W.," *New York Evening World*, 27 March 1914, quoted in *M&S*, 110–11.
15. *Washington Herald*, 11 March 1914, quoted in *M&S*, 120.
16. *Brooklyn Citizen*, 12 March 1914, quoted in *M&S*, 121.
17. Evans to Dodge, c. 5 April 1914, MDLC.
18. *M&S*, 38.
19. *CC*, 250–51.
20. *CC*, 255.
21. Lane to Stein, 31 March 1914, GLSC.
22. The exact date of Stein and Toklas's departure for London is not clear, as Mellow says they left Paris on 6 July 1914 (*CC*, 256), whereas Stein reports the date as 5 July 1914 (*AABT*, 144).
23. Quoted in Hoffman, ed., *Critical Essays on Gertrude Stein*, 31.
24. *AABT*, 144–46; *CC*, 256–58.
25. *AABT*, 147.
26. *AABT*, 149.
27. *M&S*, 291.
28. Following this estrangement brought on by Dodge's feeling abandoned by Van Vechten, the two were distant and only in sporadic contact for years. Van Vechten visited Dodge in Taos in 1927 and 1933. In 1935 Dodge sent Van Vechten a copy of *Movers and Shakers* and received no response. At her urging, he finally replied and his frank criticism caused Dodge to remain silent toward him for the next sixteen years. Van Vechten wrote: "It didn't seem very important to me to write to you about the book because I don't like it and I didn't see any sense of telling you that! You seem to belittle every character in it including yourself" (quoted in Kellner, *Carl Van Vechten and the Irreverent Decades*, 269). Finally, in 1951, the two were reconciled when they ran into each other in Santa Fe. As Van Vechten tells it: "[A] large woman plunged toward me on the sidewalk. . . . She embraced me heartily with the salutation, 'You old fool, you!' repeated several times with considerable force, led me to her car to speak to Tony, her Indian husband, and that was the conclusion of our longest feud" (Van Vechten, *Fragments From an Unwritten Autobiography*, 2:37). (The details for this account of the relationship between Dodge and Van Vechten are from Kellner, *Carl Van Vechten and the Irreverent Decades*, 85, 269, 284–85 and *GS/CVV*, 55 n. 4.)
29. *M&S*, 295.

30. Dodge, "The Secret of War,"
    Masses (November 1914): 16.
31. *AABT,* 155.
32. *AABT,* 155.

1915–1934

1. *M&S,* 303.
2. *M&S,* 319–20.
3. *M&S,* 331.
4. *M&S,* 335.
5. *M&S,* 336.
6. *M&S,* 354.
7. *M&S,* 354.
8. *M&S,* 344.
9. *GSC,* 205. For dating the following letter, I have relied upon
   Kellner's report that Hopwood
   first visited 27 rue de Fleurus
   around 1915. However, in *The
   Flowers of Friendship,* Gallup
   dates Dodge's letter from approximately early 1923 (152)
   and Jack Sharrar, in *Avery Hopwood: His Life and Plays,* suggests that although Van Vechten
   had passed along a greeting to
   Stein from Hopwood in a letter
   of 1915, he and she may only
   have heard of each other at that
   early date and met later (61).
10. Stein to Van Vechten, 15 March
    1923, CVVC.
11. *AABT,* 138.
12. Ulla Dydo sheds some light on
    the possible connection between
    Stein's and Hopwood's plays:
    "The most likely link is between
    the Mabel in the list of M names
    and the situation of Mabel Dodge
    at that time. Dodge . . . was the
    subject of much gossip in the
    letters of Stein and Van Vechten
    in 1923 about her fourth mar-
    riage, to the Pueblo Indian
    Antonio Lujan. The innumer-
    able couplings in both *A List* and
    Our Little Wife echo Mabel's
    many divorces and remarriages"
    (Stein, *A Stein Reader,* 382).
13. Stein, "All Sunday," included in
    Alphabets and Birthdays, 113,
    105.
14. *AABT,* 172.
15. *M&S,* 350.
16. *GS/CVV,* 48.
17. *New Republic* (13 January 1917):
    308.
18. *M&S,* 532.
19. *M&S,* 533.
20. *M&S,* 534.
21. Luhan, *Edge of Taos Desert: An
    Escape to Reality,* 94 (hereafter
    cited as *ETD*).
22. *ETD,* 62–63.
23. *ETD,* 94.
24. *ETD,* 231, 232.
25. Luhan, *Winter in Taos,* 66 (here-
    after cited as *WIT*).
26. Rudnick, *Mabel Dodge Luhan,*
    156–57.
27. *WIT,* 62–63.
28. Toklas, *The Alice B. Toklas Cook
    Book,* 75.
29. *ETD,* 331.
30. *PW,* 122–23.
31. *GS/CVV,* 65.
32. Luhan, *Lorenzo in Taos,* 77.
33. Stein to Van Vechten, 15 March
    1922, CVVC.
34. Stein to Van Vechten, 8 April
    1923, CVVC.
35. Rudnick, *Mabel Dodge Luhan,*
    223.
36. Dodge changed the spelling of
    Tony's name from Lujan to
    Luhan because of the difficulties
    in pronunciation that the "j"
    brought about. Tony went along
    with the change, spelling his
    own name "Luhan" (Rudnick,
    Mabel Dodge Luhan, 345 n. 29).
37. Stein to Van Vechten, May
    1923, CVVC.
38. Stein to Van Vechten, 31 May
    1923, CVVC. Edward Burns
    notes that Van Vechten had sent
    Stein a clipping from the *New
    York World* (28 April 1923) that
    quoted Dodge as explaining that
    "business considerations" had

played a role in her decision to marry Antonio Luhan. She did not elaborate further on what she meant (*GS/CVV*, 78 n. 4).

39. Stein to Van Vechten, 5 August 1923, CVVC.

40. Van Vechten to Stein, 22 October 1923, GLSC.

41. Van Vechten to Stein, 22 February 1923, GLSC.

42. Dorothy Brett, "Autobiography," 41, as quoted in Rudnick, *Mabel Dodge Luhan*, 254.

43. Luhan, "My Attitude in the Writing of Autobiography," quoted in Rudnick, *Mabel Dodge Luhan*, 255–56, as quoted in Marcia Haubold, "Mabel Dodge Luhan: An Historical Study of an American Individual and Her Social Environment" (Master's thesis, University of Iowa, 1965), 110.

44. *GS/CVV*, 152–53.

45. Stein to Van Vechten, 20 September 1927, CVVC.

46. Stein to Van Vechten, 26 April 1928, CVVC.

47. Included in *FF*, 228.

48. Loren Mozley to Stein, 29 December 1929, GLSC.

49. Sherwood Anderson, *Letters*, 295, quoted in *CC*, 426.

50. Dodge to Van Vechten, 4 October 1934, CVVC.

51. *WIR*, 153.

52. Gertrude Atherton to Dodge, 4 March 1935, MDLC.

53. Atherton to Stein, 16 March 1935, GLSC.

54. *GS/CVV*, 416.

55. Dodge to Van Vechten, 6 April 1935, CVVC.

56. Dodge to Leo Stein, 31 April 1935, GLSC.

57. *GS/CVV*, 446.

58. *GS/CVV*, 448,

59. *GS/CVV*, 460. Van Vechten does not appear in *European Experiences* since the book ends with Dodge's journey back to the United States in December 1912 and Dodge did not meet Van Vechten until the spring of 1913. A chapter of *European Experiences*, "Muriel," is devoted to Muriel Draper.

BIBLIOGRAPHY

Acton, Harold. *Memoirs of an Aesthete.* London: Methuen, 1948.

Apollinaire, Guillaume. *Anecdotiques.* Paris: Gallimard, 1955.

———. *Apollinaire on Art: Essays and Reviews, 1902–1918.* Edited by Leroy C. Breunig. New York: Viking Press, 1960.

The Armory Show: International Exhibition of Modern Art 1913. 3 vols. Reprint. New York: Arno Press, 1972.

Baedeker, Karl. *Paris and Environs.* 18th ed. Leipzig: Karl Baedeker, 1913.

Baigell, Matthew. *Dictionary of American Art.* New York: Harper and Row, 1979.

Baker's Biographical Dictionary of Musicians. 8th ed. New York: Schirmer Books, 1992.

Barr, Alfred H. *Matisse: His Art and His Public.* New York: Museum of Modern Art, 1951.

Beerbohm, Max. *Zuleika Dobson; Or, An Oxford Love Story.* London: W. Heinemann, 1911.

Berenson, Bernard. *The Italian Painters of the Renaissance. Vol. 2: The Florentine Painters, The Central Italian Painters.* 1896. Reprint. London and New York: Phaidon, 1968.

———. *Sunset and Twilight: From the Diaries of 1947–1958.* New York: Harcourt, Brace and World, 1963.

Blanche, Jacques-Émile. *Aymeris.* Paris: Librairie Plon, 1922.

———. *Portraits of a Lifetime.* Translated by Walter Clement. London: J. M. Dent, 1937.

Bridgman, Richard. *Gertrude Stein in Pieces.* Oxford: Oxford University Press, 1970.

Brooks, Van Wyck. *The Confident Years: 1885–1915.* New York: E. P. Dutton, 1952.

Brown, Milton W. *The Story of the Armory Show.* New York: H. Wolff, 1963.

Browning, Robert. *The Complete Poetic and Dramatic Works of Robert Browning.* Edited by Horace E. Scudder. Boston: Houghton, Mifflin, 1895.

Burns, Edward, ed. *Staying on Alone: Letters of Alice B. Toklas.* New York: Vintage Books, 1973.

———, ed. *The Letters of Gertrude Stein and Carl Van Vechten, 1913–1946.* 2 vols. New York: Columbia University Press, 1986.

Cambridge Biographical Dictionary. Edited by Magnus Magnusson. Cambridge: Cambridge University Press, 1990.

Camfield, William A. *Francis Picabia: His Art, Life and Times*. Princeton: Princeton University Press, 1979.

Cargill, Oscar. *Intellectual America: Ideas on the March*. New York: Macmillan, 1941.

Carrington, Charles. *Rudyard Kipling, His Life and Work*. London: Macmillan, 1955.

Churchill, Allen. *The Improper Bohemians: The Re-Creation of Greenwich Village in Its Heyday*. New York: E. P. Dutton, 1959.

Coke, Van Deren. *Andrew Dasburg*. Albuquerque: University of New Mexico Press, 1979.

Coriat, Isador H. *The Meaning of Dreams*. Boston: Little, Brown, 1915.

Crunden, Robert M. *From Self to Society, 1919–1941*. Englewood Cliffs, N.J.: Prentice-Hall, 1972.

———. *Salons: Encounters with European Modernism, 1885–1917*. New York: Oxford University Press, 1993.

Davidson, Jo. *Between Sittings*. New York: Dial Press, 1951.

Draper, Muriel. *Music at Midnight*. New York: Harper and Brothers, 1929.

Eastman, Max. *Venture*. New York: Albert and Charles Boni, 1927.

———. *The Enjoyment of Living*. New York: Harper and Brothers, 1948.

Eisler, Benita. *O'Keeffe & Stieglitz: An American Romance*. New York: Doubleday, 1991.

Evans, Donald. *Sonnets from the Patagonian*. Philadelphia: Nicholas L. Brown, 1918.

Farnham, Emily. *Charles Demuth: Behind a Laughing Mask*. Norman, Okla.: University of Oklahoma Press, 1971.

Four Americans in Paris: The Collections of Gertrude Stein and Her Family. New York: Museum of Modern Art, 1970.

Freud, Sigmund. *The Interpretation of Dreams*. 1900. Reprint. *The Standard Edition of the Complete Psychological Works of Sigmund Freud*. Vols. 4 and 5. Translated and edited by James Strachey. London: Hogarth Press, 1953.

———. *Inhibitions, Symptoms and Anxiety*. 1926. Reprint. *The Standard Edition of the Complete Psychological Works of Sigmund Freud*. Vol. 20. Translated and edited by James Strachey. London: Hogarth Press, 1953.

Gallup, Donald, ed. *The Flowers of Friendship: Letters Written to Gertrude Stein*. New York: Alfred A. Knopf, 1953.

Gedo, Mary Mathews. *Picasso: Art as Autobiography*. Chicago: University of Chicago Press, 1980.

Gide, André. *The Journals of André Gide*. 2 vols. Vol. 1 (1889–1913). Translated and edited by Justin O'Brien. New York: Alfred A. Knopf, 1947.

Goodrich, Lloyd. *Max Weber: Retrospective Exhibition*. New York: Whitney Museum of American Art, 1949.

Gowing, Sir Lawrence, ed. *A Biographical Dictionary of Artists*. 2 vols. Englewood Cliffs, N.J.: Prentice-Hall, 1983.

Green, Jonathan, ed. *Camera Work: A Critical Anthology*. New York: Aperture, 1973.

Green, Martin. *New York 1913: The Armory Show and the Paterson Strike Pageant*. New York: Charles Scribner's Sons, 1988.

Haas, Robert Bartlett, ed. *Gertrude Stein: A Primer for the Gradual Understanding of Gertrude Stein*. Los Angeles: Black Sparrow Press, 1973.

Hahn, Emily. *Mabel: A Biography of Mabel Dodge Luhan*. Boston: Houghton Mifflin, 1977.

Hanscombe, Gillian, and Virginia L. Smyers. *Writing for Their Lives: The Modernist Women, 1910–1940*. London: Women's Press, 1987.

Hapgood, Hutchins. *A Victorian in the Modern World*. New York: Harcourt, Brace and World, 1939.

Hartley, Marsden. *Adventures in the Arts: Informal Chapters on Painters Vaudeville and Poets*. 1921. Reprint. New York: Hacker Art Books, 1972.

Haskell, Barbara. *Marsden Hartley*. New York: Whitney Museum of American Art, 1980.

———. *Charles Demuth*. New York: Whitney Museum of American Art, 1987.

Heller, Adele, and Lois Rudnick, eds. *1915, The Cultural Moment: The New Politics, the New Woman, the New Psychology, the New Art, and the New Theatre in America*. New Brunswick, N.J.: Rutgers University Press, 1991.

Hobhouse, Janet. *Everybody Who Was Anybody: A Biography of Gertrude Stein*. New York: Doubleday, 1975.

Hoffman, Michael J. *The Development of Abstractionism in the Writings of Gertrude Stein*. Philadelphia: University of Pennsylvania Press, 1965.

———, ed. *Critical Essays on Gertrude Stein*. Boston: G. K. Hall, 1986.

Homer, William I. *Alfred Stieglitz and the American Avant-Garde*. Boston: New York Graphic Society, 1977.

Kellner, Bruce. *Carl Van Vechten and the Irreverent Decades*. Norman, Okla.: University of Oklahoma Press, 1968.

———, ed. *Letters of Carl Van Vechten*. New Haven: Yale University Press, 1987.

———, ed. *A Gertrude Stein Companion: content with the example*. Westport, Conn., and New York: Greenwood Press, 1988.

Lasch, Christopher. *The New Radicalism in America (1889–1963): The Intellectual as a Social Type*. New York: W. W. Norton, 1965.

Lesure, François, ed. *Igor Stravinsky, Le Sacre du Printemps: Dossier de Presse*. Geneva: Editions Minkoff, 1980.

Lowe, Sue Davidson. *Stieglitz: A Memoir/Biography*. New York: Farrar, Straus Giroux, 1983.

Ludington, Townsend. *Marsden Hartley: The Biography of an American Artist*. Boston: Little, Brown, 1992.

Luhan, Mabel Dodge. *Intimate Memories: Background*. New York: Harcourt, Brace, 1933.

———. *Lorenzo in Taos*. New York: Alfred A. Knopf, 1932; London: Martin Secker, 1933.

———. *European Experiences: Volume Two of Intimate Memories*. New York: Harcourt, Brace, 1935.

———. *Winter in Taos*. New York: Harcourt, Brace, 1935.

———. *Movers and Shakers: Volume Three of Intimate Memories*. New York: Harcourt, Brace, 1936.

———. *Edge of Taos Desert: An Escape to Reality: Volume Four of Intimate Memories*. New York: Harcourt, Brace, 1937.

May, Henry F. *The End of American Innocence: A Study of the First Years of Our Own Time, 1912–1917.* New York: Alfred A. Knopf, 1959.

Mellow, James R. *Charmed Circle: Gertrude Stein & Company.* New York: Avon Books, 1974.

Michaels, Barbara L. *Gertrude Käsebier: The Photographer and Her Photographs.* New York: Harry N. Abrams, 1992.

Miller, Terry. *Greenwich Village and How It Got That Way.* New York: Crown Publishers, 1990.

Murray, Peter, and Linda Murray. *A Dictionary of Art and Artists.* 3d ed. Middlesex: Penguin Books, 1972.

Myers, Frederic W. H. *Human Personality and Its Survival of Bodily Death.* 2 vols. New York: Longmans, Green, 1903.

Nelson, Jane. *Mabel Dodge Luhan.* Boise, Idaho: Boise State University, 1982.

The New Columbia Encyclopedia. 4th ed. Edited by William H. Harris and Judith S. Levey. New York: Columbia University Press, 1975.

The Oxford Companion to English Literature. 5th ed. Edited by Margaret Drabble. Oxford: Oxford University Press, 1985.

Parry, Albert. *Garrets and Pretenders: A History of Bohemianism in America.* 1933. Reprint. New York: Dover Publications, 1960.

Phaidon Dictionary of 20th-Century Art. London: Phaidon Press, 1973.

Richardson, John. *A Life of Picasso.* Vol. 1 (1881–1906). New York: Random House, 1991.

Rubinstein, Arthur. *My Young Years.* New York: Alfred A. Knopf, 1973.

Rudnick, Lois Palken. *Mabel Dodge Luhan: New Woman, New Worlds.* Albuquerque: University of New Mexico Press, 1984.

Samuels, Ernest. *Bernard Berenson: The Making of a Connoisseur.* Cambridge, Mass.: Belknap Press, Harvard University Press, 1979.

Schack, William. *Art and Argyrol: The Life and Career of Dr. Albert C. Barnes.* New York: Sagamore Press, 1960.

Scudder, Janet. *Modeling My Life.* New York: Harcourt, Brace, 1925.

Sharrar, Jack F. *Avery Hopwood: His Life and Plays.* Jefferson, N.C.: McFarland, 1989.

Shattuck, Roger. *The Banquet Years: The Origins of the Avant Garde in France, 1885 to World War I.* 1955. Reprint. New York: Vintage Books, 1968.

Simon, Linda, ed. *Gertrude Stein: A Composite Portrait.* New York: Avon Books, 1974.

———. *The Biography of Alice B. Toklas.* Garden City, N.Y.: Doubleday, 1977.

Souhami, Diana. *Gertrude and Alice.* London: Pandora Press, 1991.

Steegmuller, Francis. *Apollinaire: Poet Among the Painters.* New York: Farrar, Straus, 1963.

Steffens, Lincoln. *The Autobiography of Lincoln Steffens.* 2 vols. New York: Harcourt, Brace, 1931.

Stein, Gertrude. *Geography and Plays.* Boston: Four Seas, 1922.

———. *The Making of Americans.* 1925. Reprint. New York: Something Else Press, 1966.

———. *The Autobiography of Alice B. Toklas.* New York: Vintage Books, 1933.

———. *Matisse Picasso and Gertrude Stein with Two Shorter Stories.* Paris: Plain Edition, 1933.

———. *Portraits and Prayers.* New York: Random House, 1934.

———. *Lectures in America.* New York: Random House, 1935.

———. *Everybody's Autobiography.* New York: Random House, 1937.

———. *What Are Masterpieces.* Los Angeles: Conference Press, 1940.

———. *Selected Writings of Gertrude Stein.* 1945. Reprint. Edited by Carl Van Vechten. New York: Vintage Books, 1962.

———. *Two: Gertrude Stein and Her Brother and Other Early Portraits.* New Haven: Yale University Press, 1951.

———. *As Fine As Melanctha.* New Haven: Yale University Press, 1954.

———. *Alphabets and Birthdays.* New Haven: Yale University Press, 1957.

———. *Gertrude Stein on Picasso.* Edited by Edward Burns. New York: Liveright, 1970.

———. *Fernhurst, Q.E.D., and Other Early Writings.* New York: Liveright, 1971.

———. *Reflection on the Atomic Bomb.* Edited by Robert Bartlett Haas. Los Angeles: Black Sparrow Press, 1973.

———. *The Yale Gertrude Stein.* New Haven: Yale University Press, 1980.

———. *A Stein Reader.* Edited by Ulla E. Dydo. Evanston, Ill.: Northwestern University Press, 1993.

Stein, Leo. *Appreciation: Painting, Poetry and Prose.* New York: Crown Publishers, 1947.

———. *Journey Into the Self: Being the Letters, Papers, and Journals of Leo Stein.* Edited by Edmund Fuller. New York: Crown Publishers, 1950.

Steiner, Wendy. *Exact Resemblance to Exact Resemblance: The Literary Portraiture of Gertrude Stein.* New Haven and London: Yale University Press, 1978.

Sterne, Maurice. *Shadow and Light: The Life, Friends and Opinions of Maurice Sterne.* Edited by Charlotte Leon Mayerson. New York: Harcourt, Brace and World, 1952.

Stewart, James McG. *Rudyard Kipling: A Bibliographical Catalogue.* Toronto: University of Toronto Press, 1959.

Strachey, Barbara, and Jayne Samuels, eds. *Mary Berenson: A Self-Portrait from her Letters and Diaries.* London: Victor Gollancz, 1983.

Toklas, Alice B. *The Alice B. Toklas Cook Book.* 1954. Reprint. New York: Harper and Row, 1986.

———. *What Is Remembered.* New York: Holt, Rinehart and Winston, 1963.

Van Vechten, Carl. *Music After the Great War and Other Studies.* New York: G. Schirmer, 1915.

———. *Peter Whiffle: His Life and Works.* 1922. Reprint. New York: Alfred A. Knopf, 1927.

———. *Fragments From an Unwritten Autobiography.* 2 vols. New Haven: Yale University Library, 1955.

Vorse, Mary Heaton. *A Footnote to Folly.* New York: Farrar and Rinehart, 1935.

Walker, Jayne L. *The Making of a Modernist: Gertrude Stein from Three Lives to Tender Buttons.* Amherst, Mass.: University of Massachusetts Press, 1984.

Watson, Steven. *Strange Bedfellows: The First American Avant-Garde.* New York: Abbeville Press, 1991.

Webster's Biographical Dictionary. Springfield, Mass.: G. & C. Merriam, 1976.

White, Eric Walter. *Stravinsky: The Composer and His Works.* 2d ed. Berkeley and Los Angeles: University of California Press, 1979.

Whitman, Walt. *The Leaves of Grass.* 1855. Reprint. New York: Thomas Y. Crowell, 1933.

Who Was Who in America. Volumes: Historical Volume (1607–1896), 1963; vol. 1 (1897–1942), 1942; vol. 2 (1943–50), 1950; vol. 3 (1951–60), 1963; vol. 4 (1961–68), 1968; vol. 5 (1969–73), 1973; vol. 6 (1974–76), 1976; vol. 7 (1977–81), 1981. Chicago: A. N. Marquis.

Who Was Who in American Art. (Compiled from original 34 volumes of *American Art Annual: Who's Who in Art, Biographies of American Artists Active 1898–1947.*) Edited by Peter H. Falk. Madison, Conn.: Sound View Press, 1985.

Zurier, Rebecca. *Art for the Masses: A Radical Magazine and Its Graphics, 1911–1917.* Philadelphia: Temple University Press, 1988.

INDEX

rior design consultant, 244; as newspaper columnist, 19; and her memoirs, 253–54; and psychoanalysis, 17–20, 85n, 129, 146, 245; as salon hostess, 8–9, 128, 155–57. *See also* Dodge, Edwin; Evans, Karl; Evenings; Luhan, Antonio; "Portrait of Mabel Dodge at the Villa Curonia," Stein; Reed, John; Sterne, Maurice

Dove, Arthur, 14, 15, 17, 58, 159n

Draper, Muriel, 2, 9, 56, 62, 75, 153, 170, 201–2, 244, 262

Draper, Paul, 2, 56, 100, 153, 170, 201, 202

Draper, Ruth, 100, 153n, 158

Dreiser, Theodore, 159n, 184n

du Bois, Guy Pène, 167

Duchamp, Marcel, 191

Duncan, Elizabeth, 239–40, 243

Duncan, Isadora, 97, 239–40

Duse, Eleanora, 34

Eastman, Max, 9, 19, 93, 206, 207n

Edes, Robert, 18–19

Edge of Taos Desert, Mabel Dodge Luhan, 142, 143

Edgerly, Myra, 95n, 155, 156, 209, 210, 217, 244

Edstrom, David, 204, 205, 207

Elektra, Strauss,173-74

Ellis, Havelock, 19

Enemies, Hapgood and Boyce, 133

English Review, 43, 154, 169, 170

"Esthetic Significance of the Motion Picture, The," Hartmann, 15

European Experiences, Dodge, 25, 28, 31, 78, 162, 224, 262

Evans, Donald, 83n, 210, 216n, 217, 218, 220, 223, 227, 229, 232, 247

Evans, John, (Mabel Dodge's son), 26, 46-47, 54, 61, 62, 126, 141, 142, 157, 197, 234, 239; pictured, 104, 105, 110, 140; painting of, 111

Evans, Karl, 6, 7, 99n

Evenings, Mabel Dodge's, 8–9, 17, 128, 132, 155-57, 208n, 251; without Dodge, 211

Everybody's Autobiography, Stein, 7, 149, 262

Everybody's Magazine, 19

"Exploring the Soul and Healing the Body," Eastman, 19

Faÿ Bernard, 6

Ferber, Edna, 184n

Field, George, 64, 65, 68, 92

Finney Farm, Dodge at, 244, 245

Flaubert, Gustave, 5, 42

Fleming, George, 36. *See also* Fletcher, Julia Constance

Fletcher, Julia Constance, 2, 36-40, 53, 82; letter to Stein from, 60; Stein's portrait of, 39, 63, 86, 92, 159, 180; mentions, 50, 52, 56, 57, 64, 65, 67, 70, 74, 87, 94, 96, 183, 191

Fontainebleau, France, Dodge at, 201

"Food," Stein, 218

Foote, Mary, 54, 55, 71, 72, 85, 92, 189, 202, 227, 232; portrait of Mabel Dodge by, 115

Ford, Ford Madox, 43

Forum, 82, 176

Four Saints in Three Acts, Stein, 256

Francesca, Piero della, 40n

Fraser, Jimmy, 143

French-Lemon Bank, 37

Freud, Sigmund, 17-20, 243

Freudian Wish, The, Holt, 19

Fry, Roger, 154, 168, 169, 170

"G.M.P.," Stein, 38, 168, 175n

Galvin, Miss, 197, 199

Gans, Bird, 166, 243

Gauguin, Paul, 12

"Gentle Lena, The," Stein, 42

Geography and Plays, Stein, 39, 168, 186n, 188n, 191n

Gertrude Stein, Picasso, 26, 123,

91n, 187, 191, 207, 231; Stein's word portrait of, 186
To Mabel Dodge No. 2, Dasburg, 117
Toklas, Alice B., 44, 63-64, 70, 83, 162, 224, 242, 257, 258n; cited, 36, 61, 91n, 258n, 260; letters from Dodge to, 70–71, 84, 100; letter to Dodge from, 154-55; Dodge's possible nickname for, 44, 46, 64, 65, 70; pictured, 120, 124, 148, 149; mentioned, 1, 2, 5, 7, 25, 26, 28, 30, 34, 36, 38, 38n, 39, 51, 57, 66, 95n, 98, 189, 193, 212, 233, 243, 250, 258, 259, 261, 262
Toulouse-Lautrec, Henri de, 15
Tristan und Isolde, Wagner, 174
Twain, Mark, 55n
Two: Gertrude Stein and Her Brother and Other Early Portraits, Stein, 50, 88, 168, 188n, 204n, 206n, 232
291, Stieglitz's gallery, 3, 10, 13–17, 58, 134, 135, 165–67, 176, 204, 206, 220, 221n. *See also* Stieglitz, Alfred

Ullman, Eugene, 183
"Unconscious in Art, The," Casser-es, 15
United States, Gertrude Stein in the, 5, 37, 149, 257, 260-62
Universalities, the, one named, 46

Vallombrosa, 225
Van Gogh, Vincent, 12, 15
Van Vechten, Carl, 11, 126, 166n, 174n, 185n, 208n, 217-18, 241, 257, 259n, 261; cited, 9, 31, 128, 243, 251, 262; letter to Stein by, 262; Dodge meets, 164-65; Dodge's poem about, 165; Dasburg's portrait of, 118–19; photographs by, 138, 147, 148,

149; pictured, 131, 147, 149; Stein meets, 2, 193-97, and writes to, 198, 252-56, 262; mentioned, 4, 34, 83n, 119, 126, 128, 138, 166–67, 181, 200-203, 234, 235, 254, 258, 259, 260, 262
Varieties of Religious Experience, The, James, 19
Vaughn, Herbert, 56
Venture, Eastman, 9
Villa, Pancho, 210
Villa Curonia, 9, 30-34, 201; ghosts at, 53-56; pictured, 106, 107; Stein at, 36-37, 60-65
Vivekananda, 79, 90
Vollard, Ambroise, 12

Wagner, one named, 51
Wagner, Richard, 174
Washington Square Gallery, 218
Watson, Grant, 77, 78, 84, 92, 153, 154, 170, 181, 229
Watts, Mrs., 50
Watts, one named, 52
Weber, Max, 11, 12, 14, 15, 17, 134, 183, 220; critical writing on Stein by, 178, 182; imitation of Stein's writing, 194
Weeks, Mabel, 60, 91, 94, 97, 152, 153, 154, 157, 166, 172, 173, 187, 212, 213, 244
Wells, H. G., 43, 153, 154, 187n
West-eastern Divan, Goethe, 44
"What Happened. A Five Act Play," Stein, 186n
What is Remembered, Toklas, 61, 260
"What is the Object of Art," Bergson, 15
Whistler, James, 15
White, Clarence H., 14
Whitehead, Alfred North, 233, 234
Whitehead, Evelyn, 233
Whitman, Walt, 27n, 33, 102
Wilde, Oscar, 15